Penguin Masterstudies

Geography

Susan Mayhew, B.A., was educated at Leicester University. She gained a double distinction in her Postgraduate Certificate of Education at London University. She has taught in a number of schools in both the public and private sectors and is currently Geography Supervisor at Beechlawn Tutorial College in Oxford. She has also written the guide to geography in the Penguin Passnotes series.

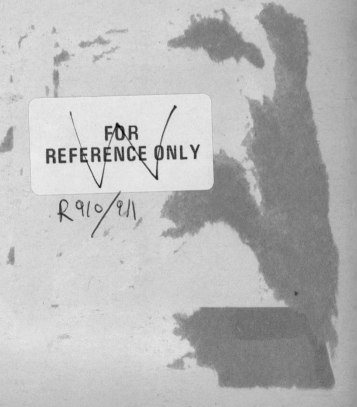

Penguin Masterstudies
Advisory Editor: Stephen Coote

Geography

Susan Mayhew

Penguin Books

Penguin Books Ltd, Harmondsworth, Middlesex, England
Viking Penguin Inc., 40 West 23rd Street, New York, New York 10010, U.S.A.
Penguin Books Australia Ltd, Ringwood, Victoria, Australia
Penguin Books Canada Ltd, 2801 John Street, Markham, Ontario, Canada L3R 1B4
Penguin Books (N.Z.) Ltd, 182–190 Wairau Road, Auckland 10, New Zealand

First published 1986

Copyright © Susan Mayhew, 1986

Made and printed in Great Britain by
Cox & Wyman Ltd, Reading
Filmset in 9/11 pt Linotron Times by
Rowland Phototypesetting Ltd, Bury St Edmunds, Suffolk

For Vicki Gregory

Contents

Introduction

1. Make sure you know which Board you are taking; the precise requirements of the syllabus; and the special or regional options and case-study areas, where relevant.

2. If necessary, get in touch with the Examination Boards. All ten listed on pp. 10–11 will supply past papers. In addition, AEB, CAM, JMB, LON and NI produce a yearly report – the *Examiners' Report* – which gives a question-by-question account of what they expected and where candidates went wrong. If you read these in conjunction with the examination papers concerned you will be helped enormously. Your teacher should have copies, but you can buy them. In all transactions with the Boards, phone first to find out the availability and cost of the items you want, plus postage/packing prices. You can then send a cheque or postal order for the right amount.

3. About this book:
 (i) Two abbreviations are frequently used: 'op. cit.' means 'the book by this author which I have already named'; 'et al.' means 'and other people'. Both these abbreviations are used in referring to other books; you can take it that these books are recommended further reading. If you cannot buy them, order them from your local library.
 (ii) The questions in this book have been chosen as the most representative examples. Many come from the Welsh and Northern Ireland Boards – this does not mean they are not relevant to English and Scottish candidates. On the contrary, Boards frequently adopt one another's types of questions. Even if questions from your particular Board do not appear in the book, you will find that your syllabus requirements have been fully covered.
 (iii) Every word in **bold** type is a word whose definition you should know. Make a vocabulary book from these and learn them.
 (iv) Read the whole book. No one will need it all, but the extra breadth of knowledge gained thereby will certainly not be wasted.
 (v) Work with this book as soon as you can. There are many suggestions on how to improve techniques and extend your knowledge; you can't do these things if you start using this book one week before your A-level.

4. During the examination:
 (i) If you are using a calculator, do a rough sum to check that the calculated answer is likely to be right. Thus, if you have to multiply 436×18, the answer should be close to 400×20, i.e. 8,000.
 (ii) Check that you are answering the correct number of questions from the right sections.
(iii) Obey instructions carefully. Pages 16–19 and 120–25 will explain just what the examiner means by each different command.
(iv) Use your time sensibly. The first marks in the question are often the easiest ones to get. Make sure you have done something on the full number of questions required.
 (v) Use any outlines given you. You may mark the map extract, photograph or question paper in any way you wish and also make rough notes.

The Examination Boards

The addresses given below are those from which copies of syllabuses and past examination papers may be ordered. The abbreviations (AEB, etc.) are those used in the text to indicate the source of an exam question.

Associated Examining Board,   [AEB]
Wellington House,
Station Road,
Aldershot,
Hants GU11 1BQ   0252-25551

University of Cambridge Local Examinations Syndicate,   [CAM]
Syndicate Buildings,
17 Harvey Road,
Cambridge CB1 2EU   0223-61111

Joint Matriculation Board,   [JMB]
(Agent) John Sherratt & Son Ltd,
78 Park Road,
Altrincham,
Cheshire WA14 5QQ   061-973 5711

University of London School Examinations Department,   [LON]
52 Gordon Square,
London WC1E 6EE   01-636 8000

Northern Ireland Schools Examinations Council, [NI]
Examinations Office,
42 Beechill Road,
Belfast BT8 4RS   0232-704666

Oxford Delegacy of Local Examinations, [OXF]
Ewert Place,
Summertown,
Oxford OX2 7BZ   0865-54291

Oxford and Cambridge Schools Examination Board, [O and C]
10 Trumpington Street,
Cambridge CB2 1QB   0223-64326
or
Drill Hall,
Elsfield Way,
Oxford OX2 8EP   0865-54547

Scottish Certificate of Education Examining Board, [SCO.T]*
(Agent) Robert Gibson & Sons Ltd, [SCO.A]†
17 Fitzroy Place,
Glasgow G3 7SF   041-248 5674

Southern Universities Joint Board, [SUJB]
Cotham Road,
Bristol BS6 6DD   (ex-directory)

Welsh Joint Education Committee, [WEL]
245 Western Avenue,
Cardiff CF5 2YX   0222-561231

* T – Traditional Higher.
† A – Alternative Higher.

Part One: Geographical techniques

1. Maps and photographs

> Geography is about maps
> But biography is about chaps.
> (E. C. Bentley)

This is an old rhyme, and geography has changed greatly since it was written. Today there is much more emphasis on human geography. Unfortunately, examination candidates seem to have forgotten that the first half of this couplet still holds good. Your performance at A-level will be greatly improved if you can both read maps – Ordnance Survey, Geological Survey, Soil Survey, Land Utilization Survey – and draw sketch maps wherever they make your point clearer. The best way to achieve these skills is to use maps throughout every stage of your A-level course.

1. Reading Ordnance Survey maps

At A-level, O.S. mapwork questions are not usually compulsory, except on the Scottish Traditional Higher paper. Nevertheless, you will almost always find a map interpretation question somewhere on your examination paper. This question is, on average, worth over 10% of the total examination mark.

It will be assumed that you have mastered certain technical abilities at O-level. These include:
– recognition of symbols for 1:50,000 and 1:25,000 sheets
– determining four- and six-figure grid references
– calculation of distances, bearings and gradients
– construction of cross- and sketch-sections.
You will rarely be asked to do these *directly* at A-level, but should be ready to use any of these skills if they will make your answer clearer. It is obvious from examiners' reports that some very basic errors are still being made:

(i) Reversed grid references
Grid references should refer first to the easting (vertical line), then to the northing (horizontal line). If you have difficulty remembering this, use the expression 'VEry HaNdy', which contains the initial letters of Vertical, Easting, Horizontal, Northing in the correct sequence.

(ii) Confusion over map symbols

This occurs even when candidates are given map keys (AEB; LON; JMB). If you have a key, study it carefully, and check what you say against it. Otherwise, learn your symbols thoroughly. The most common complaints were that candidates could not distinguish between motorways and canals, nor recognize parish boundaries, shown now only on 1:25,000 sheets.

(iii) Difficulties over scales

The map scale, either 1:50,000 or 1:25,000, will be given on the map. Look for it.

At 1:50,000, 1 cm represents ½ km (500 m).
At 1:25,000, 1 cm represents ¼ km (250 m).
All Boards now use metric maps.

(iv) Confusion between east and west

This is astonishingly prevalent among A-level geographers. The simple mnemonic is 'WE', as in '*We* know the difference between West and East!'

(v) Inadequate use of map evidence

Make sure you give a six-figure grid reference for every feature you discuss. Support every statement you make with map evidence. Many candidates do very badly on maps of areas they have been taught about, as they tend to regurgitate their lesson notes, which may well not be relevant, and ignore the map evidence. Sometimes you will be given diagrams and an O.S. map extract. Use the map evidence, even if you feel you could answer the questions from the diagrams alone.

(vi) Failure to follow instructions

Here is a list of 'command words' used in mapwork questions, followed by an outline of what the examiner wants you to do.

Account for: attempt to explain the development of a feature, taking care not to be too dogmatic. Use words like 'may', 'might', 'could have'. If you have to account for physical features, diagrams are usually vital. For human features, a sketch map will sum up the important factors.

Comment on: generally entails some explanation, or recognition of relationships.

Compare: means, strictly speaking, note the similarities (but is more often used as 'compare *and* contrast').

Contrast: means note the differences. If you are asked to contrast two features, you must do this point by point, interlarding your writing with words like 'but' and 'whereas'. Try to find a logical system for the order in which you put your points. For example, for a comparison between relief regions you might use size, average land height, gradients, drainage pattern, drainage density, probable geology. Two separate accounts of the features you are to contrast will score no marks at all.

Discuss: as 'comment on'.

Outline the relationships: means show the possible links which exist between features of physical and/or human geography shown on the map. Fig. 1 shows some of the relationships you might be able to suggest from O.S. map evidence. You may be given other data, like geology maps, to use in your outline of relationships. Failure to use all the data given will result in lost marks.

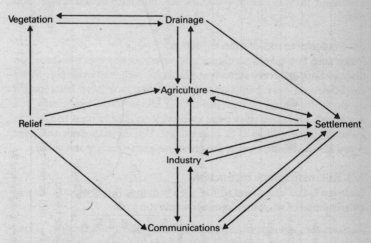

Fig. 1 *Relationships suggested by O.S. map evidence*

Draw a transect diagram: means that you should draw a section and annotate it systematically, according to relief (**physiography**), drainage, vegetation, routeways and settlement. Sometimes you are asked to do this directly:

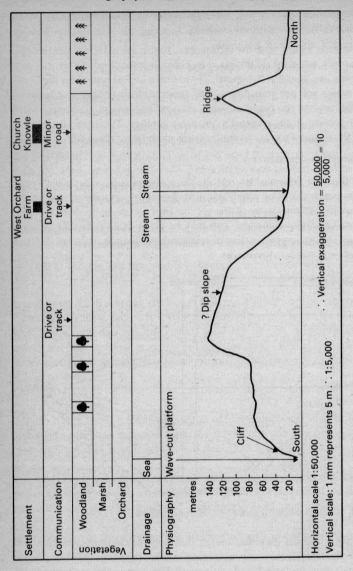

Fig. 2 *Transect along easting 94*

Q. 1. Study the O.S. map extract provided (1:50,000: Corfe Castle – see cover). Draw a transect diagram showing the relationship between physical and human geography.

Fig. 2 shows the type of answer you might produce.
  Note that:
– features of which you are unsure may be marked in with a query
– the vertical (side) scale is much larger than the horizontal scale
– the vertical exaggeration has been calculated.

If you have to draw a transect of a 1:50,000 map, without a grid to help you, use a side scale of 1 mm per 10 m. This is a scale of 1:10,000 and will give you a vertical exaggeration of 5. On a 1:25,000 map, use a side scale of 2 mm per 10 m, i.e. 1:5,000; also a **vertical exaggeration (V.E.)** of 5. If you always use these side scales then you need never calculate the V.E., but you must always state it.

On other occasions, you may not be asked directly for a transect, but a sketch-section transect would be helpful; for example, in:

*Q. 2. Describe and explain **rural** land-use, past and present, in the area west of easting 96.*

First divide the area into physical regions by eye (see p. 22, point 5) and make sure your transect crosses each kind of area. For the Corfe extract you would be wise to run your transection through the ancient field systems (956780). Then mark in the different kinds of land-use, using categories like villages and farms, fields, woodland and orchards. Note that:
(a) the examiner has highlighted the word 'rural', so do not write about industry
(b) all land has some use. Do not simply label it 'open space'. In the absence of any other evidence (such as marsh, spoil tips, buildings, etc.) you can mark rural land-use as 'agricultural', adding '? grazing' to the steeper slopes.
Such a transect will bring certain points out clearly. Fig. 2 will show you that the deciduous woodland is above 80 m and the coniferous woodland is on the northern flank of the ridge. The farm and village are at around 50 m.

A transect will be especially useful if you are also given a geology map (Fig. 3, overleaf).

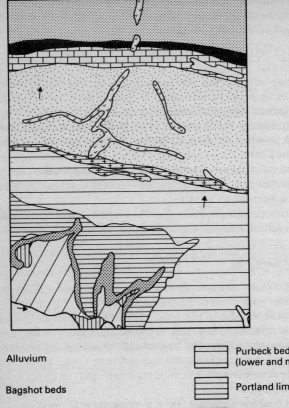

Key

Alluvium		Purbeck beds (lower and middle)	
Bagshot beds		Portland limestone	
London clay		Portland sand	
Chalk		Kimmeridge clay	
Wealden and greensand (sandstones, clays and grit bands)		Landslip	
Purbeck marble		Dip arrows	

Fig. 3 *Sample geology map*

*Q. 3. Use the O.S. 1:50,000 map extract of the area around Corfe and the accompanying geological diagram (Fig. 3) to write an explanatory account of the relief and drainage of the area lying **west** of easting 95. What further information beyond that supplied by the O.S. map and geological diagram would be of value in accounting for the features you describe?* [O and C; adapted]

In this case, you could draw a transect as for Fig. 2, but giving only the relief, geology and drainage. Those rocks which form uplands, those which make up lowlands, those which support drainage, and so on, will now be clear.

The vast majority of mapwork questions fall into one of the following categories:

A. *Landforms:*
 (i) recognition
 (ii) explanation
(iii) relationship to geology
(iv) analysis of drainage patterns.
(Questions combining the first three of these aspects are among the most commonly set mapwork questions.)

B. *Settlements:*
 (i) patterns
 (ii) site, position, form and functions.

Less frequently occurring are questions on:

C. *Land-use*, including conflicts in land-use

D. *Communications*

E. *Industry* (rarely).

Many questions combine two of these categories.

A. Landforms

(i) Recognition

The simplest questions ask you to identify landforms:

Q. 4. Label the outline map to show the major features of the relief and drainage of the O.S. map area.

Fig. 4 shows the kind of outline map to expect, but you will not always be given an outline. Questions like this must always be answered with an annotated map, so if you are not given one, draw one:

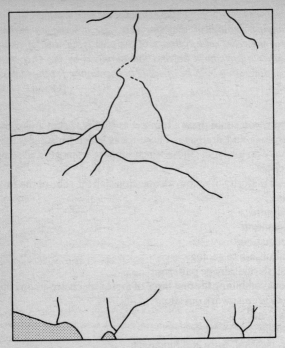

Fig. 4 *Outline map sample*

Table 1.   Sketch-map construction from O.S. extracts

1) Draw a rectangle to half-scale.
2) Label the grid-lines which bound your extract.
3) Put in perhaps two or three eastings and northings; do not put in every grid-line.
4) Mark in major drainage features.
5) Add significant contours – those which divide the area into different physical regions. You should subdivide for marked changes in average altitude and changes in surface relief features.
6) Mark in landforms, using symbols like the ones in Fig. 5.

The following definitions of landforms may be helpful here:

COMMON LANDFORMS

Col: a lowland pass in a line of hills.

22

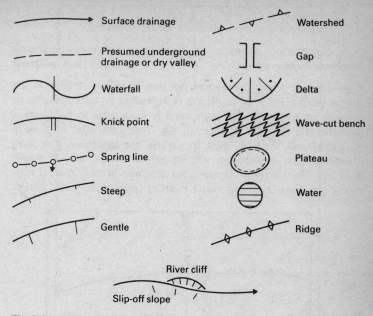

Fig. 5 *Morphological map symbols*

Escarpment: a steep **scarp** slope together with a gentler **dip** slope. Also known as a **cuesta**.

Hill: higher land, but below 600 m.

Mountain: high land, over 600 m in Britain.

Plateau: area of comparatively flat land at height. May be an **erosion surface**.*

Ridge: long, narrow stretch of upland.

Spur:† a projection of a hill into a lowland area.

Valley:† a long depression between highland areas, usually occupied by a stream.

---

* Erosion surfaces are identifiable by the flatness of the land and the similarities of spot heights, but you should be very diffident in suggesting the presence of any. There should always be some other evidence of uplift, e.g. waterfalls, raised beaches.

† Frequently confused by A-level candidates. Compare height at edges and in centre to confirm correct identification.

(ii) Explanation

More difficult are questions which ask for explanations:

Q. 5. Describe and attempt to explain the principal geomorphological features in the map extract. [NI; half; adapted]

'The extent to which the student can pass from map reading to the correct interpretation of landforms is dependent on his knowledge of physical geography.'* The basic need is to be able to recognize a landform (see 'Further reading', p. 40). Your knowledge of physical geography will then be used to explain the landforms you have identified. This explanation will be helped by the use of simple diagrams. Do not try to duplicate the diagrams in most A-level texts unless you have a strong visual memory and artistic skill. Simple

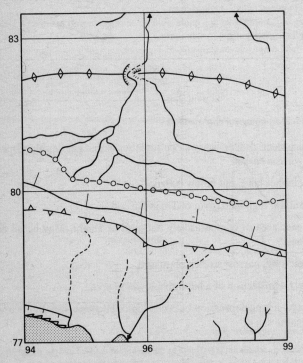

Fig. 6 *Morphological map of Corfe Castle area*

* Speak, P., and A. H. C. Carter, *Map Reading and Interpretation*, Longman, 1981.

diagrams are found in R. B. Bunnett, *General Geography in Diagrams* (Longman, 1977), an O-level text which is an excellent revision book for A-level. A morphological map will help in answering Question 5. Fig. 6 shows a morphological map of the Corfe Castle area, using the symbols in Fig. 5.

If you have time, you might clarify your explanation by drawing an enlarged portion of the map.

Table 2.   Enlarging a map area

1) Select your area and draw a rectangle round it on the O.S. extract. Divide each O.S. square into four, using a pencil.
2) On your examination script, draw a rectangle twice the size. Put in grid squares and the quartering guide-lines on the same scale.
3) On the enlargement, mark the points at which contour-lines, roads and rivers intersect guide- or grid-lines.
4) Using the O.S. extract as a guide, join up contours, roads and rivers. Use colours to distinguish between them.
5) Now add other relevant features.

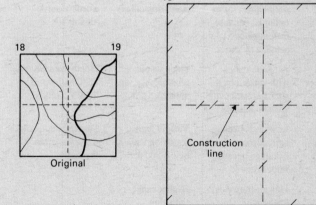

Fig. 7 *Enlarging a map area*

(iii) Relationship to geology

Question 3 typifies those which ask you to link geology and landforms. To link the two satisfactorily you need some basic geological knowledge:

Table 3.   Sedimentary rocks on O.S. maps

Rock type	Characteristics	Landforms	Other map evidence
Limestone			
(1) Carbon-iferous (north of Notting-ham)	Jointed, and so permeable; forms uplands, because little surface erosion by water	Pot-hole, swallow-hole, dry valley, gorge, scar	Little surface drainage. Mostly above 300 m
(2) Jurassic (south of Middles-brough)	Not jointed but permeable; forms uplands, because little surface erosion by water	Wooded scarps; some dry valleys	Usually lower elevation than (1), e.g. around 200 m
Chalk	Porous, and so permeable; forms uplands, because little surface erosion by water	Scarps and dips, many dry valleys	Tumuli, hill forts; words 'bourne', 'downs'
Sandstone	Altitude varies with variations in rock hardness; dry valleys possible	Steep slopes *possible*, e.g. on millstone grit	Heath symbols on 1:25,000; words 'heath', 'sandy'
Clay (sometimes called marl)	Lowlands because soft; copious drainage because impermeable	Valleys, vales; elevation usually below 200 m	Drainage cuts; old clay pits, often flooded
Shales	Harder than clay, but also impermeable	Higher relief than clay	

If you are trying to guess the geology of an area from O.S. map evidence alone, you should look for at least three pieces of evidence before *suggesting* one rock type. Do this only for sedimentary rocks: it is too difficult to deduce igneous or metamorphic rocks from O.S. map evidence.

Q. 6. With reference to the 1:50,000 map extract (Corfe) and a geology map (Fig. 3) of the same area,
 (i) write an explanatory account of the landforms and drainage of the area;
(ii) comment on the cross-sectional form of the valleys.

This is a useful revision question. Check the word 'comment' on p. 16, and remember that, before you explain, you must first describe. All geographical descriptions of landforms should include size, shape and slope. These you can determine from the map. Use the scale. Your answer should include a morphological map, plus key, at least one profile, and an enlarged portion to show a typical valley. The 'dip' arrows on the geological map should help you to determine whether there is a dip slope on the extract.

(iv) Analysis of drainage patterns
Questions on drainage are generally incorporated in a general discussion of landforms (Questions 3, 4, 5, 6 – above). Increasingly, examiners want you to describe and analyse drainage patterns. The following skills may be helpful here.

(a) FINDING THE WATERSHED, i.e. the limit of the drainage basin. You can do this on the map, in pencil. In this way, you can describe and count the number of basins (whole or part) in the extract.

(b) ESTIMATING THE AREA OF THE DRAINAGE BASIN. On a 1:50,000 sheet, each grid square covers $\frac{1}{4}$ km^2. When you have pencilled in your watershed, count the number of whole squares, then halves, and then, very roughly, collect up enough portions of squares to make up a whole. Total up the number of whole squares achieved by this method, and divide by four, to give the approximate area of the drainage basin in km^2. This can be useful in comparison questions.

Q. 7. Compare the relief and drainage of the area between northings 80 and 82 with the area south of northing 82 (Corfe O.S.).

(c) RECOGNIZING DRAINAGE PATTERNS. You should know **dendritic**, **trellis**, **radial**, **sub-parallel** and **rectangular** (p. 166) drainage patterns, but only the first two will be identifiable on an O.S. map. If the rivers don't show up clearly, go over them in pencil.

(d) RECOGNIZING RIVER CAPTURE. This is tricky. Only suggest that capture has occurred *if:*

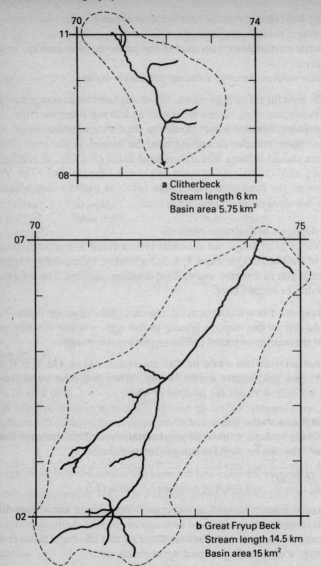

a Clitherbeck
Stream length 6 km
Basin area 5.75 km²

b Great Fryup Beck
Stream length 14.5 km
Basin area 15 km²

Fig. 8 *See Question 8*

1) the river changes course very dramatically and . . .
2) there is at least one 'wind gap' visible and . . .
3) there is evidence of rejuvenation *downstream* of the elbow of capture (see p. 172).

Further evidence is given if the downstream tributaries are 'hanging'.

Q. 8. With the aid of Figs. 8a and 8b which sketch the stream patterns in the drainage basins of Clitherbeck and Great Fryup Beck:
 (i) number the streams in the figures to show the stream orders;
(ii) complete columns IV and V in the table below.

	I Total stream length (km)	II Basin area (km²)	III Drainage density	IV No. of streams in each order 1st 2nd 3rd	V Bifurcation ratio 1st/2nd 2nd/3rd
Clither- beck	6.0	5.75	1.04		
Great Fryup Beck	14.5	15.0	0.97		

[LON; part]

To do this, you may use either the Horton or the Strahler system (see p. 169), but you *must* state the system used.

Drainage: some minor points
1) River terraces are not usually recognizable on 1:50,000 maps because they are smaller than the contour interval, i.e. 10 m.
2) A waterfall may be a knick point, but could be due to a more resistant rock layer.
3) Parish boundaries (shown only on 1:25,000 sheets) often follow rivers. Where the boundary diverges from the river, the course of the river *may* have changed.
4) **Long profiles** may often be drawn to illustrate the characteristics of a river. Cross profiles should be used frequently. An asymmetrical profile may indicate a fault which the river is exploiting.
5) You will rarely have time to calculate drainage density, but you can

estimate it. Fig. 9 shows the three terms used. All the extracts are on the same scale.

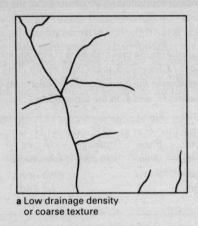

a Low drainage density
or coarse texture

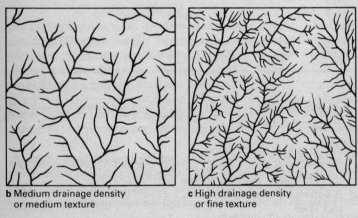

b Medium drainage density
or medium texture

c High drainage density
or fine texture

Fig. 9 *Drainage densities at 1:50,000*

Coasts

Much of the chapter so far applies also to coastal geomorphology. In addition you should know the following:

1) The **coast** is the zone extending landward from the low tide mark (L.W.M.M.T.). There is no standard definition of its inland limit.
2) The **shore** extends between the high and low tide marks.

3) Coasts may be described as straight, irregular or crenulated (very irregular).

4) You should look for evidence of drowning (submergence) on irregular coasts, and of uplift – raised beaches and silt-choked meandering rivers.

5) Where you have a flat-topped cliff stretching some way inland, you may have an erosion surface. Further evidence is given by the presence of shingle, stacks and caves. The strongest pointer would be the fact of the surface extending uniformly across different types of rock.

6) Always remember that marine forces (p. 177) are not the only ones shaping the coastline. Sub-aerial processes (p. 159) are also at work.

Q. 9. Describe the forces at work in shaping the coastline shown on the O.S. map extract (Corfe). [SCO. A]

B. Settlements

(i) Patterns

Examiners' reports suggest that there is much confusion over the meaning of the term 'settlement pattern'. Unfortunately, the textbooks do not agree with one another. Charles Whynne-Hammond* makes the following distinction: **settlement pattern** concerns the character of the settlements '. . . whether they are nucleated (as villages), or dispersed (as isolated dwellings)'; **settlement distribution** concerns the location of settlements of any size across the landscape. But Peter Haggett† would class both these definitions under the same umbrella: settlement pattern.

Geographers frequently disagree, and you should be aware of this. As in stream-order questions (p. 29), decide on the definition you are going to use and name the authority whose system you are to follow. Then outline simply the other system and cite the authority for it, before you go on to answer the question.

(ii) Site, position, form and functions

Precise understanding and use of vocabulary is more important than ever in this section.

---

* Whynne-Hammond, C., *Elements of Human Geography*, George Allen & Unwin, 1979.
† Haggett, P., *Geography: A Modern Synthesis*, Harper & Row, 1984.

Table 4.   Vocabulary in 'human' mapwork

City: a settlement of over 100,000 people (or covering more than 20 grid squares*)

Conurbation: a built-up area exceeding 30 grid squares and incorporating several towns

Dense rural settlement: some settlement in the majority of grid squares

Dispersed settlement: settlement mainly composed of isolated dwellings (can be dense)

Form: *in rural settlements,* this means shape, and includes **linear**, **loose-knit**, **nucleated**, **open-space**; *in towns,* look for varieties of street patterns: medieval, nineteenth-century grid, twentieth-century curves and cul-de-sacs, as well as shape and size

Functions: services provided by town: economic, social, communication. Most settlements have several. *All towns are route centres*

Hamlet: a small group of houses, possibly including a church without a spire or tower, or an inn

Isolated dwelling: in Britain, usually a farm or manor house by itself in the middle of the countryside

Location (or **position**): the relationship of the settlement with surrounding human and physical features. If you refer to the location of a large settlement on an O.S. map, give the grid square in which the core is located

Rural: sometimes means any place in the countryside, but you would do well to exclude mining villages from this classification. Rural settlements will be based on agriculture and forestry, but may also have non-rural workers living there (commuters, retired persons)

Site: the actual land occupied by the settlement. Spot heights can give extra detail here. If a geomorphological feature is within the site, e.g. an incised meander, identify it

Situation: relationship of the settlement to the surrounding physical features

Sparse: fewer than 25 people per km^2, i.e. one or no dwellings in each grid square

Town: more than 2,000 people. Built-up area covering six or more grid squares

Urban settlement: settlement in towns or cities

Village: settlement of up to 2,000 people – built up over 1–5 grid squares

---

* Numbers of grid squares are approximate.

Typical questions in this section, adapted for use on the extract on the book cover, are:

Q. 10. Contrast the form of Kingston (Corfe extract 957797) with that of Worth Maltravers (974775).

Question 11 is typical of those on patterns and distribution:

Q. 11. Using the O.S. map extract provided (Corfe), give a reasoned account of the location and distribution of settlement. [OXF; adapted]

Do not neglect the importance of agriculture in settlement: information on slopes and drainage is found on every O.S. map. If you are given a geology map, use it for evidence of probable soil types developed on, e.g. clay, sandstone, chalk, and look for any alluvial deposits. Give also the negative factors.

As with landform questions, you may have to make divisions:

Q. 12. On a grid suggest a subdivision of the area, based upon the pattern of settlement. Add explanatory annotation to your map.

[13 marks] [LON; part]

Note the mark allowance. Always take care to use your time in relation to the marks available. In this question you must define what you understand by 'pattern of settlement' (p. 31).

Some Boards are trying to incorporate human geography theory into mapwork, notably the Alternative Scottish Higher and London. Thus:

Q. 13. With the aid of a diagram, compare Brighton and Hove with a model of a coastal holiday resort, bringing out similarities and differences. [SCO. A; part]

You would need to draw:
 (i) a model of a resort
(ii) a diagram of Brighton and Hove, using the same key,
then devote a paragraph to the similarities. The second section, on the differences, should be peppered with terms like 'whereas' (see p. 17). Map references should be given to illustrate every point you make. Note that you are not asked to account for the differences.

Nearest-neighbour analysis (see pp. 114–15) questions are beginning to appear on London Paper I, and might conceivably be set in conjunction with an O.S. map.

A small number of questions refer to settlement through time:

Q. 14. Explain how physical geography has influenced the development of settlement from earliest times until the present.   [NI]

Table 5.   Historical evidence on O.S. maps

Approximate date	Historical era	Evidence
2000 B.C. →	Neolithic (New Stone Age)	cairns, long barrows
1500 B.C.	Bronze Age	stone circles, tumuli (round barrows)
500 B.C.– A.D. 0	Iron Age	hill forts, field system (Corfe extract 956781)
A.D. 0–400	Roman	FORT VILLA CAMP ('Roman' type); Roman road, 'way'; place-name element: '-caster'
A.D. 400–1000	Anglo-Saxon	Place-name elements: '-wick', '-ham', '-ing' (Danish place-name element '-by')
1000–*c.*1500	Middle Ages	castle, abbey, town walls

Remember that ridgeways were important routes in pre-Roman times. Extra settlement detail on 1:25,000 sheets includes field sizes and parish boundaries. Finally, in answering a settlement mapwork question do not be too deterministic. For example, Church Knowle (Corfe extract 9481) *is* a scarp-foot village – but why did it develop at that particular point at the base of the scarp? Always indicate that you are aware of the many human factors which will have operated.

C. Land-use

Table 6 summarizes the information given by map symbols on the 1:25,000 and 1:50,000 sheets which may indicate land-use, or the factors affecting it.

In addition, the 1:25,000 sheets have a great deal of written information. Look out for words like 'pit', 'factory' or 'works'. Most 1:25,000 sheets used by examiners do not have much tourist information, so you must try to pick out tourist attractions as indicated by historic sites (in Gothic lettering), remembering that tourists rarely walk very far; and by National Trust signs. You must also be able to work out whether the countryside would be particularly attractive.

You should be looking for all the indications given in Table 6 when trying to determine the land-use. Make sure you are able to recognize these features.

Table 6.   Indications of land-use from O.S. map symbols

Type of information	1:25,000	1:50,000
Water supply	Marsh	Marsh
	Reeds	—
	Spring	—
	Well	—
	Dam	—
	Reservoir	—
	Wind pump	Wind pump
Agricultural	Field boundary: size and shape	—
	Orchard	Orchard
	Glasshouse	Glasshouse
	Rough grassland	Rough grazing*
	Bracken, heath*	—
Woodland	Coniferous	Woodland (no distinction on some sheets)
	Non-coniferous	
	Coppice	—
	Scrub	—
Industrial	Narrow-gauge line	Freight on mineral line
	Chimney	—
	Gravel pit	Open pit
	Sand pit	—
	Disused pit	—
	Quarry	Quarry
	Slag heap	Spoil heap*
Tourist	Youth Hostel	Youth Hostel
	National Trust property	National Trust property
	Site of Antiquity	Picnic, camp, caravan site
		Information Centre
		National Park boundary
Military	Danger areas	Danger areas

* On some sheets only.

Questions on land-use occur less frequently than those on landforms and settlement and require one or more of the following skills:

(a) DESCRIPTION OF LAND-USE. Deal with each category in turn. Here is a mnemonic for the categories you are likely to encounter: WATCH IT, i.e. Water – Agriculture – Trees (woodland) – Communications – Housing – Industry – Tourism and recreation. For each category, do not list the location of every single example but try to find a pattern of location either by bearing or height, slope, geology, etc. Then indicate its relative importance on the map in terms of the area of land used.

(b) EXPLANATION OF LAND-USE. You must be careful here to show that the explanations you put forward are possibilities, i.e. use 'may' and 'might have'. You should be looking first for physical factors: Relief, Drainage, Soils, Vegetation, Natural resources, Geology (if given). The initials of these are found in the word ReDiScoVeriNG. Secondly, there are the human factors that show up on an O.S. map. Power (rarely), Raw Materials (limited on map evidence to minerals and agricultural output, unspecified, except for orchards), Labour and Markets (both occur in towns and cities), and Transport. These initials appear in the word PeRaMbuLaTe. Questions 15 and 16 are typical:

Q. 15. Study the Corfe extract. Describe and suggest reasons for the distribution of the vegetation and agricultural land-use in relation to both the physical and the human factors that are evident on the map.

[JMB; adapted]

Q. 16. Describe and attempt to explain the distribution of the various types of woodland shown. [NI]

(c) DELIMITATION OF LAND-USE AREAS.

Q. 17. Divide the area on the Corfe extract into land-use zones.

For this, the categories in WATCH IT should be sufficient. You might divide the agricultural into intensive and extensive, and add 'military' should the map evidence indicate it.

(d) LAND-USE CONFLICTS. If you go through your land-use categories (above), it will be clear that there will be competing uses for the land.

Q. 18. Indicate clearly and discuss three areas of probable conflicts in land-use.

Try to find three different problems; don't rewrite the same problem in another form.

  Here is another 'conflict' question:

Q. 19. (a) In an area such as southern England (see O.S. map extract) or the Highlands of Scotland, traffic problems are created by the variety of road-users. With reference to the varying requirements of users such as farmers, truck drivers, and different types of holiday-makers, discuss the problems that can arise.

(b) The schemes listed below have been used in some places as ways of reducing particular traffic problems in holiday areas:

(i) construction of motorways;

(ii) creation of traffic-free areas;

(iii) bus or minibus links within and around beauty spots;

(iv) diversion of different types of traffic to different routes.

Choose two of these schemes and, for each, explain its advantages and disadvantages. [SCO. T]

By the time you have read this question, you may have forgotten that it is a 'map question'. Refer to the map, first when you choose, and then when you discuss, the feasibility of the schemes you choose. For example, in answer to (b) (iv), '. . . it would be difficult to divert traffic from Corfe Castle, 9681, because the chalk ridge running E–W from 935823 to 990817 at around 100 m blocks movement N–S'.

D. Communications

Most questions centre on the relationships between routes and relief. Gradients are important here, and you could improve your answer by calculating gradients along named sections. If you have time, you could draw long profiles of relevant sections of routes.

  Map exercise: Compare the routes taken eastwards from Corfe by the A-road and the railway (now disused) by drawing long profiles of these routes. (Hint: go over the contours in pencil and sort out which is which *on the map* before you start. Label all embankments, cuttings and tunnels.)

  When describing routes you should refer to:

(i) direction

(ii) distance – remember that roads which undulate greatly actually cover a much greater distance than appears on the map:

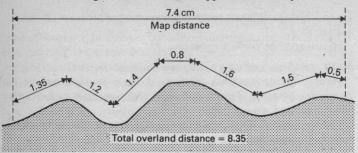

Fig. 10

(iii) elevation
(iv) slope (gradient)
 (v) constructional features: bridges, embankments, cuttings, tunnels.
When you consider the physical influences, remember:
 (i) geology. Cuttings are difficult to make in granite; and have to be reinforced in chalk. Bridges need firm foundations. Alluvium and clay can be badly drained
(ii) negative areas. Point out, and explain, the existence of areas with poor communications.

E. Industry

Map interpretation questions on industry are rare, probably because the information on an O.S. map is insufficient for a full explanation of industrial location.

Q. 20. Describe and explain the location of industry on the Corfe extract, using a labelled sketch map.

The procedure is the same as in any 'describe and explain' question.
 When you 'describe', do not give a minutely detailed, unstructured list. Try to group industry by type if you can, e.g. primary, secondary heavy, secondary light, tertiary and quaternary (p. 296). For each type, state its location in terms of *position* (p. 32), as well as grid reference.
 If you cannot distinguish the type of industry, use a classification based on location, e.g.:
 (i) dock-side
(ii) canal-side
(iii) rail-side

(iv) road-, especially motorway-side
 (v) C.B.D.-based (pp. 65–6) – this will mostly be tertiary and quaternary
(vi) other: e.g. tourism.

Industrial location is usually explained in terms of five basic factors: power, raw materials, labour, markets and transport. You can also mention multiplier effects (p. 334) and functional linkages.

As in all 'human' mapwork questions, do not be too **deterministic**, i.e. do not give a picture of man's activities being dominated by the factors you can see on the map.

Finally, remember that you must practise all the skills and try out all the hints in this section if you are to use any of them efficiently and quickly in the examination.

2. Reading other maps

Most mapwork questions are set on O.S. maps. The Southern Universities' Joint Board Paper III is a problem-solving paper which uses physiographic, **drift** (superficial geological deposits), soil and land classification maps, among others. If you are taking this Board, it is most important for you to have seen one of these papers. Do not be overawed: simply write your report on the problem set, following the instructions to the letter and using the structure given by the examiners. Thus, in Question 21, you can use points (a) to (d) as your headings.

Q. 21. Suppose that a development plan for York includes the creation of a new industrial estate with an accompanying housing scheme with leisure facilities and open space including a lake, newly planted woodland and a stadium. The whole scheme requires about 1½ sq. km of land (about a grid square and a half) and you can assume that the land you require, if not already developed, will be made available. You should try to avoid using land of high food-producing capability.

Suggest a suitable site for this major urban development proposal, paying attention to: (a) access; (b) site conditions (as far as you can infer them); (c) construction difficulties; (d) effect on agricultural land-use and on existing communities.

Write a brief report justifying your choice of area. Remember that good-quality farmland will be much more expensive to obtain than poor-quality land and its loss will mean a greater reduction in food output. On the other hand, difficult site conditions will raise the cost of the completed development.   [SUJB]

Refer to all the data given, under the appropriate headings. Do not neglect the O.S. extract, and use sketch maps to clarify any points you make.

Candidates taking other Boards will be expected to have seen Land-use, Geological and Soil Survey maps, and to be aware that they give information which an Ordnance Survey map cannot furnish.

3. Interpreting photographs

You should practise looking at maps with the relevant photographs as much as possible. Candidates often find it difficult to orientate an aerial photograph with a map. The basic procedure is as follows:
1) Draw a line down the centre of the photograph.
2) Pick out two features on or near this line, one in the background and one closer. Choose the most distinctive features you can: a church with a spire or tower, or a bridge, for example.
3) Find the chosen features on the map. Draw a pencil-line to join them up. This line from the nearer to the further feature shows you which way the camera was pointing.

You can improve the way you use any photograph in several ways:
1) You can deduce the absolute size of a feature if there is anything to take a scale from, e.g. a human or animal figure. Estimate in metres.
2) You can estimate relative sizes, e.g. of one cliff to another, by proportion (but do allow for perspective). Thus, for example, you might say 'the chalk cliff appears to be four times higher than the limestone cliff'.
3) You can refer to locations on the photograph by use of the terms 'foreground', 'middle-ground', 'rear-ground', 'right', 'left' and 'centre'. Or you can mark the photograph in ink, A, B, etc., and refer to these reference points. If you do, you must remember to put your name, number and centre number on the photograph and *give it in.*

Further reading

Speak, P., and A. H. C. Carter, *Map Reading and Interpretation*, Longman, 1981.
Russell, D. F. E., *Landforms and Maps*, Pergamon Press, 1975.

2. The collection of data

> He began, at school, in that fecund romance, Geography.
> (Thomas Wolfe, *Look Homeward, Angel*)

1. Published sources

A. Census returns

In 1801, Britain had its first full census. There were three occupational classifications: trade, manufacturing and handicraft; and ages were not recorded. There has been a census in every succeeding decade except 1941. Information on age and migration increased and the number of occupational categories rose to seven, and changed. In 1966 there was a mid-term census of a 10% sample of the population which gave even more detail.

The 1971 returns, now fully processed, will be in the main branch of your library. There is a review of the United Kingdom by county. Here you will find details of age, place of birth, sex, marital status, socio-economic group, housing conditions, household composition, car ownership and workplace given for 'administrative units' like county boroughs, rural districts, etc. Separate reports comment on commuting, migration, and so on. You would be well advised to use census returns from your local area to test the theories you learn in human geography, e.g. ZIPF* on migration; gravity models and commuting theories; or you can investigate changes through time in the age–sex or socio-economic structure of your town. Make a list of what you need to know, and ask the librarian for help.

The census has certain limitations:
1) Delay in publication. The processing of the 1981 census took over two years.
2) The administrative units used may take in large parts of countryside together with a town, making rural/urban contrasts difficult to unscramble.

---

* Names you must know are printed in capitals. An index of important geographers will be found on p. 421.

3) The boundary changes of the early 1970s make comparisons between the 1981 and earlier censuses difficult.

4) Employment classification in the censuses is not the same as the system commonly used by human geographers (p. 258).

5) The original returns (**enumerators' reports**) give detail for much smaller units. They are in the keeping of your local authority, but you need the permission of the Registrar-General to see them. Earlier enumerators' books are in the Public Record Office at Kew. From these you could reconstruct the social geography of your area, street by street, a century ago.

6) People sometimes lie on census returns!

B. Electoral registers

Also in the library is a house-by-house list of all registered voters. You will have to ask where the past electoral registers are. This can give an indication of population densities within a town, if used in conjunction with 6-inch O.S. maps to give you the sizes of the streets.

Not everyone registers, and minors (under 18 years old) are not listed.

C. Local-authority rate-books

These are in the Treasurer's department of the local Town Hall, and list the rateable value of property. You can use these in a number of ways:

(a) to make a morphological map of housing standards in a town

(b) to detect changes in the location of better-class housing over time

(c) to delimit the C.B.D. (pp. 65–6)

(d) to test the distance-decay curve (p. 268).

Re-rating occurs at odd intervals, so your material may be outdated.

Q. 1. Assess the usefulness for local studies in historical geography of either the official population census of the United Kingdom, or local-authority rate-books. [O and C]

Q. 2. Assess the value for geographical studies of the population censuses conducted in the United Kingdom. [NI]

We will see later how other publications, e.g. timetables and newspapers (p. 61), can be used in mapping urban fields.

The information in this chapter is often tested as part of a question.

Question 3 below is one-quarter of the whole question, but reflects the type of question which is being asked on AEB and JMB.

Q. 3. You are given the opportunity of doing six weeks' fieldwork on any aspect of British physical or human geography in which you are interested. You may work on your own or as leader of a group of ten people.
(a) What aspect of geography would you select to study and how might your work improve existing knowledge? [5 marks]
(b) What principal sources of information would you consult before commencing fieldwork? [5 marks] [NI; part; adapted]

D. Parish registers

Parish registers record births, deaths and marriages, and many pre-date the earliest census. Evidence of migration, epidemics, fertility and infant mortality can be found in them. Ask your vicar for help. E. A. Wrigley lists published parish registers in *An Introduction to English Historical Demography*. Remember that Catholics, Jews and Nonconformists are not listed.

Street directories, found in the library, describe the functions of each building in a town. Other statistical sources include the Registrar-General's *Quarterly Reports*, and the *Monthly Digest of Statistics*.

Only when you have made use of these sources will you be able to tackle questions on them. Quote your own experience wherever relevant.

2. Fieldwork

> His presence in the field made the difference of 40,000 men.
> (Wellington, on Napoleon)

Your presence in the field, gaining first-hand experience, may not be quite so crucial, but can sway the balance between pass and fail.

A. Sampling

In most investigations, the geographer has too much material – whether from published sources or his own fieldwork. He therefore

samples, i.e. studies a certain percentage of the material available to him.

In **systematic sampling** every *n*th item, point or quadrat is used. Thus, in a settlement study of an area, an alphabetical list of the settlements is made and every, say, tenth place is selected. For landscape investigations, either **point sampling** (a grid), **linear** or **transect sampling** (lines), or **quadrat sampling** (squares) can be used on the relevant map (see Fig. 11).

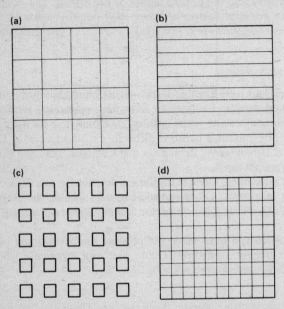

Fig. 11 *(a) Point samples, (b) linear sampling, (c) discontinuous quadrats, (d) continuous quadrats*

With the grid, the intersections mark the sample sites. For the linear sample, the proportions of different categories of, for example, land-use are recorded for each line, and subsequently totalled. Quadrats can be used similarly. Quadrats and lines must be parallel and equidistant, but their orientation is not important.

Random sampling uses irregular intervals, and can be based on grid co-ordinates, or pre-numbered items. Do not invent the intervals yourself – you might make a pattern unwittingly.

In Question 4, every house could be numbered for a real investigation (but not when answering the examination question), and then

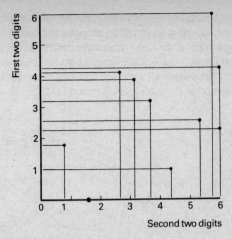

Fig. 12a *Sampling using random co-ordinates*

2360	4260
1807	2653
6057	3931
4126	0016
3237	1043

Fig. 12b *Random numbers used in Fig. 12a*

10% selected, using random-number tables. These numbers have four digits, as in Fig. 12b. There are 469 houses in the sample, so you would use the last three digits only and ignore any over 469.

Q. 4. Fig. 13 (overleaf) shows part of a British town which contains 469 households living in a variety of housing districts. You are about to carry out a field survey to examine the relationship between house type, age of house and the number of persons under the age of sixteen years.
(a) Describe the types of sampling that you can use.
(b) What are the advantages and disadvantages of the sampling methods which you have described. [AEB; part]

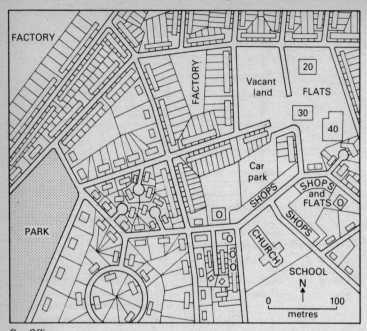

O = Offices

30 = Number of flats in a block

Fig. 13 *See Question 4*

Stratified sampling could also be used in Question 4. In this method, the area under investigation is divided into relevant zones or **strata**.* For Question 4, the strata might be house type; for a land-use question the strata might be rock type. Samples are then taken from each stratum according to its importance. In Question 4 there are 90 flats, i.e. 90/469 × 100 = 19% of the housing total. Therefore 19% of the sample should come from the flats.

To answer sampling questions well, you *must* show diagrams. Quote your own practical work in illustration wherever relevant.

Q. 5. (a) Describe what is meant by the following techniques: random point sampling, systematic linear sampling, stratified point sampling.

* Do not confuse with geological strata.

(b) For each of the three selected techniques, describe in detail one geographical example to show how it might be used.

(c) Identify the strengths and weaknesses of each of the three techniques as methods of obtaining geographical data.   [NI]

A 'geographical example' may be taken from your own fieldwork or from a classroom exercise you have done – even a practical question from a past paper is acceptable. The strengths and weaknesses of the techniques are outlined in Table 7:

Table 7.   Sampling types: strengths and weaknesses

Sampling type	Advantages	Disadvantages
Systematic	Simple. Linear sampling most time-effective sampling method. No previous knowledge of area required	Sampling interval can coincide with regular geographical variations: biased sample results
Random	Representative sample achieved	Total numbers in sample must be known first. Chance numbers *can* coincide with geographical variations
Stratified	Highly representative sample. Fewer samples needed	Preliminary survey needed to determine categories (strata)

Entire questions on sampling are rare, but many questions incorporate sampling techniques. For the value of sample data, see Chapter 5.

Further reading

Toyne, P., and P. T. Newby, *Techniques in Human Geography*, Macmillan, 1971, pp. 1–14.

B. Topographical surveying

Cambridge asks detailed survey questions and O and C, SUJB and AEB ask more general questions, but anyone doing fieldwork should be able to survey.

(i) Linear (flat outline) surveys

(a) CHAIN TRAVERSE.* **Chains** (iron bars, joined by oval links) are better than measuring tapes: they do not stretch. Two people are needed in order to turn the chain forward and record the number of turns. The best chain surveys:

1) cover the survey area with triangles, as nearly equilateral as possible
2) have lines closely passing the features to be mapped
3) have the angles between each traverse checked (forward and back bearings) with a sextant: compasses are easily deflected by nearby iron, and are inaccurate on slopes
4) can be tested by a **check line** (B–D on Fig. 14), constructed and measured after the map is drawn. The corresponding line on the ground is then measured. The two lengths should agree.

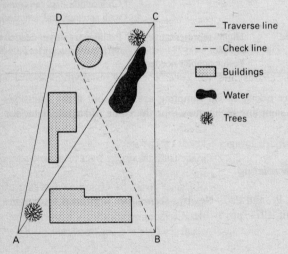

Fig. 14 *Traverse lines and check line*

---

* A traverse is a survey line.

Right-angled measurements are then taken from the traverse to the features being surveyed (Fig. 15).

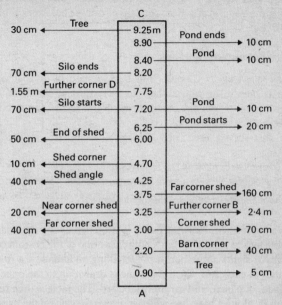

Fig. 15 *Part of a traverse from line A–C, Fig. 14*

The strengths and weaknesses of this surveying method are as follows:

Chaining: advantages – simple to undertake and to understand
                              – cheap
              disadvantages – needs two people
                              – inaccurate on slopes over 5°, unless step chaining is used*
                              – obstacles must be circumnavigated with care and measurements sometimes have to be calculated trigonometrically: a major source of inaccuracy (see Fig 16, overleaf).

---

* Consult a specialized book.

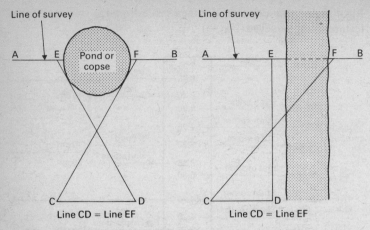

Fig. 16 *Avoiding obstacles in chaining (after Garner)*

(b) PLANE TABLING. Drawing paper is stretched over a flat board with adjustable legs to level it. From a point near one of the bottom corners, the surveyor sights a number of points along an **alidade** – a ruler with sight vanes at each end. Each sight-line is drawn on to the paper along the alidade, in pencil, and carefully labelled. The table is then removed to station B, along a base-line which is drawn to scale on the paper. The stations should be 'fixed points' from an O.S. map, the table being orientated with a trough compass. The same objects are then re-sighted. Each object's position is found at the intersection of the two relevant rays.

Plane tabling: advantages – 'instant' map
– sightings can pass over water obstacles
– only one linear measurement necessary
disadvantages – rain distorts the paper
– inaccurate where triangles are badly shaped.

Question 6 underlines the need for first-hand experience if you are to answer satisfactorily.

Q. 6. Choose a simple topographical surveying technique.
(i) Describe how it was used in a project or exercise.
(ii) Discuss its strengths and weaknesses.   [JMB; half]

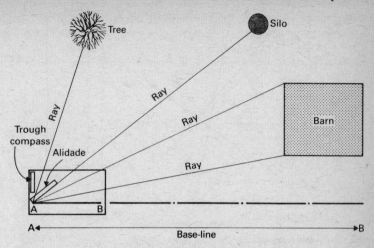

Not to scale

Fig. 17 *Plane tabling*

RESECTIONING WITH A PLANE TABLE: If the table is not at a 'fixed point', its location can be found by **resection**: the table is orientated with a trough compass, the alidade pivoted in turn on three fixed points, and rays are drawn. The fixed points should be chosen so that the angles of intersection of the rays lie between 30° and 150°. The meeting point of the rays determines the location of the table.

Often, the rays do not meet exactly, but form a 'triangle of error'. To find your true position, move the table either right or left and lightly re-draw the rays. If *all* the rays have rotated in the *same* direction (i.e. clockwise or anti-clockwise), you are inside the triangle. If so:

1) choose a point inside the triangle
2) rub out all preceding rays
3) run the alidade from this 'trial point' to the furthest fixed point
4) draw rays from the other two points. They should all meet. If they don't, repeat from (1) until the triangle of error has shrunk to a dot.

If you are outside the triangle of error, you are in one of six segments (see Fig. 18, overleaf). You are either to the right of *all* the points, i.e. segment III, or left of them *all*, i.e. segment VI. Locate your trial point in the segment where the longest ray must move the furthest distance (in this case VI), then proceed as from (2) above.

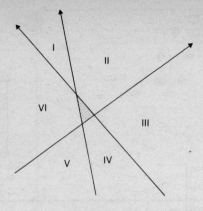

'Triangle of error' shaded

Fig. 18 *Trial point outside the triangle of error*

Resection is quicker than location by linear measurement, and more accurate. It enables the surveyor to fix a spot without having to visit any other points, or to mark it.

Q. 7. (a) *What are the advantages of resection in mapping topographical detail?*

   (b) *Fig. 19a shows an area to be mapped by plane table. Point Z is to be fixed by resection. Why were control points A, B and C particularly suitable?*

   (c) *Resection from A, B and C produced the triangle of error in Fig. 19b.*

   (i) *Estimate and mark the true map position of Z.*

   (ii) *How did you determine this position?*

Once you know whether you are inside or outside the triangle of error, you can estimate your position by drawing back-rays (Fig. 20). Each ray should be proportional to the length of the sight-line it is taken from.

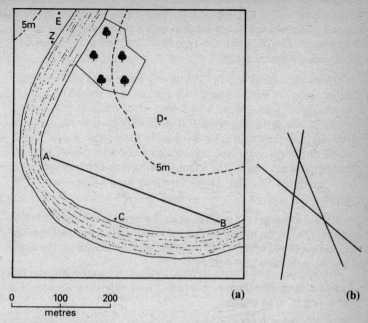

(a)

(b)

Fig. 19 *See Question 7*

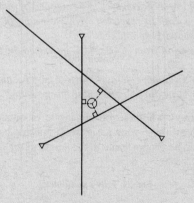

Fig. 20 *Fixing by means of back-rays*

(ii) Slopes

If a theodolite is used in conjunction with a plane table, heights can be surveyed. This, however, is expensive. Two common methods of angular measurement are by:

(a) SCIENTIFIC INSTRUMENTS. The survey line should run along the steepest slope, at right angles to the contour, and should be marked with chains or tapes. Start at the bottom of the slope. A second surveyor stands at the first **break of slope** (abrupt gradient change), and you should aim your sight at his eye level to allow for your own height. Record the slope angle and take forward and back sights for subsequent points as a check. The Suunto clinometer is easier to use, but is only accurate to ½°. The Abney level can record differences of 10 seconds.

(b) PITTY'S PANTOMETER consists of an H-shaped frame with rotatable uprights. One of the uprights has a spirit level, also a protractor at the intersection of the upright and crossbar, thereby measuring the angle of each step (usually 1 m) directly.

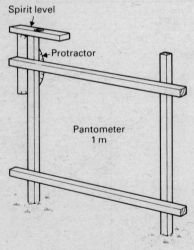

Fig. 21 *Pitty's pantometer*

For a valley area, random sample slopes should be surveyed. The profiles should be drawn with a V.E. of 2.

These morphological mapping techniques can give detail which does not show on 1:25,000 maps, particularly the following slope elements:

straight (rectilinear); over 45° (free face); concave (waning slope); convex (waxing slope). Concave slopes become flatter as they descend from you, while convex slopes become steeper. Breaks of slope are shown by a V-shaped symbol on the steeper side of the slope. These slope elements are of importance to geomorphologists since each is said to reflect the process at work.

These techniques are also useful for studies of valley asymmetry (p. 29) and river terraces, which are too small to feature at a scale of 1:25,000.

In Question 8, 'other information' might include artificial drainage; or vegetation and geology, if you are to use stratified sampling.

Q. 8. How would you undertake a study of slope morphology in a valley (about 8 km long) and what apparatus, maps and other information would you need for your fieldwork? [SUJB]

Q. 9. For the drainage basin illustrated below (Fig. 22), how would you test in the field the theory that the average slopes of successively higher-order streams decrease as you go up the order?

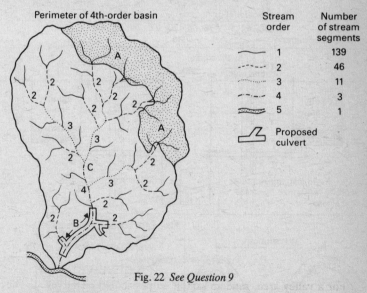

Stream order	Number of stream segments
1	139
2	46
3	11
4	3
5	1

Proposed culvert

Fig. 22 *See Question 9*

One major difficulty in investigating first-order streams is actually finding where the stream begins in the field. No one has decided the point at which a **rill** becomes a stream.

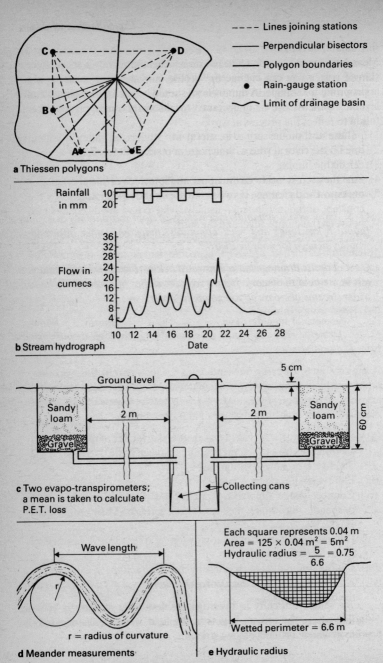

a Thiessen polygons

- - - - Lines joining stations
——— Perpendicular bisectors
■■■ Polygon boundaries
● Rain-gauge station
〜 Limit of drainage basin

Rainfall in mm

b Stream hydrograph

Flow in cumecs

Date

c Two evapo-transpirometers; a mean is taken to calculate P.E.T. loss

Ground level

Sandy loam

Gravel

2 m

2 m

Sandy loam

Gravel

5 cm

60 cm

Collecting cans

d Meander measurements

Wave length

r = radius of curvature

e Hydraulic radius

Each square represents 0.04 m
Area = 125 × 0.04 m^2 = 5m^2
Hydraulic radius = $\frac{5}{6.6}$ = 0.75

Wetted perimeter = 6.6 m

Fig. 23 *Terms and techniques in river investigations*

(iii) Beach surveys

Measuring tapes are difficult to use on beaches; simply by walking over shingle ridges you can change the profile, and the pantometer is not appropriate for shingle. A dumpy level should be used with a tripod and levelling staff. A tape is not necessary, as distances can be calculated as follows:

1) put the staff on the spot to be surveyed
2) line up the central wire with the centre mark of the staff
3) centre the bubble
4) take the recordings from the upper and lower wires
5) multiply the difference between the upper and lower readings by the constant of the instrument – usually 100 – to find the direct distance between the dumpy level and the staff.*

Other beach fieldwork includes sieving samples of material to find the distribution of particle sizes, testing pebble sizes along a shingle spit and analysing the roundness of the shingle particles – do they get progressively rounder with distance from a river mouth?

(iv) River investigations

Q. 10. Describe how you would investigate the hydrological characteristics of a small stream. [LON]

A major source of error for candidates is illustrated in this question, i.e. a technical term which, if misunderstood, can produce irrelevant answers. **Hydrological** means to do with water, especially its movement. Relevant investigations are summarized below.

(a) RIVER-WATER INPUT: PRECIPITATION WITHIN CATCHMENT AREA:
  (i) Determine size of catchment area (drainage basin).
  (ii) Site five rain-gauges within basin.
  (iii) Plot these sites on base map.
  (iv) Connect gauge sites with straight lines. Bisect these lines with perpendiculars which meet to form a series of **Thiessen polygons** (Fig. 23a).
  (v) Determine the area of each polygon. Express it as a fraction of total catchment area.
  (vi) Multiply rainfall at each gauge by its area fraction.
  (vii) Add the results from each polygon to give total precipitation over the catchment area.

* A cheaper surveying method is given in full in King, C. A. M., *Physical Geography*, Basil Blackwell, 1980, pp. 74–5.

Rainfall figures can be collected hourly, daily or weekly, according to the nature of the information required.

If you do this exercise, or even think carefully about it, you will realize that there will be many practical problems. You should be aware of these, as examiners often ask about them.

(b) RIVER FLOW:

(I) Discharge:

(i) Record channel depth at ½-m intervals.

(ii) Plot river cross-section on squared paper.

(iii) Calculate cross-sectional area in m^2.

(iv) Determine velocity in m/sec by

(a) timing a floating object over a measured distance and multiplying result by 0.8 (since surface flow is faster than mean flow), or

(b) using a current meter held at two-thirds of the depth. Several readings should be taken for either method.

(v) Discharge in cumecs = velocity in m/sec × cross-sectional area.

(II) Variations in velocity at different points in the channel.

Investigations (a) and (b)(I) can be combined to make a hydrograph (Fig. 23b).

(c) RIVER-WATER LOSS: EVAPORATION. This cannot be directly measured from the river, but **potential evapo-transpiration** can be calculated as precipitation minus percolation (see Fig. 23c).

(v) Other river investigations

(a) LOAD:

(I) Dissolved load is determined by chemical analysis of the river water. For dissolved limestone, E.D.T.A. tablets are added to 100 ml of water until the colour changes from purple to blue. 'Hardness' is expressed in the number of tablets used.

(II) Suspended load is measured by taking samples of water at various depths. Sediment is filtered out.

(III) Bed load cannot be measured without expensive technology.

(b) STREAM-COURSE ANALYSIS. Data can be taken from maps but, where these are inadequate, use a traverse (p. 50). Measure wave length, river width and radius of curve. You can investigate the following relationships:

- hydraulic radius (ratio of cross-sectional area to wetted perimeter; see Fig. 23e) and load
- wave length and discharge (Fig. 23d)
- radius and depth (Fig. 23d).

Sinuosity is the amount a river meanders within its valley, and is calculated by dividing total stream length by valley length. Different sinuosity values for different rivers might be due to differences in discharge.

Q. 11. What sources of information, criteria, and methods of analysis would you use in making a quantitative comparison between two contrasting rivers? [SUJB; adapted]

*Q. 12. What techniques could **you** use to determine the characteristics of a sediment?* [O and C]

(vi) Soil investigations
Questions on fieldwork in soils are rare; soil theory is very frequently questioned (pp. 224–7). However, you should be aware of the following field investigations:

(a) EXAMINATION OF SOIL PROFILE:
  (I) Soil pit. The turves are removed for eventual replacement and the pit is dug down to the parent rock. The profile is cleaned with a knife and the colour and depth of each horizon noted. Notes should be made of the nature of the boundaries (sharp or blurred); and their shape (smooth, wavy or discontinuous).
  (II) Augering. The auger brings up soil samples but does not indicate the horizons as clearly as the soil pit.

(b) DEPTH OF SOIL is most easily determined using an auger and metre-rules.

(c) SOIL TEXTURE is determined by using soil sieves and plotting the result on a soil triangle.* A field assessment can be made: sand can be seen as individual grains; silt feels slippery but not sticky; clay is sticky when wet but hard when dry; humus-rich soils feel greasy.

*Q. 13. Explain how **you** would collect data so as to establish the nature of the relationship between slope angle and depth of soil within a small valley.* [O and C; part]

* For a full explanation, see Strahler, A. N., *Physical Geography*, 4th edn, Wiley, 1975, p. 295.

3. Fieldwork in human geography

A. Questionnaires

In many investigations of human geography, relevant published information is not available; published statistics do not give detail for small areas, and opinions are rarely recorded. For studies on spheres of influence, shopping patterns, planning decisions and central-place status, among others, questionnaires are an important data source. Thus, a questionnaire is one method of data collection in:

Q. 14. A new superstore is due to open in six months' time at a peripheral urban location. Describe how you would collect appropriate data to assess the impact of this store on the existing spatial shopping patterns.

[O and C; part]

You should therefore know that a good questionnaire:
  (i) samples a representative proportion of the population. This means judging socio-economic class by eye. Never ask!
 (ii) has clear, concise questions: people do not want to linger
(iii) has a majority of questions answerable by YES or NO to facilitate processing
(iv) has questions which can easily be answered in the absence of the informed investigator
 (v) gives clear options for replies so that data can be compared easily; e.g. in a 'status' survey, ask, 'Have you travelled: (a) less than 1 mile; (b) 1–5 miles; (c) 5–10 miles; or (d) further?' Don't simply ask, 'Where do you come from?'

Q. 15. Consider in detail some of the problems likely to be encountered in undertaking a questionnaire survey to determine the sphere of influence of a small market town. [O and C]

Among your problems might be:
(a) acquiring the relevant census information on age and socio-economic status for the appropriate area (pp. 41–2). You will need this for stratified sampling – and should describe this technique in your answer
(b) finding statistically suitable subjects. You can ask for details of jobs and ages, but people can refuse to answer . . . or lie! You may wait endlessly for a 25-year-old group-B male
(c) getting a correspondence in your answers. One person's 'rarely' is another's 'often'. Use a range of answers as in (v) above.

Other difficulties are found in trying to satisfy the requirements of points (ii), (iii) and (iv) above. When writing about these you must think of examples to illustrate your answer, preferably from your own experience. You should know the strengths and weaknesses of all the geographical techniques you use.

B. Sphere of influence

This is the area surrounding a town or city within which that urban centre has major cultural, social and economic influence, and can also be called the **umland** or **urban field**.

There are two methods of delimiting a sphere of influence:
(a) by fieldwork:
    (i) questionnaire surveys of shoppers, film-goers, workers, etc., in the town
   (ii) delivery area of major stores
  (iii) catchment areas of schools, hospitals
  (iv) newspaper circulation areas
   (v) frequency of bus services.

You will find that these 'fields' do not overlap neatly.
(b) theoretically. This involves the 'break point' formula:

$$\text{distance of break point from A} = \frac{\text{distance between A and B}}{1 + \sqrt{\dfrac{\text{population B}}{\text{population A}}}}$$

where A and B are two towns.

Check past papers to see if your Board will give this equation on the practical paper; Oxford examiners do not.

Q. 16.   *(i) Using the formula of the 'gravity model' provided and the data on the worksheet, calculate the 'break point' distance between Norwich and King's Lynn and between Norwich and Bury St Edmunds. (Calculate to the nearest whole kilometre.) Plot your results on the map and draw in the theoretical sphere of influence of Norwich.*

     (ii) Suggest why the size of towns in terms of population may not be a suitable index of a town's attraction. What alternative indices may be used?

   (iii) An alternative delimitation of the sphere of influence of Norwich is shown on the map based on the frequency of bus services. Suggest why this method may have less relevance to present-day patterns than when it was devised in the 1950s.

> (iv) *Outline and discuss two further methods by which the sphere of influence of Norwich could be determined.* [SCO. A]

As a revision exercise you should attempt Question 16, part (i), based on your local area. Crude measures of population are not really good enough: 'Just as the weights of molecules of different elements are unequal, so should the "weights" of different kinds of people be different.'*

Some geographers multiply population by mean per capita income; others use numbers of retail outlets. You must know the weakness of using population as a factor. 'Distance' can mean very different things when measured by cost or time rather than by simple mileage.

With this, as in all fieldwork techniques in this book, JMB tend to ask you, (a) how you used the technique, and (b) what weaknesses and strengths you found. This stresses the importance of undertaking the exercise above.

C. Shopping surveys

Spheres of influence can also be plotted for shopping centres within a town. You might investigate 'orders' of shopping centres (Fig. 24) or the variation in the field of one centre according to the nature of the good or service. To answer a question on this topic well, you must be able to explain the procedure, illustrating wherever possible from your own experience, and you must know the strengths and weaknesses of your method.

D. Central-place status

A **central place** provides goods and services to the surrounding area. This is part of central-place theory, but note that you are *not* required to discuss this theory in Question 17.

Q. 17. Critically examine possible ways of measuring central-place status. [LON]

You are asked to 'critically examine', i.e. describe, giving strengths and weaknesses. Try underlining the 'command words' in a question: it will focus your thoughts on to the correct approach.

---

* Isard, W., *et al.*, *Methods of Regional Analysis*, 1960; but quoted in the accessible Haggett, P., *Locational Analysis in Human Geography*, Edward Arnold, 1977.

Table 8.   Ways of measuring central-place status

Central-place-status measurement	Advantages	Disadvantages
1) Number and variety of businesses	Indicates economic importance	Difficult to establish numbers employed
2) Size of population	Figures easily accessible	Crude figures do not indicate economic importance (p. 62)
3) Size of 'field'/'umland'	Shows extent of influence	Fields vary with function
4) Population of umland	Good indicator in human and economic terms	Fields difficult to delineate
5) Range of retail outlets	Easily investigated	Can be artificially inflated by seasonal tourism

The last method in Table 8 was further developed by Everson and Fitzgerald, who produced a method of establishing relative status using 'ranked' services as in Fig. 24.*

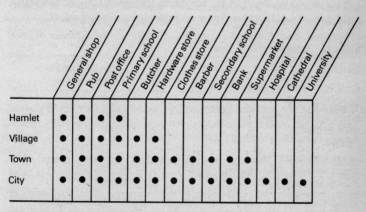

● indicates presence of function

Fig. 24 *Settlement status defined by indicator functions*

* Everson, J. A., and B. P. Fitzgerald, *Settlement Patterns*, Longman, 1969.

CHRISTALLER himself defined **centrality** as the ratio between all the services provided by a town and the services provided for the residents only. Let us take telephones as an example.

1) A town has 25,000 inhabitants and 5,000 telephones.
2) The umland has 1 phone per 50 persons.
3) Therefore expected number of phones $= \dfrac{25,000}{50} = 500$.
4) Ratio of actual to expected: 5,000:50, i.e. 10:1.
5) Therefore index of centrality $= 10$.

Settlement indices use another technique to measure status:

1) Count the numbers of one service function in all the towns in the area under investigation.
2) Find the **functional centrality value** for that function using the formula F.C.V. $= 1/n \times 100$, where n = total number of functions. (Thus, if there are 34 dentists in the area, F.C.V. for dentists $= 1/34 \times 100 = 2.9$.)
3) Find the F.C.V. for a range of functions.
4) For each town, multiply the relevant F.C.V.s by the number of outlets in that town, e.g. if the town has 17 dentists, $17 \times 2.9 = 49.3$.
5) Sum the values derived from (4), for each town (= **standard index**).
6) Towns can now be ranked: the higher the S.I., the higher the status.

You should be aware of the minimum (**threshold**) population which justifies a service function. Some examples are given in Table 9:

Table 9.   Threshold populations

Function	Threshold population of catchment area
Doctor's surgery	3,500
Shops, primary school	4,500
Main post office	7,000
Library	15,000
Bank, secondary school	18,000
Swimming pool, disco, cinema	60,000
Technical college	90,000

Source: Bradford, M. G., and W. A. Kent, *Human Geography: Theories and Their Applications*, Oxford University Press, 1977.

E. Delimitation of the central business district

This, the **C.B.D.**, is the commercial, social and cultural core of a city, where the chief shops and offices are concentrated. It is usually the focus of the urban transport system. You should incorporate this definition when answering *any* question on the C.B.D.

The most commonly used method of mapping the C.B.D. was devised by Vance and Murphy* as follows:

1) Obtain a large-scale map of the city centre.
2) By fieldwork – writing to or visiting businesses, etc. – find
   (i) total floor area of each building
   (ii) total floor area devoted to C.B.D. activities, i.e. retailing, entertainment, finance, business administration.

Using this information:

3) Derive the **height index**:

   i.e. $\dfrac{\text{area devoted to C.B.D. functions}}{\text{ground-floor area}}$.

4) Deduce the **intensity ratio**:

   i.e. $\dfrac{\text{area devoted to C.B.D. functions} \times 100}{\text{total floor area}}$.

E.g. a building has a ground-floor area of 40,000 m^2 and a total floor area of 156,000 m^2, of which 90,000 m^2 is devoted to C.B.D. activities:

$$\text{height index} = \frac{90,000}{40,000} = 2.25$$

$$\text{intensity ratio} = \frac{90,000 \times 100}{156,000} = 57.7\%.$$

The C.B.D. occurs where the height index is greater than 1 *and* the intensity ratio is over 50%. These figures are calculated for every building in the city centre and the extent of the C.B.D. is determined. Obviously this information will be difficult to find and will take a long time to collect and process.

Additionally, visit your town planning department and ask them for their maps of the planning areas of the town. This is much quicker.†

* See Yeates, M. H., and B. J. Garner, *The North American City*, 3rd edn, Harper & Row, 1980, Chapter 12.

† J. Taussik suggested this time-saving, and perfectly valid, method.

Q. 18. Discuss, from examples of fieldwork which you have carried out, the problems involved in identifying the 'central business district'.

[OXF; part]

It is problems like these that you should outline clearly in Question 18, as well as the method. Vance and Murphy's method works best with American city 'blocks'; but these are rarely found in England.

With another method, you can use the rateable values of all the properties in the area. This information is readily available from the Town Hall.

1) List rateable values of city-centre properties.
2) Calculate from maps, or measure, the street frontage of each property.
3) Calculate 'foot frontage value' for each building by using the formula:

$$\frac{RV \times 3}{L \times 10}$$

    where RV = rateable value
           L = length of frontage in metres.

4) Find the **peak land value** (highest foot frontage value).
5) All buildings with a foot frontage value of 5% or more of the peak are said to be within the C.B.D.

This figure of 5% is one derived from a number of American experiments, and may well not apply to your town.

With a large town, it may be necessary to **sample**, using transects.

Other areas of a town can be delimited, e.g. social areas. Housing conditions are reflected in rateable values. With the aid of a large-scale plan and a local-authority rate-book you can mark the rateable value of every dwelling in a town.

Q. 19. Discuss, from examples of fieldwork carried out, the problems involved in identifying social areas of a town. [OXF; part]

Question 19 would be an excellent fieldwork exercise. The difficulties of getting up-to-date maps, classifying highly rated but multiply occupied dwellings, establishing figures of rateable values to correspond to 'poor', 'middle-class' and 'high-class' housing, and working with out-of-date rateable values (p. 42) may readily be imagined; but only when you attempt this exercise will other problems emerge – which you will be able to write about with conviction!

Further reading

For studies based on building density, see Toyne, P., and P. T. Newby, *Techniques in Human Geography*, Macmillan, 1971, pp. 122–4.

3. Visual representation of data: graphs, cartography and weather maps

> . . . the pictures for the page atone.
> (Alexander Pope, *The Dunciad*)

Almost all geographical writing is improved by maps, diagrams and graphs. You may be directly examined on the techniques necessary for these on a practical paper; in any case attention will be paid to how data are represented in order (a) to make your own writing clearer; (b) to answer data-response questions (see Chapter 7).

Graphs

Values on graphs are called variables. One set is usually **independent** of the other (e.g. time, class groupings). The other variable fluctuates (e.g. rainfall, number of occurrences), and is **dependent**. The Dependent variable is always plotted on the Vertical, or Ordinate, Y, axis; the Independent variable is on the Abscissa or X axis (mnemonic: Drinking Very Old Yoghurt Is Always eXcruciating). Never neglect this convention.

The type of graph used depends on the nature of the data. **Discrete**, or **non-continuous**, data can only take certain values: numbers of people are discrete; you can't have half-people. **Grouped** data are those which have been compressed into classes, in the way teachers group marks (e.g. 60–70% = class B), and are also discrete. Non-continuous data are shown on **histograms**.

If the groups are very small, or the data are **continuous**, continuous lines can be drawn to construct **frequency polygons** and **cumulative-frequency polygons**. Continuous data could have *any* value within a given range. Thus temperatures can be 5.1°C, 5.2°C, 5.3°C and so on. Any figures involving an exact measurement are deemed to be continuous data.

A. Histograms

First choose your classes:

(i) This can be done by drawing a **scatter diagram**, where every figure of the data set is plotted as a point. If any obvious groupings show up, they are the **ideal** class limits (Fig. 25a).

(ii) However, classes should be of regular size, either in **arithmetical progression**: 0–2; 3–4; 5–6; or in **geometrical progression**: 0–1; 2–4; 5–8; 9–16.

(iii) The number of classes should not exceed 5 times the log of the number of observations. Thus, for 49 observations, the maximum number of classes would be $5 \times \log 49 = 5 \times 1.690 = 8.45$; suggesting 8 groupings.

It is often difficult to satisfy the conditions in points (i), (ii) and (iii), and compromises are often made.

The **frequency** (or number) of occurrences is always plotted on the ordinate axis, which must start from zero. The classes are marked on the abscissa and the graph shows up as a series of blocks (Fig. 25b).

Remember: no statistical grouping = no histogram. A histogram is *not* the same thing as a bar graph, which represents *different* items by a series of columns.

Frequency polygons

These use **class marks**, i.e. the mid-point of each class. Thus the class mark for a grouping of 0–20 is 10, and the marks occupy the abscissa, frequency again being recorded on the ordinate. Join the points up as straight lines: only statisticians can calculate the curves correctly to create frequency curves.

Q. 1. Below are totals of annual rainfall in mm (to the nearest 25) for Minot (North Dakota) for a recent period.

550, 425, 475, 475, 475, 550, 575, 500, 500, 500, 475, 600, 525, 450, 450, 475, 500, 450, 400, 525, 375, 500, 475, 450, 500, 575, 525, 500, 550, 450.

(a) On graph paper plot a histogram to represent these data. Using the same axes, draw a frequency polygon. Which of the histogram or the frequency polygon gives the better representation of the data, and why?

(b) By comparing areas beneath the histogram, answer the following questions.

    (i) How many years in every ten received the modal rainfall in the period of the record?

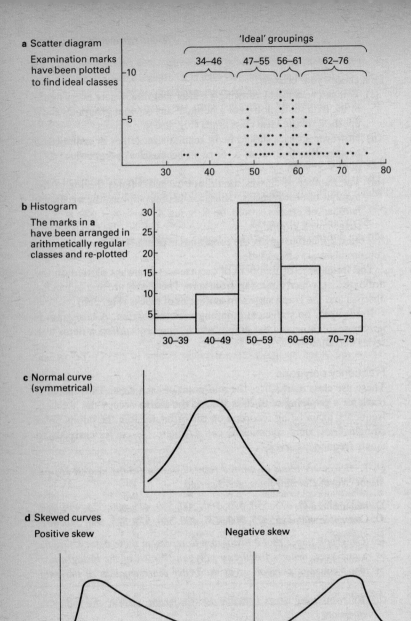

Fig. 25 *Data in graph forms*

(ii) *Wheat farmers in the area know that they get their highest crop yields when the rainfall total lies between 450 mm and 525 mm. How frequently did such rainfall totals occur?*

(c) *What limitations does this form of statistical analysis have for the wheat farmer of the area and how might these limitations be lessened?*

[SCO. A]

Frequency curves

These have characteristic shapes. Fig. 25c shows the symmetrical curve which is normally found most often. It is therefore known as a **normal curve**.

Asymmetrical or **skewed** curves are shown in Fig. 25d. A skew to the left is a **positive** skew, one to the right is a **negative** skew.

Relative-frequency histograms

These can be drawn by expressing the frequency in each class as a percentage of the total frequency of occurrences. The ordinate scale now shows percentages.

Cumulative-frequency polygons

These are based on figures like those in Tables 10 and 11 (below and overleaf).

Table 10. Employment structure of selected countries

Employment category	U.S.A. (1976)	France (1975)	Czechoslovakia (1975)	Pakistan (1975)
			(millions)	
A. Agriculture and fishing	2.84	2.01	1.12	11.22
B. Mining and construction	5.20	1.84	0.72	0.20
C. Manufacturing	18.80	6.33	2.83	2.83
D. Commerce and servicing	39.28	6.15	0.75	3.61
E. Transport	5.19	0.83	0.71	0.37
F. Public administration	4.20	3.05	1.02	1.72
G. Armed forces	2.33	0.49	0.18	0.42
H. Other occupations	4.21	0.36	0.08	0.05
Total employed	82.05	21.06	7.41	20.42

This is how Table 11 was calculated (look at the columns for Pakistan in both tables):

Table 11.   Rank orders and cumulative percentages of workers employed in various employment categories

U.S.A.		France		Czechoslovakia		Pakistan	
rank	cum. %	rank	cum. %	rank	cum. %	rank	cum. %
1 (D)	47.87	1 (C)	30.05	1 (C)	38.19	1 (A)	54.95
2 (C)	70.78	2 (D)	59.25	2 (A)	53.30	2 (D)	72.62
3 (B)	77.11	3 (F)	73.73	3 (F)	67.06	3 (C)	86.48
4 (E)	83.43	4 (A)	83.27	4 (D)	77.18	4 (F)	94.91
5 (H)	88.56	5 (B)	92.01	5 (B)	86.89	5 (G)	
6 (F)	93.68	6 (E)	95.95	6 (E)	96.47	6 (E)	
7 (A)	97.14	7 (G)	98.27	7 (G)	98.90	7 (B)	
8 (G)	99.98	8 (H)	99.98	8 (H)	99.98	8 (H)	

N.B.:   (i) figures do not always sum to 100% due to rounding
        (ii) cum. % = cumulative %

1) Group A has the largest number of workers.
2) The number of workers has been expressed as a percentage of the total:

$$\frac{11.22}{20.42} \times 100 = 54.95\%.$$

3) This percentage is entered under rank 1.
4) Group D is the next largest: 3.61.

5) Percentage group D $= \dfrac{3.61}{20.42} \times 100 = 17.67\%.$

6) This figure is added to percentage group A: 54.95 + 17.67 = 72.62%, the figure for rank 2.

If JMB candidates have to draw a cumulative-frequency polygon, they will be given clear instructions. However, you can be given such a polygon to interpret, and you will be expected to know the principles upon which it has been drawn up.

Examiners' major complaints on the execution of graph questions are:
  (i) poor scaling: usually values are too cramped on the ordinate
 (ii) inaccurate plotting
(iii) failure to interpret graphs (see Chapter 7).

Question 2 demonstrates clearly the way examiners want to see an understanding of the data you have worked on. This understanding often draws on other parts of the syllabus.

Table 12.

	J	F	M	A	M	J	J	A	S	O	N	D
Rainfall (mm)	55	45	40	40	46	49	55	66	52	54	66	55
	Annual total: 623 mm Range: 520–710 mm											
Potential transpiration (mm)	1	10	32	57	85	95	95	78	50	22	5	0
	Winter total: 70 mm Summer total: 460 mm											
Sunshine (hours/day)	1.7	2.4	3.9	5.5	6.7	6.9	6.2	5.6	4.7	3.5	2.0	1.6
Air temp. (°C)	2.9	3.4	5.4	8.4	11.2	14.4	16.1	16.0	14.4	11.0	6.6	4.3
Day length (hrs)	9.5	11.0	13.0	15.2	17.3	18.5	17.9	16.0	13.9	11.8	10.0	9.1
	Growing season 248 days: 26 Mar.–29 Nov.											

Source: Ministry of Agriculture, with permission.

Q. 2. *Table 12 gives climatic data for north Norfolk.*
(a) *How could the data be represented to bring out important features and relationships?*

(b) *Comment on the probable seasonal drainage and irrigation needs of Norfolk farmland.*

(c) *How far might the data help a farmer to decide on the type of agriculture to practise on his land, and what other climatic data might he require?* [SUJB]

Part (a) indicates a written answer, but it is vital that you clarify your answer with a diagram.

The independent variable is time, so the months are plotted on the abscissa. Then the various items of data are sorted into types. Rainfall and potential transpiration use the same units (mm), so can be plotted together as the variable at the foot of the ordinate: rainfall can be shown in columns, drawn with a continuous line; potential transpiration as columns drawn with a broken line. Above these two a break is indicated (Fig. 26) and the two variables measured in hours – length of sunshine, length of day – can be shown as a compound line graph. The ordinate is again 'broken' and the remaining variable, air temperature, is plotted as a line graph. Your diagram need be no neater than Fig. 26: YOU ARE NOT ASKED TO PLOT THE DATA.

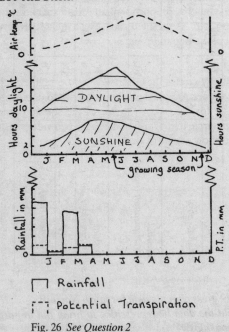

Fig. 26 *See Question 2*

Age–sex pyramids

These are basically paired histograms, set on their sides and plotted back to back. The class interval is usually five years, and the male data are on the left of the ordinate, which is set centrally.

Should you need to draw one, even in a sketch, remember that the frequencies on the abscissa are *percentage* frequencies.

Q. 3. With the aid of sketch population pyramids, describe the difference in age structure of the population of a developed country and a developing country. [SCO. A; part]

Age–sex populations do not show the fertility of a population, the death rates or the population policies of the state concerned.

B. Symbols

Newspapers frequently depict statistics by using picture symbols. Car output, for example, can be shown by a series of car drawings, each drawing representing, say, 1,000 cars. Occasionally, these symbols are drawn proportionately to the value of the figures. Generally, only the height of the symbol is proportional and this exaggerates comparisons when the width, etc., is also increased. 'Such manipulation is, of course, not unknown in the popular press.'*

Area symbols

These are usually circles or rectangles. To be mathematically sound, calculate the square root of the value you wish to depict and use this at a suitable scale for the radius, or side of the square. You cannot mix the square and circle if you wish to compare two values visually.

You should show a scale of circles (Fig. 27).

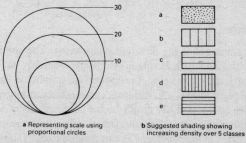

a Representing scale using proportional circles

b Suggested shading showing increasing density over 5 classes

Fig. 27 *Scale and shading*

* Toyne, P., and P. T. Newby, *Techniques in Human Geography*, Macmillan, 1971.

Volumetric symbols

Here the circle becomes a sphere, the square a cube, and the radius or side length is based on the cube root of the value.

The advantage of volume over area representation is that the range of values you can show by the former is much greater in the same available space. However, if the symbols are subdivided, the volume symbol is unrepresentative because perspective distorts the size of the sectors.

C. Pie graphs – divided circles

Method:
1) Work out the sum of all values.
2) Then, for each subdivision, calculate the angle of the sector, thus:

$$d = \frac{v \times 360}{T}$$

where d = angle at centre of sector
v = value
T = sum of all values.

3) Site the largest sector immediately to the right of the '12 o'clock' position. Any grouping of 'others' goes to the left of '12 o'clock'.
4) Pencil-lines dividing the segments use up some of the space in the circle. Accordingly, leave the largest sector until last – it can absorb the slight loss of area best.
5) If you are drawing two or more divided circles, follow the same order in placing the segments.

Divided circles can be made proportional, e.g. to show total employment and the breakdown into classes, and placed within different areas on a map to show regional variations.

D. Bar graphs

These are columns showing different phenomena. The columns are of uniform width, the width having no statistical meaning, but the height being proportional to the value. Compound bar graphs are used to show a number of phenomena, e.g. different commodities in an export trade. Two or more compound bar graphs make comparisons of totals easy, but it is difficult to determine individual values. Bar graphs can be located on maps, in the same way as can divided circles (above).

Q. 4. Using the data in Table 13, draw divided circles for each parish to show the relative importance of each of the three land-uses shown.

Table 13.   Land-use in hectares

Parish	Crops	Grass	Rough grazing, woodland and other	Total land
Marvell	1,920	1,870	350	4,140
Drayton	720	610	100	1,430
Selburn	930	370	340	1,640

In Question 4, make the circles proportional to total area, then sub-divide them according to the formula on p. 76.

E. Choropleths

These are maps where areas are shaded differently according to the frequency of a particular phenomenon.
   Method:
1) If necessary, process the data until they are in the required form. For example, density figures are calculated from:

$$\frac{\text{number of phenomena}}{\text{area}}.$$

2) Break up the data set into classes. Although the rule for class numbers in histograms is 5 times the log number of investigations, at A-level you will find 4 or 5 classes enough – more can be confusing and pose difficult choices over shading. For a wide range of data, consider using a geometrical progression of classes.
3) Write class names in pencil in each unit. When two adjoining units fall into the same class, you should make the shading continue without a break across the boundary or boundaries.
4) A key should be constructed showing *every* class, even if one class does not actually occur in your example. The higher the density figures, the more dense your shading or the darker your colour should be (see Fig. 27, p. 75). Avoid solid black which obscures detail or plain white which gives a completely empty appearance.
   Choropleths are easy to 'read' but incorporate problems:
(a) the data are usually obtained for administrative units. The average

77

    value for the administrative unit may conceal important concentrations of population

(b) the impression given from the choropleth is that the characteristics portrayed stop at the boundary line. A line of ribbon development outside a city boundary may 'disappear' when average values for the rural area it extends into are calculated.

  Cambridge examines practical cartography very frequently and asks for an assessment of the methods.

F. Dot maps

An alternative method of showing distribution is by marking each occurrence of a phenomenon with a dot. If you were to do this for the population of your county you would quickly come across two problems:

(i) where to locate the dot. This is usually solved by plotting dots on settlements

(ii) trying to fit the thousands of dots from a town into a small space. Accordingly the dot is usually given a scale value, e.g. 1 dot represents 50 persons. This makes problem (i) more difficult in very desolate areas.

  Dot maps give a better impression of clusters of population than do choropleths. At times, dots are used as the basic unit, and proportional circles or spheres are used for the towns.

G. Flow-line graphs (routed flows)

When volumes of movement are to be mapped, the width of the route line can be made proportional to the volume of flow. If the range of values is very great, the width of line can be drawn in proportion to the square root of the value; but this misleads the eye when two flows meet, as the combined flow will be calculated by the square root of its value and will not appear to be wide enough, although mathematically correct. Some routed flows carry so much traffic that details of the route are lost, so instead **desire lines** are constructed. The widths of these lines are also proportional to the volume of movement, but all the origins and destinations are joined 'as the crow flies'. Too many desire lines on one map can lead to an awful mess.

H. Isopleths

These are lines joining any points where a phenomenon has the same value. For example, a line on a map joining places of equal:

    pressure = **isobar**
    water depth = **isobath**
    transport time = **isochrone**
    transport costs = **isodapane**
    sunshine hours = **isohel**
    rainfall = **isohyet**
    intensity of earthquake shock = **isoseismal line**
    travel (people) costs = **isophore**
    transport costs per weight unit = **isotim**.

Some exam questions require the candidate to construct one such isoline from a number of points. Often it is necessary to estimate where a required value might fall (**interpolation**). If you have four points, find a central point, equidistant from all four, and attribute to it the mean value of the four points.

It is not often, except for the Cambridge Board, that you are required to use cartographic skills during the examination. They are important in three areas:

(i) in illustrating fieldwork data if you attempt a project or local study
(ii) in answering fieldwork questions which also require you to 'present' your results:

Q. 5. (a) With reference to a specific town or city, describe and evaluate the fieldwork necessary, and the information you would hope to derive from it, in order to delimit the 'central business district' of the town.

(b) Suggest, with sketched examples, a variety of cartographic methods for presenting the information you have amassed. Discuss the relative merits and demerits of the methods.

[SCO. A]

(iii) in answering questions which require you to evaluate cartographic techniques. A selection is given below:

Q. 6. Assess the relative merits of different cartographic techniques which might be used to map the distribution and density of population.

[LON]

Q. 7. With reference to examples drawn from physical geography, discuss the relative advantages, disadvantages and problems associated with the use of choropleths and isopleths as means of portraying quantitative data in map form. [O and C]

In Question 7, above, remember that contours are isopleths. Refer also to other isopleths which relate to physical geography.

Q. 8. Study Figs. 28a and 28b which relate to world population increase, and comment on the clarity and effectiveness of the two figures. Suggest other ways in which the facts of world population increase could be given. [SUJB]

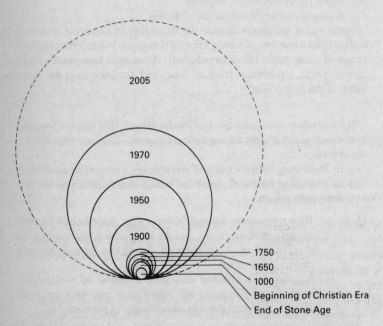

Fig. 28a *World population growth (from Lowry, J. H.,* World Population and Food Supply, *Edward Arnold, 1977)*

In Question 8, you must consider the 'clarity' of the diagrams, i.e. can you clearly and accurately gain precise information on world population through time? If not, why not? If the diagrams are 'effective' they will convey the correct impression of how world population is growing. Do they?

World population

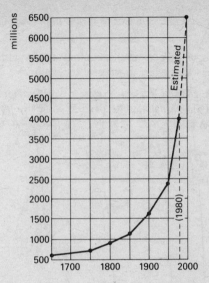

Fig. 28b *World population growth (after Dasman and Hanshard)*

Weather maps

Weather maps are examined in data-response questions: very rarely will you need the techniques used in constructing one of these **synoptic charts**. Since some of the skills are occasionally tested, it will be helpful to show how raw data can be turned into a synoptic chart. (The steps below refer to Fig. 29, overleaf.)

(a) Use pressure readings in Fig. 29a to construct isobars. Isobars are plotted at 4-mb intervals: 992, 996, 1000, 1004, 1008, 1012, 1016, 1020, 1024 and 1028 are the normal range from LOW to HIGH in the U.K. Retain any readings which have these values, and find more values by interpolation. Fig. 30 shows how some of the interpolated values were found. The western reading of 1008 is joined by a light pencil-line to reading 1014. Since 1012 is numerically half-way between 1008 and 1014, the 1012 reading is interpolated half-way along the construction line. Note that the eastern reading of 1008 has been used twice. Use Fig. 31 to practise isobar interpolation.

81

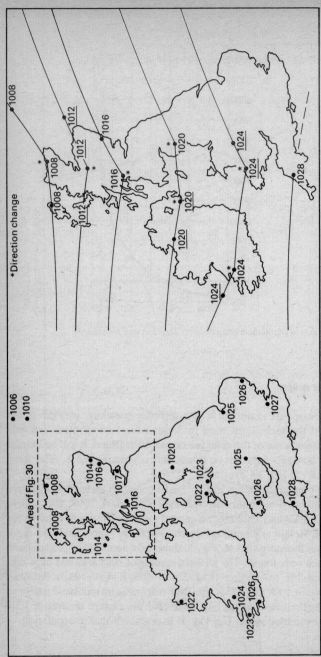

a Actual pressure readings

b Figures on 1004, 1008, 1012 series retained.
Interpolated figures thus: <u>1024</u>

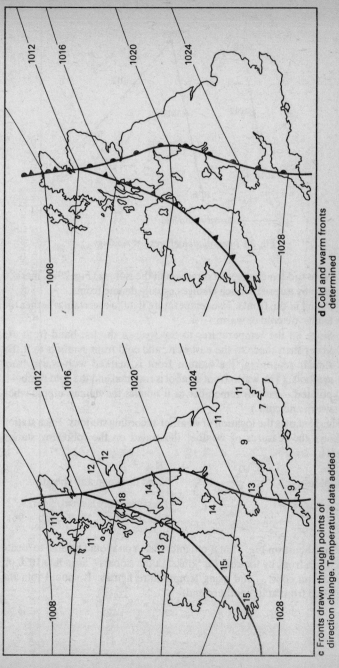

c Fronts drawn through points of direction change. Temperature data added

d Cold and warm fronts determined

Fig. 29 *Construction of a synoptic chart*

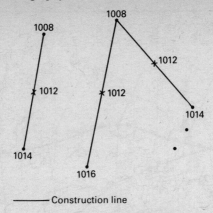

—— Construction line

Fig. 30 *Interpolation of pressure readings*

(b) Note sudden changes of direction in the isobars (Fig. 29b), marked here by asterisks. Such changes usually denote fronts.

(c) Pencil in the fronts. Use temperature data to ascertain whether the fronts are cold or warm.

(d) Since all the temperatures to the west of the left-hand front are lower than those to the east of it, add cold front symbols to it. By similar reasoning, the eastern front is marked with warm front symbols. (The warm front symbol is rounded and the cold symbol is pointed – easy to remember as it mimics the human nipple when warm and cold.)

Fig. 31 shows the location of weather-recording stations. Each station displays the features of weather illustrated on the following station model:

Temperature °C		Wind direction and speed
Present weather		Pressure (only last two figures, e.g. 1016 mb = 16, 996 mb = 96)

Plot isobars on Fig. 31 at 8-mb intervals. You should be able to locate the warm front by looking for 'kinks' in the isobars – as in line 1020 off the Devon coast – and using temperature figures. It should join the occluded front at its southern end.

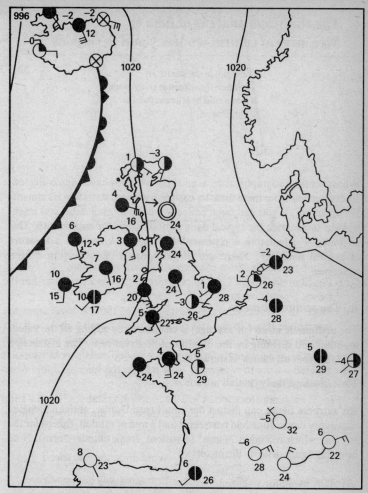

Fig. 31 *Selected weather features over part of Europe*

4. The statistical analysis of data 1: Measures of central tendency and deviations

> Though it in the centre sit
> Yet when the other far doth roam
> It leans, and hearkens after it.
> (John Donne)

Whatever the geographical data, and however they have been collected, all deductions from them must be based on a sound statistical treatment. For example, if you had been collecting daily rainfall data, you might wish to summarize the typical daily rainfall figure for each month. This is done by calculating a representative figure, known as a **measure of central tendency**. There are three methods of measuring central tendency:

A. The arithmetic mean

The **arithmetic mean** (or **average**) is calculated by adding all the values together and dividing by the number of observations. (The instruction 'add together all values' is shown as Σ.)

Thus, average daily rainfall in June $= \dfrac{\Sigma \text{ daily totals}}{30}$.

An extreme figure can distort the result (see Donne, above). Imagine that every day in June had between 2 and 3 mm of rainfall, except for the last day which recorded 79 mm* (a violent, freak thunderstorm). Note how this figure distorts the mean:

(i) daily mean for 1–29 June $= \dfrac{\Sigma x}{29} = \dfrac{77.2}{29} = 2.6$ mm

(ii) daily mean for 1–30 June $= \dfrac{77.2 + 79}{30} = \dfrac{156.2}{30} = 5.2$ mm.

That freak day has doubled the mean daily figure. In such cases, the **median** is a better indicator of central tendency.

* 95 mm of rain fell between 11 a.m. and 3 p.m. on 5 June 1983 at Poole, Dorset.

B. The median

This is determined by arranging all the values in order of magnitude, and choosing the middle number. In the case of an even number of items, the mean of the middle two values is taken.

Here are production figures for Belgian iron ore in thousands of tonnes:

YEAR:	1945	1946	1947	1948	1949	1950	1951
TONNES:	11	14	21	34	15	16	28

YEAR:	1952	1953	1954	1955	1956	1957
TONNES:	47	35	29	37	50	48

Rearranging in order of magnitude:

11 14 15 16 21 28 29 34 35 37 47 48 50
↑
median

In this method, every value has equal importance: only the occurrence of the figure is significant. So we can envisage a very different set of figures which would have the same median, e.g.

1 2 3 4 5 6 29 40 50 60 70 80 90
↑
median

The median gives us some idea of what to expect, but you cannot assume that two countries with the same median figure of iron-ore production over the same period have any similarity in their present or past production.

C. The mode

The **mode** is the figure occurring most often in a set of data. Imagine that the following angles had been recorded on a chalk scarp traverse:

30° 30° 30° 30° 31° 31° 32° 36° 37° 38°

30° is the mode: the most frequently occurring slope angle. The geomorphologist could then state that the scarp mostly sloped at 30°.

It is often very difficult to find a clear mode – there isn't one in the Belgian iron-ore figures above. A mode is more easily found if you group these figures into classes (see Chapter 3):

Belgian iron ore 1945–57

Classes (thousand tonnes)	No. of occurrences	
11–20	4	← **modal class**
21–30	3	
31–40	3	
41–50	3	

Change the classes, however, and a new mode appears:

Classes (thousand tonnes)	No. of occurrences	
0–12.5	1	
12.6–25	4	
25.1–37.5	5	← modal class
37.6–50	3	

To add to your difficulties, it is possible to have two modes occurring in one set of figures: 'the mode is not a method to be highly recommended'.*

You cannot answer questions like Question 1 without figures to illustrate your points. If you understand what has been written in this chapter you need not memorize the figures given; practise making up your own figures. This is a much better test of understanding than simply quoting the figures in this section.

Q. 1. Explain the terms 'mean', 'median' and 'mode', and give examples of the importance of each as a measure of central tendency in a geographical context. [O and C]

Most questions on central tendency require you to calculate means, medians and modal classes, and further require you to comment on your findings. You will never be given very many figures without being allowed to use a calculator. Cross off each figure in pencil as you enter it into the calculator, and add the figures up at least twice. Double-check that you are dividing by the correct number of items.

---

* Gregory, S., *Statistical Methods and the Geographer*, Longman, 1978.

To speed up the identification of the median, draw up a grid on a rough sheet, starting from the lowest and ending with the highest figure:

0	30	60	90	120
1	1	1	1	1
2	2	2	2	2
3	3	3	3	3
4	4	4	4	4
5	5	5	5	5
6	6	6	6	6
7	7	7	7	7
8	8	8	8	8
9	9	9	9	9
10	40	70	100	130
1	1	1	1	1
2	2	2	2	2
3	3	3	3	3
4	4	4	4	4
5	5	5	5	5
6	6	6	6	6
7	7	7	7	7
8	8	8	8	8
9	9	9	9	9
20	50	80	110	140
1	1	1	1	1
2	2	2	2	2
3	3	3	3	3
4	4	4	4	4
5	5	5	5	5
6	6	6	6	6
7	7	7	7	7
8	8	8	8	8
9	9	9	9	9

Write each figure in the appropriate place, crossing it off (at a different angle from the first time) each time you do so. When you have inserted all the figures, count them on your grid, as a cross-check.

Deviation from the mean

Here are the month-by-month figures of mean daily discharge for two different rivers:

Table 14.   River discharges

Month	J	F	M	A	M	J	J	A	S	O	N	D	Yearly mean
Mean daily discharge in cumecs A:	12.5	9.8	4.4	1.4	1.5	1.0	1.6	0.9	7.1	7.7	11.3	12.1	5.9
B:	5.7	6.0	5.8	6.2	6.7	6.8	6.3	6.6	5.4	5.1	5.2	5.0	5.9

Both have the same mean daily discharge, measured over the year, but river A differs, or **deviates**, very greatly from this mean of 5.9 cumecs. Clearly the mean does not tell us enough. We also need to know how much the discharge rates deviate from the mean. The simplest way to do this is to find out how much each figure differs from the mean. This can be done in a table. Using the data for river A:

River A: deviations from mean

Values (x)	Deviations (d)
12.5	6.6
9.8	3.9
4.4	1.5
1.4	4.5
1.5	4.4
1.0	4.9
1.6	4.3
0.9	5.0
7.1	1.2
7.7	1.8
11.3	5.4
12.1	6.2
12)71.3	12)49.7
Average ($\bar{x}$) = 5.9	4.1

Then the average amount by which the individual values deviate from the mean is calculated. This figure is known as the **mean deviation**.

Notice that plus and minus signs have been ignored in calculating the deviation. This is not 'cheating', but is mathematically awkward. A better method is to show plus or minus deviations. You'll remember that 'a minus times a minus is a plus'. That is why a second method to measure deviation is used in which all the deviations are squared. Thus the minus signs are removed in a mathematically 'correct' fashion.

Returning to river A:

x	d	Deviation squared (d^2)
12.5	+ 6.6	43.56
9.8	+ 3.9	15.21
4.4	− 1.5	2.25
1.4	− 4.5	20.25
1.5	− 4.4	19.36
1.0	− 4.9	24.01
1.6	− 4.3	18.49
0.9	− 5.0	25.00
7.1	+ 1.2	1.44
7.7	+ 1.8	3.24
11.3	+ 5.4	29.16
12.1	+ 6.2	38.44
$\bar{x} =$ 5.9		12)240.41 = 20.03

The average of d^2 is known as the **variance**. But this is an average of the deviations *squared*. To get back to the average deviation, we must therefore take the square root of the variance; in this case:

$$\sqrt{20.03} = +/- 4.4.$$

The square root of the variance is the **standard deviation**, and is sometimes given the sign σ (sigma). Now we can say that river A has a mean daily flow of 5.9 cumecs with a standard deviation of +/− 4.4. The figures for σ are always in the same units as those for the mean. River B has a standard deviation of 0.6.

Even with a calculator, working out σ takes time. Fortunately there is a short cut:

Instruction	Instruction in mathematical terms
1) Square each reading.	$x \ldots x^2$
2) Add the squares.	Σx^2
3) Take the mean of the squares.	$\dfrac{\Sigma x^2}{n}$
4) Calculate the mean of the readings.	$\bar{x}$
5) Square this figure.	$\bar{x}^2$
6) From the mean of the squares, subtract the mean reading squared.	$\dfrac{\Sigma x}{n} - \bar{x}^2$
7) Find the square root of the result of calculation (6).	$\sqrt{\dfrac{\Sigma x}{n} - \bar{x}^2} = \sigma$

IMPORTANT NOTE: MARKS ARE SQUANDERED EACH YEAR BY INACCURATE SUMMING AND SQUARING – THE MOST COMMON FAULTS IN STATISTICS QUESTIONS.

In any question requiring you to calculate standard deviation you will be given this formula. (Mathematical symbols will always mean the same whenever you are given any formula to calculate.)

Should you be asked to explain the meaning of standard deviation, you need not go into a worked example, *unless that comprises the whole question*.

The best way to remember the quick method is by practice. Use four numbers and keep them small. Set it out like this:

Readings	Readings squared
1	1
2	4
3	9
4	16

Total	= 10	Total	= 30
Mean	= 2.5	Mean	= 7.5
Mean^2	= 6.25		

You do the *same* for both columns *until* you square the average of the readings. Then subtract the right-hand figure from the left,

$$\text{i.e.} \quad \frac{\Sigma x^2}{n} - \bar{x}$$

$$\text{i.e.} \quad 7.5 - 6.25 = 1.25$$

and find its square root: $\sqrt{1.25} = 1.118$.

Deviation from the median

So far we have considered the way data vary – or are scattered – from the mean, or average. If we use the median as our measure of central tendency, a different system comes into play. Just as in the calculation of the median, the data are ranked in order of magnitude. This can be done on a dispersion diagram, as in Fig. 32 (overleaf), which uses data from Table 15.

Table 15. Sample figures for a dispersion diagram

Year	°C	Year	°C	Year	°C
1951	5.0	1958	5.1	1965	5.1
1952	4.2	1959	3.7	1966	4.7
1953	6.6	1960	5.5	1967	5.7
1954	5.8	1961	5.4	1968	4.9
1955	3.9	1962	6.1	1969	6.4
1956	4.4	1963	3.7	1970	4.8
1957	6.8	1964	7.3	1971	6.1

In this example, there are 21 values. The median is therefore the eleventh value. *It does not matter that the tenth value is the same as the eleventh.*[*] The 'halves' produced by drawing the median line are then halved again to produce the quartiles. Since there is an even number of values in the lower half – ten – the quartile is constructed at the half-way point between the fifth reading (4.4) and the sixth reading (4.7), i.e. at 4.55. The upper quartile is to be found half-way between the sixteenth and seventeenth readings. In Fig. 32 these have the same value. This does not matter. Set the quartile at that value, i.e. 6.1.

This method is much quicker than computing deviations from the mean. The interquartile range indicates the usual extent to which

---

[*] I am indebted to Rev. J. S. T. Woolmer for this clarification, which does not emerge from any of the texts on statistics for geographers.

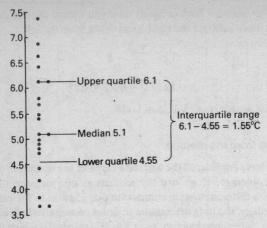

Fig. 32 *Dispersion diagram from figures in Table 15*

temperatures deviate from the median, and this is not distorted by the extreme figure of 7.3 (see p. 86).

For the figures in Table 15, the median temperature is 5.1°C and the interquartile range is 1.55°C. This is a small deviation and shows that the median is a good measure of central tendency in this case or, in simpler language, that the median temperature is fairly typical.

You would be well advised to determine the interquartile range in part (ii) of the next question. Do not trouble to draw a dispersion diagram; just jot down the figures in order of magnitude.

Q. 2. Table 16 shows rainfall data (in millimetres) for five stations in England and Wales. Study the information carefully, then discuss:

(i) the variations in the ten-year mean between each station,

(ii) the variation in annual rainfall within each station,

(iii) the extent to which the data support the claim that the 1970s were a dry decade. [OXF]

Thus, for Moel Gwynedd, from Table 16:

Reference figures:	16	17	18	19	20	21	22	23	24	25	26		27
Values:	1,646		1,819		2,002	2,111	2,261	2,332		2,541	2,620	2,660	2,735
Rank of value:	1.		2.		3.	4.	5.	6.		7.	8.	9.	10.

	lower quartile ↑ 2,002	median ↑ 2,296.5	upper quartile ↑ 2,620

the interquartile range is 2,620 – 2,002 = 618 mm.

Table 16. Rainfall data (in mm), 1970–79, for five stations in England and Wales

Station:	Moel Gwynedd	Hause Gill	Oxford	Norwich	Canvey Island
Location:	Mid-Wales	Lake District	South Midlands	East Anglia	Thames Estuary
Height a.s.l.:	350 m	267 m	63 m	35 m	1 m
Year					
1970	2,660	1,432	640	630	525
1971	1,819	1,227	741	593	457
1972	2,111	1,333	576	525	370
1973	2,332	959	495	558	421
1974	2,735	1,602	784	681	598
1975	2,002	1,235	538	594	577
1976	1,646	1,198	509	516	390
1977	2,541	1,407	710	565	475
1978	2,261	1,394	577	646	502
1979	2,620	1,415	752	678	572
Ten-year mean	2,273	1,320	632	599	489
Long-term mean	not available	1,561	651	660	556
Median	2,296.5	1,365.5	608.5	593.5	488.5
Modal class	2,501–2,750	1,251–1,500	526–600	526–600	526–600
Standard deviation	355	166	102	56	76

Here is an interesting question:

Q. 3. 'Measures of central tendency have limited use in geographical studies. The scatter in any data set is of far greater interest.' Discuss. [NI]

First, you should define the term 'measure of central tendency'. Then you can indicate the cases where typical figures are of great value, for example averages of G.N.P., per capita income, calorie intake, birth rates, death rates, etc., giving figures from named countries. (See p. 384.)

It is true, however, that extreme conditions can be very important in some geographical contexts. Some instances are: flooding in desert environments (p. 189), droughts (p. 223), and the importance of periglacial conditions in forming dry valleys (pp. 152–3). You should expand on one of these.

5. The statistical analysis of data 2: Errors and correlations

> Sole judge of truth, in endless error hurled:
> The glory, jest and riddle of the world.
> (Alexander Pope, *An Essay on Man*)

This is an excellent description of statistics, written before the subject was invented. Sampling techniques are prone to error, and no statistical conclusions are complete without taking this into account.

The standard error of the mean

The figure for the mean discharge of river A (Table 14) was computed from sample readings. How likely is it that this mean based on sampling – the **sample mean** – exactly reflects the **true mean** based on every discharge level throughout the year? The difference between the two is the **standard error of the mean** calculated as $\dfrac{s}{\sqrt{n}}$

where s^* = standard deviation of the sample data

n = number of occurrences in the sample.

Therefore:

1) The true mean lies between $\bar{x} \pm \dfrac{s}{\sqrt{n}}$, where $\bar{x}$ = the sample mean.

   Substituting the figures derived from Table 14, the true mean lies between $5.9 \pm \dfrac{4.4}{\sqrt{12}}$, i.e. $5.9 \pm \dfrac{4.4}{3.5}$, i.e. 5.9 ± 1.3.

   This means that the true mean lies between 7.2 (i.e. $5.9 + 1.3$) and 4.6 ($5.9 - 1.3$).

   This formula has a 68% **confidence level** (probability of being correct).

2) For a 95% confidence level the formula is:

   $$\text{true mean} = \bar{x} \pm \frac{2.s}{\sqrt{n}}$$

---

* For an explanation of the use of s rather than σ, see Gregory, op. cit., pp. 87–8.

3) and for a 99.7% confidence level:

$$\text{true mean} = \bar{x} \pm \frac{3.s}{\sqrt{n}}.$$

Standard errors can be expressed as percentages. Table 17 is based on a JMB question.

Table 17.

Land-use	Arable		Market gardening		Grassland		Woodland		Other	
	Total in sample	%	Total in sample	%	Total in sample	%	Total in sample	%	Total in sample	%
	6	40	3	20	4	26.66	1	6.66	1	6.66

Total of samples = 15.
Thus, from sampling, we can estimate that 40% of the land is arable. How 'true' is this estimate? The formula for the standard error of the estimate is given by the examiner:

$$\sqrt{\frac{p \times q}{n}}$$

where p = percentage of land in a certain category
    q = percentage of land not in that category
    n = number of points in the sample.

Thus, for arable, standard error $= \sqrt{\dfrac{40 \times 60}{15}} = 12.6$.

This means that the estimate of arable lies between 52.6% (40 + 12.6) and 27.4% (40 − 12.6) at the 68% confidence level. (*Not* a very confident estimate, but this reflects the very small numbers in the sample.)

In any exercise where you have to make calculations, you will be given the formula. *Always show your working.* Oxford and O and C tend to set generalized questions where an ability to quote formulae is an advantage (see Question 1).

Q. 1. Explain, using precise geographical examples, what is meant by any four of the following statistical terms: (a) continuous and discontinuous data; (b) population and sample; (c) standard deviation; (d) significant difference of means; (e) correlation.   [O and C]

Differences between means

Since a sample mean may not represent the true mean (**population mean**), it follows that we have to be very careful when comparing two such means. For example, look at the information in the following table:

Table 18.

Type of settlement	No. of settlements in sample	Total of filling stations in sample	Sample mean no. of filling stations per settlement
Small villages	26	39	1.5
Large villages	18	36	2.0

The mean number of filling stations per settlement, as deduced from a sample, is greater for large villages than for small ones. This could be due to oddities and chances in the sample. **Student's t-test*** shows whether the difference between the two means is:

(a) **probably significant**: 95% certain that chance is not involved
(b) **significant**: 99% certain that chance is not involved
(c) **highly significant**: 99.9% certain that chance is not involved.

Thus in Question 1, part (d), 'significant' is a technical word indicating a precise degree of certainty.

The chi-squared test

Table 18 suggests that there is a link – or **correlation** – between settlement size and the number of filling stations. The **chi-squared (χ^2) test** is designed to discover whether this apparent link is due to random factors – chance – or whether there is some **causal**† factor involved in the correlation.

The test depends on the **null hypothesis**: that there is no factor affecting the distribution of any phenomena. In the case of the filling stations in Table 18, the null hypothesis would be that nothing influences the number of petrol stations in a settlement. Specimen figures are given in Table 19:

---

* For the methods used in this test, see Gregory, op. cit., pp. 153–4, but you should not need to use it at A-level.
† Causal – causing something, *not* casual!

Table 19.

Settlement	Population (in thousands)	No. of filling stations
A	9	11
B	7	9
C	6	10
D	2	3
E	2	2
F	1	1

The total number of filling stations is 36. If population does not affect their distribution, we would expect these to be shared evenly between the six settlements, i.e. $\frac{36}{6} = 6$ each. This is the **expected frequency**. The χ^2 test compares this expected frequency with the **observed** (actual) **frequency**. Thus:

Table 20.

Settlement	Observed frequency of filling stations (O)	Expected frequency of filling stations (E)	O − E	(O − E)²	$\frac{(O-E)^2}{E}$
A	11	6	5	25	4.17
B	9	6	3	9	1.5
C	10	6	4	16	2.67
D	3	6	−3	9	1.5
E	2	6	−4	16	2.67
F	1	6	−5	25	4.17

$$\frac{\Sigma(O-E)^2}{E} = 16.68$$

This value of $\Sigma(O - E)^2/E$ is χ^2, which is now one of the co-ordinates on the χ^2 graph (Fig. 33). The other co-ordinate on this graph is the degree of freedom. You find this figure by subtracting 1 from the number of observations; in this case $6 - 1 = 5$. The graph can be used to test how likely distribution is due to chance. A low probability value on the graph indicates that the null hypothesis does not apply and that there is a causal factor at work. The probability figure derived from plotting $16.68 = \chi^2$ against 5 (degrees of freedom) lies between 0.1% and 1%, showing that

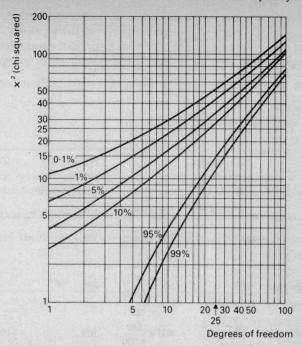

Fig. 33 *Chi-squared graph*

there is a causal link between settlement size and filling stations from the data in Table 19.

Q. 2. A survey of shopping habits sets out to determine if people in Bangor, Downpatrick and Kilkeel have different preferences for shopping in Belfast. Field survey produces the following figures:

Table 21.

Town	No. of persons interviewed	No. of persons who visit Belfast at least once a week
Bangor	400	232
Downpatrick	500	260
Kilkeel	400	197

The total sampled is 1,300, of whom 689 visit Belfast weekly.

The null hypothesis for this question would be that nothing influences the proportion of people from each town who visit Belfast weekly. That is – and now you will use the null hypothesis to predict the **expected value** – for each town the proportion visiting Belfast weekly will be the same as for the whole sample, i.e. $\dfrac{689}{1,300}$ (from the values in the preceding paragraph).

Set out the figures in cells, thus:

Table 22.

Town	No. of weekly shoppers to Belfast		No. not visiting Belfast weekly	Total
	Observed (O)	Expected (E)	Observed	
Bangor	232	$400 \times \dfrac{689}{1,300}$ = **212**	168	400
Downpatrick	260	$500 \times \dfrac{689}{1,300}$ = **265**	240	500
Kilkeel	197	$400 \times \dfrac{689}{1,300}$ = **212**	203	400
Total	689		611	1,300

All the figures are set down – including the non-weekly shoppers – so that you can cross-check the totals.

The question continues:

(i) *Use the chi-squared (χ^2) test to establish if the proportions of people visiting Belfast at least once a week from each town are significantly different. The chi-squared formula is:*

$$\chi^2 = \Sigma \frac{(O - E)^2}{E}$$

where O is the observed frequency and E the expected frequency. A graph for the chi-squared test is shown in Fig. 33.

(ii) *Outline your reasoning at each stage of the analysis.*

(iii) *Comment on your results.*

[NI]

(ii) Filling-station deviations:

A	11	–	6 =	5
B	9	–	6 =	3
C	10	–	6 =	4
D	3	–	6 =	–3
E	2	–	6 =	–4
F	1	–	6 =	–5

4) Multiply each pair:

A	4.5 ×	5 =	22.5
B	2.5 ×	3 =	7.5
C	1.5 ×	4 =	6.0
D	–2.5 ×	–3 =	7.5
E	–2.5 ×	–4 =	10.0
F	–3.5 ×	–5 =	17.5

5) Sum the products: 71.0

6) Divide sum by number of pairs: $\dfrac{71}{6} = 11.83$ (= co-variance).

7) $\sigma^x = \sqrt{\dfrac{\Sigma(x - \bar{x}^2)}{n}} = \sqrt{\dfrac{53.5}{6}} = \sqrt{\dfrac{8.92}{6}} = 2.98.$

8) $\sigma^y = \sqrt{\dfrac{100}{6}} = \sqrt{16.6} = 4.08.$

9) Multiply σ^x by σ^y: $2.98 \times 4.08 = 12.16.$

10) Divide this figure into co-variance $= \dfrac{11.83}{12.16}$

$$r = 0.97.$$

Spearman's coefficient was 0.936. Pearson's shows a higher degree of correlation between population and filling stations.

Regression lines

A quick way of showing a correlation is to plot the two variables on a scatter diagram (Fig. 34). If there is a close association between the two variables, it may be possible to draw a line through the cluster of points so that they are distributed symmetrically about the line. This is a **best-fit**, or **regression**, **line**. This can be done by eye at A-level, although there is a mathematical* (**least squares**) and a graphical method.

Regression lines can indicate a relationship between two variables

* Gregory, op. cit., p. 191.

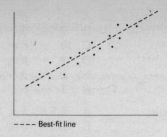

---- Best-fit line

Fig. 34 *Scatter diagram and best-fit line*

and can be used to make predictions. In this case, the line is extended either way to estimate unknown values.

Q. 4.   *(i) Describe two techniques which you could use to establish statistical association between sets of observations.*

      (ii) How would you distinguish between causation and correlation?

      (iii) Give examples from human geography of how you would apply your techniques.   [OXF]

Even when the most stringent tests show a correlation between two sets of data, there may be no causal link, i.e. one might not cause the other. Here are two sets of statistics:

Table 26.   South African agricultural production and Belgian iron ore

Year	South African agricultural production (in million Rands)	Belgian iron-ore production (in thousand tonnes)
1946	14	150
1947	21	170
1948	34	200
1949	15	160
1950	16	200
1951	28	270

The value of Spearman's coefficient for these two sets of data is 0.8142, i.e. a very strong positive correlation. But no one would argue that the production of Belgian iron ore affected the farm output of South Africa.

Questions 4, 11, 13 and 14 in Chapter 2 also required you to explain how you would analyse the data found in fieldwork. Furthermore, if you have carried out a local study project, you will be expected to analyse your results and assess their value statistically.

6. Locational analysis in human geography: techniques

> How many roads must a man walk down?
> (Bob Dylan, *Blowing in the Wind*)

Networks

The pattern of routes or **network** of any region underlies the whole of its human and economic activity.

Try to avoid the generalization that 'town X grew because it had good communications': some of the networks you observe will post-date the establishment of the town; some will pre-date it.

Mathematical analysis of networks uses the following terms:

 (i) **vertices** (v): points, or settlements served
 (ii) **edges** (e): routes between points
(iii) **nodes**: points where two or more edges meet
(iv) **connectivity**: the degree to which the nodes are directly connected. One measurement of connectivity is:
 (v) the **beta** (β) **index** where $\beta = e/v$. The higher the figure for β, the better the connectivity.

Topological maps

The analysis of a network is greatly aided if a model, known as a **graph**, is made of the real system. Graphs identify the terminals and junctions (points and nodes) of the network and the routes (edges) between them, but they are not concerned with the distance between points, the precise paths taken or the size of the areas. The best-known example of a **topological map** – another term for the graph described above – is the London Underground map.

The numbers of edges between points can be set out in a table, known as a **connectivity matrix**, as in Fig. 35 overleaf.

A connectivity matrix may, in turn, be used to construct a topological map. To construct one from Fig. 35, you may locate your five points in any convenient pattern, since distance and direction are not important here. Now link the nodes, working *from* each in turn (Fig. 36a).

	a	b	c	d	e
a	–	0	1	1	0
b	0	–	0	0	1
c	1	0	–	1	1
d	1	0	1	–	1
e	0	1	1	1	–

Fig. 35 *Connectivity matrix representing network between five vertices*

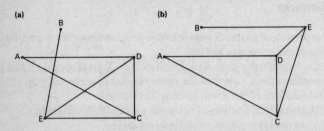

Fig. 36 *Construction of a topological map from a connectivity matrix*

The first 'plot', (a), has routes intersecting, e.g. BE intersects AD. This gives an impression of cross-roads for which there is no evidence in the matrix. Simply move point E to any point which will 'untangle' the routes: Fig. 36b.

Should you be given both topological and topographical maps of the same area, do not neglect to use the information displayed about distance and direction and circuits provided by the latter.

Most examination questions concentrate on the description of networks:

Q. 1. Figs. 37a and b show communications networks at various dates. Study them and answer the following:

(a) Compare the railway network open by 1845 with the motorway network proposed for the early 1980s.

(b) Which industrial cities had the highest degree of accessibility to ports in the 1845 and 1980s networks? Explain your answer.

(c) Comment on the pattern of accessibility of Wales and East Anglia as revealed by the two maps. [SUJB]

The networks in Figs. 37a and b are too complex for mathematical treatment. You should answer part (a) in terms of:

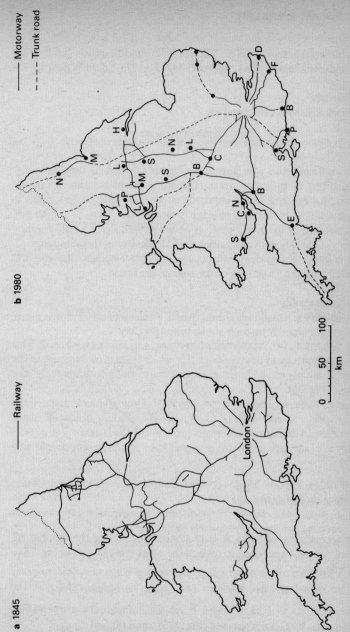

Fig. 37 *(a) Railways in 1845, (b) motorways in 1980*

a 1845

b 1980

——— Railway

——— Motorway
‐ ‐ ‐ ‐ Trunk road

London

0   50   100
km

(i) Form

Use terms like 'radial' (Figs. 37a and b: around London), 'grid' (Fig. 37a: industrial north-east), 'sub-parallel' (Fig. 37a: South Wales).

(ii) Density

Network density is calculated as:

$$\frac{\text{total length of network}}{\text{area}}.$$

You would improve your answer enormously by making simple density calculations of specimen areas. Use the scale to measure a sample square, for example in the industrial north-east; with dividers, make a rough estimate of the total mileage in that square. Thus: '. . . high rail densities are in the north-east, at about 80/400, i.e. 0.5 miles/square miles . . .' This type of calculation should take two or three minutes.

It is important to demonstrate, by using place-names, that you are familiar with the geography of the area on the maps.

(iii) Accessibility

Accessibility is usually measured over a whole network, but it is more easily understood if we look at one town (Fig. 38).

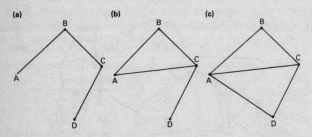

Fig. 38 *Accessibility of town A*

The accessibility of town A is reckoned by counting the number of routes (edges) used to get to each of the other three towns. In Fig. 38a, the 'edge-count' is

	to	B	to	C	to	D	total, i.e. **Shimbel index.**
A		1		2		3	= 6

When edge A–C is constructed (Fig. 38b), the situation changes:

112

	to	B	to	C	to	D	total
A		1		1		2	= 4

and when edge A–D comes in (Fig. 38c):

	to	B	to	C	to	D	total
A		1		1		1	= 3

Thus, the more routes, the lower the index and the more accessible the town. A table dealing with all the towns in the network is called an accessibility matrix. The average value of the Shimbel index for all the towns in a network can be calculated. This is the **mean Shimbel index** of the network and is one way in which geographers measure the degree of economic development in a country.

This technique can be used to answer part (b) of Question 1. Before you begin, however, two important definitions must be clarified:

(i) What is meant by 'ports'? The major British ports, by tonnage, are: London, Liverpool, Milford Haven, Southampton, Medway, Manchester, Glasgow, Middlesbrough, Hull and Newcastle. You can omit those ports which were not connected to the railway system for 1845, and leave out the ones not on the motorway/trunk-road network for 1980.

(ii) What is meant by 'industrial cities'? Some ports, like London, are also industrial cities. It will be much simpler to omit from the 'industrial' group the towns which fall into both categories.

In both these questions of definition you *must explain your reasoning*

PORTS

INDUSTRIAL CITIES	London	Liverpool	Southampton	Manchester	Middlesbrough	Hull	Newcastle	
Leeds	1	3	3	2	3	2	4	= 18
Sheffield	2	3	4	1	3	4	5	= 22
Birmingham	1	2	3	2	4	4	4	= 20
Coventry	1	3	3	3	5	4	4	= 23
Leicester	2	5	5	3	5	4	5	= 29
Stoke	2	2	5	2	7	5	6	= 29
Nottingham	2	4	5	3	5	4	6	= 29

Fig. 39 *Rough calculation of Shimbel indices for inland cities on motorway/trunk-road network*

and decision to the examiner. Then you can devise a rough-and-ready set of Shimbel indices.

From Fig. 39, Leeds needs fewer edges (routeways) than any other nodes to get to the major British ports, followed by Birmingham and Sheffield. These are therefore, *in terms of the Shimbel index*, the most accessible inland industrial cities. This, however, takes no heed of distance.

In part (c) you should name those parts of Wales and East Anglia which have most edges (routes) and explain the pattern in terms of the economic geography of the two regions. Do not confuse connectivity ('roads per town') with accessibility ('How many roads must a man walk down/To get from town to town?').

Settlements as regular lattices: nearest-neighbour analysis

In 1938, Walter Christaller suggested that, over a uniform surface, settlements would develop on a regular lattice or grid. The technique of **nearest-neighbour analysis** attempts to find evidence of regularity in the settlements of an area by comparing the existing (observed) distribution with an entirely random distribution. Thus:

1) trace off the settlement points from a map of the area to be studied
2) measure the straight-line distance between every point and its nearest neighbour. Convert these distances from scale to actual values
3) sum the distances and calculate the mean. This is the **observed mean distance**: d_o (sometimes d)
4) calculate the density of points used in the study, by dividing the number of points by the area. In this technique, density is shown as p
5) calculate the expected (random) mean, d_e, where $d_e = \dfrac{1}{2\sqrt{p}}$
6) from the values of d_o and d_e, the nearest-neighbour index (Rn) can be computed, since $Rn = d_o/d_e$.

Value of Rn	Meaning
near or equal to 1	random distribution
equal to 0.00	clustered distribution
equal to 2.15	regular distribution

Setting out the method like this shows the thinking behind the technique; but you should be aware of the fact that some mathematicians consider this test to be unsound. Furthermore, it is a lengthy business.

A short-cut formula for Rn exists and is often used by JMB:

$$Rn = 2\bar{d}\,n/A$$

where $\bar{d}$ = mean nearest-neighbour distance in metres
      n = total number of points
      A = area of the C.B.D. in square metres.

You might be given a map from which to take 'nearest-neighbour' measurements, together with a graph, like Fig. 40. The graph enables you to interpret the meaning of the value of Rn that you have calculated. It is very easy to miscalculate in questions like this. Your values of Rn should fall within the parameters of the relevant graph.

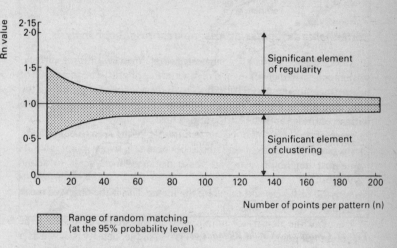

Fig. 40 *Graph for nearest-neighbour analysis*

The commonest error made by candidates on this type of question is to miscalculate the relevant area. Count the total of grid squares as a cross-check.

Rank-size relationships

Settlements can be ranked by size classes, or orders. AUERBACH devised the **rank–size rule** which states that the second-ranked town should have half the population of the first, and so on. Thus the nth town has a population of $1/n \times$ population of the first town. This rule is further discussed on pp. 330–32.

An extension of this idea is that the numbers of towns in each class will increase down the hierarchy. This is the thinking behind part (i) of Question 2.

Q. 2. Study Fig. 41 showing the system of central places in the Rhondda valley, South Wales. Taking statistical information from the map, present analytical accounts of the system in terms of:*
(i) hierarchy
(ii) spacing of centres.   [LON; part]

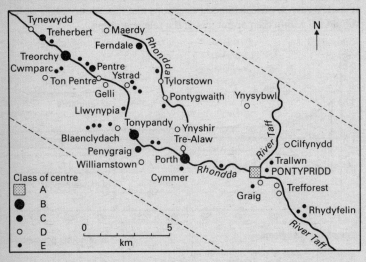

Fig. 41 *Central places in the Rhondda valley*

The quickest and clearest way to begin your answer is with a table:

Class	No. of settlements	Increment
A	1	
B	3	+ 2
C	4	+ 1
D	17	+13
E	25	+ 8

* Source: Davies, W. K. D., 'Centrality and the central place hierarchy', *Urban Studies*, Vol. 4, 1967.

and a summarizing sentence: 'Numbers of settlements increase consistently from 1 in class A to 25 in class E, but the rate of increase is very irregular.'

Part (ii) of this question seems to require a nearest-neighbour analysis, but it is worth 6 marks only. Clearly the examiners expect a less ambitious answer. From the map, it can be seen that the smaller the settlement, the lower is the mean nearest-neighbour distance of that class. You are given a scale, so illustrate your answer using figures from classes B and C. Use a paper strip with the scale marked on it, for speed. Again, a table is indicated.

Class B centres	Distance to nearest B centre (in km)	Class C centres	Distance to nearest C centre (in km)
Treorchy	6	Treherbert	4
Tonypandy	3.5	Ferndale	3
Porth	3.5	Pentre	3
Total	13	Penygraig	5.5
Mean	13/3 = 4.3 km	Total	15.5
		Mean	15.5/4 = 3.87 km

Location quotients

These are used to determine whether a particular industry has an importance to a town greater than the importance of that industry in the employment structure of the nation. Importance here is measured in terms of jobs:

1) the number of workers in one industry is calculated as a percentage of the total workforce of that specified region
2) the national percentage for that industry is calculated with reference to the total workforce of the nation
3) the value obtained in (1) is divided by the value obtained in (2).

Thus if 58% of a town's workforce is engaged in manufacturing, this figure is divided by the national figure of 29%.* Its locational quotient for manufacturing = 58 ÷ 29 = 2. Any quotient over 1 indicates that the

---

* Source: *Annual Abstract of Statistics*, H.M.S.O., 1976.

employment category for which it has been calculated is more important in the area under study than it is nationally.

Location quotients can be made of quadrats over an industrial area, and plotted on a choropleth map. This will show areas of specialization.

Q. 3. The data given below show the numbers of people in broad categories of manufacturing industry in the United Kingdom and the West Midlands for June 1974.

(a) Complete the table of location quotients.

(b) Comment on the resulting statistical comparison of employment between the West Midlands and the United Kingdom as a whole.

(c) In what other sorts of investigation would you find the location quotient useful? [OXF; adapted]

Table 27.

Industry	West Midlands		United Kingdom		Location quotient for West Midlands
	Employees (in thousands)	*% of total*	*Employees (in thousands)*	*% of total*	
Food, drink and tobacco	60	8.18	739	12.39	0.66
Chemicals and allied industries	21		432		
Metals, engineering and vehicles	573		3,260		
Textiles, clothing, footwear	47		950		
Paper, printing, publishing	32		582		
Total	733	99.98	5,963	99.99	

Bid-rent curve analysis

Bid-rent is the rent-paying ability of a land-user. From fieldwork, graphs of the rent paid by various categories of land-user, e.g. retailers, offices, can be plotted against distance from the town centre (Fig. 42).

You may be asked:

1) how is this graph obtained?

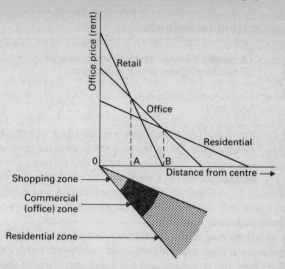

Fig. 42 *Bid-rents*

2) at which distance from the town will housing be most likely to develop? At any distance along the abscissa, the likely land-use will be the one which at that point has the highest bid-rent value. Simply drop a perpendicular from the point at which residences have the highest bid-rent

3) to comment on the slopes of each category, i.e. the **rent gradient**. Shops have the steepest rent curve because they depend on central locations. Industries, which would prefer central locations, cannot afford them, so their bid-rent is lower at the centre but declines less slowly than that of shops since a central location is not as vital.

Other techniques of locational analysis in human geography have already been discussed in Chapter 2. They are: population thresholds (p. 64); gravity models (p. 61); investigation of urban zones (p. 66); measures of central-place status (pp. 62–3); spheres of influence (pp. 61–2); delimitation of the C.B.D. (pp. 65–6).

7. Examination techniques

> Geography is no cure for what's wrong with you.
> (Ernest Hemingway, *Islands in the Stream*)

The most common fault in examinations is not a lack of geographical knowledge.* It is the failure to understand and answer the question that is the main shortcoming. When you consider this extract: 'The marks allocated in the examination as a whole will be divided as . . . follows: [geographical] knowledge: 40–45%; comprehension and application: 55–60%,'† you will understand how important it is for you to deal competently with essay questions.

Essay questions may be divided into ten categories at A-level. Learn to recognize each type with its associated 'command words'. At this stage, note how the command word is used: don't worry about the question.

A. Types of essay question

1. Definitions

These usually occur as part questions, viz.:

Q. 1. **Define** the term 'endogenetic process'. [WEL; part]

Q. 2. **What do you understand by** the term 'primary energy budget'? [AEB; part]

Q. 3. **Describe precisely** what is meant by: birth rate; death rate; natural increase; marriage rate; age-dependency ratios. [NI; part]

Every word in **bold** print in the text of this book is accompanied by a definition. You would be well advised to make your own geographical dictionary from these: writing them out will help you to learn them and you can check whether you really understand your definition.

---

* Associated Examining Board, *Reports of the Examiners*, 1978.
† Joint Matriculation Board, Examinations Council, *G.C.E. Regulations and Syllabuses*, 1983.

Note the variety of command words which indicate 'define'. A further refinement is:

*Q. 4. **Distinguish between** the concepts of overpopulation and dense population.* [OXF]

This simply requires two separate definitions, and you would be well advised to give examples.

You should make it a general rule to define your terms in every essay, whether or not you are asked to. For example, in Question 5 you must decide what 'desirable' means, i.e.
– desirable to whom
– desirable in what terms: economic developments; quality of life; per capita income, etc.

Q. 5. Is some form of economic co-operation between the countries of northern Europe desirable?

2. Summaries

There are no 'catches' in these questions: either you know the material or you don't. Examiners use a variety of words when they want a summary, but they always require examples: place-names, facts, figures. Thus:

*Q. 6. **Discuss** the factors which may influence soil development . . . during the period of tundra conditions which follow deglaciation.*

[JMB; half]

*Q. 7. **Examine** the conditions under which (a) rock type, (b) drainage characteristics are dominant in the determination of vegetation complexes.* [O and C]

*Q. 8. **Identify** the strengths and weaknesses of . . . three methods of obtaining geographical data.* [NI; part]

*Q. 9. **Outline** the main characteristics of the hot desert climate.*

[SCO.T; part]

*Q. 10. **Review** the distribution of the major types of world grassland.*

[NI; half]

3. Descriptions

'Describe' may mean write an account, or summary:

Q. 11. Describe and explain the world distribution of tropical grass-lands. [SCO. A]

It often indicates that a sketch map or diagrams will be helpful. Do not neglect to incorporate details of geographical location, aerial extent, quantity and specific place-names wherever relevant in a 'describe' question. At other times, the need for a diagram is strongly indicated:

Q. 12. Sketch three idealized age–sex pyramids to show stable, expanding and contracting populations. [NI; part]

Q. 13. Illustrate the life-cycle of a mid-latitude depression in the northern hemisphere. [NI; part]

4. Explanations

Explanation includes **how** and **why**. If both are required, deal with them in turn.

Q. 14. Account for the large volume and wide range of manufacturing industry in New Jersey.

Q. 15. Analyse the factors influencing the distribution and character of 'natural' vegetation in tropical latitudes.

Q. 16. Explain the origin, development, form and associated upper-air motion of the Indian monsoon. [WEL; part]

Q. 17. Give an explanatory account of the problems that may result from poor land-management of chernozem soils. [JMB; part]

Q. 18. How and why are villages in Great Britain becoming more urban and less rural in form and function? [AEB]

Q. 19. In what ways can climatic hazards in tropical and subtropical areas influence man's activities? [AEB; half]

Again, explanations need examples. This instruction is given by the word **exemplify**. If you explain and exemplify a statement, you have **elaborated** it:

Q. 20. 'The Common Market allows goods, services, people and capital to circulate freely throughout . . . the member countries' (G. N. Minshull). Elaborate this statement. [OXF; half]

5. Comparisons and contrasts

Strictly speaking, 'compare' means 'pick out similarities', and 'contrast' means 'note the differences'. Examiners do not always observe this technicality, and if you are asked to compare you should note (a) similarities and (b) differences. The next question illustrates this lack of precision in the use of the word 'compare':

Q. 21. **Compare** *the south-west region with other regions in respect of dependent population, and suggest reasons for the differences.*

[SUJB; part]

When the wording is 'contrast', you may safely confine yourself to differences (although a more difficult question might ask you to explain the contrasts):

Q. 22. **Contrast** *the pioneer stage of any one plant succession with its climatic climax.* [LON]

6. Relative importance

This type of question is a pitfall for many candidates. If you are asked to assess the contribution of any one factor, you *must* outline the contribution of the other factors involved. Thus in Question 23:

Q. 23. **To what extent** *has the economic activity in Pembroke been largely the result of its physical geography?* [SCO. A; part]

you should outline the physical factors which have had an impact. Use the same order in every answer where physical factors are involved: Relief, Drainage, Soils, Climate, Vegetation, Natural resources (remember the mnemonic: ReDiSCoVeriNg). Omit those factors which do not apply.

In the second part of Question 23, outline any relevant economic factors from: Power, Raw materials, Mechanization, Labour, Transport, Demand (markets) (mnemonic: PeRaMbuLaTeD – you may use the B in 'perambulated' for Banking, to remind you of the importance of finance, i.e. capital).

Questions requiring an account of all the contributory factors come in other guises:

Q. 24. *With reference to a named glaciated area . . .* **assess the particular contribution** *of glacial and periglacial processes in sculpturing the landscape.* [WEL]

This question requires you to write an explanatory account of the landforms produced by glaciation and periglaciation and to outline the other factors which may have contributed to landscape development (pp. 179–85).

Q. 25. Examine the importance of ground ice and permafrost in the development of landforms in periglacial areas. [O and C]

Other factors in Question 25 might be rock type (lithology), structure, fluvio-glacial processes.

Q. 26. Discuss the view that present-day landforms in dry deserts are the result of past processes. [SUJB; adapted]

Outline also present processes.

Q. 27. 'Locational decisions in manufacturing industry are taken in order to minimize costs' – discuss. [LON]

Give also other factors affecting locational decisions in manufacturing.

Q. 28. 'The process of urbanization in the Third World is significantly different from that experienced in developed countries' – discuss. [OXF]

Give similarities also.

7. Critical evaluations

Here you are being asked to judge how true a statement is. Thus you must give evidence for and against the statement.

Q. 29. Out-migration represents the haemorrhaging of the regional body. To what extent do you agree? [NI]

Q. 30. 'The causes of migration . . . are varied and complementary, involving both "push" factors . . . and "pull" factors.' Illustrate and evaluate this statement. [WEL]

'Illustrate' here means 'give examples' – which you should do always.

Often you are asked to criticize a theory or model. Once again, give both strengths and weaknesses. Criticism in an essay is not always negative.

Q. 31. Critically evaluate Rostow's model of the four stages of economic development. [OXF]

Of course, you must summarize the model or theory first.

Q. 32. '*It is always unrealistic to make separate studies of landforms, climate, vegetation and soils.*' **Do you agree with this statement?**

Give the arguments pro and con before you decide whether to agree or disagree.

Q. 33. **Examine the view** *that in India it is the seasonality rather than the amount of rainfall that causes so many economic problems.* [OXF]

8. Implications

When an examiner asks, 'What are the implications?', he wants to know the meaning and likely results of a set of affairs:

Q. 34. '*The Common Market allows goods, services, people and capital to circulate freely.*' **Consider the implications** [of this quotation].

[OXF; half]

9. Justifications

Not as scary as it sounds:

Q. 35. *Make and* **justify** *a classification of tropical climates.* [LON]

This simply means: explain the basis of your classification.

10. Write an essay on . . .

This, conversely, is harder than it looks. It does not simply mean, 'Write all you know about . . .' You must decide whether the subject matter involves a simple account, or whether assessment or critical evaluation are involved. Whatever the case, you must make a logical structure for your essay. Thus:

Q. 36. *Write an essay on the geomorphology of hot deserts.* [NI]

This should be tackled in terms of (a) process, (b) landforms.

Q. 37. *Write an essay on the role of weathering in landform development.* [NI]

You should note different types of weathering in each paragraph, and a short précis of the other factors in landform development is needed to complete the essay, since this is, to some extent, an 'assessment' question.

B. Answering the question

Having decided what the command words mean, it is vital that you restrict yourself to the subject specified. Some examples may be helpful:

Q. 38. By what processes do valley glaciers erode, transport and deposit material?

This does not involve a description of the resulting landforms.

Q. 39. Describe the ocean-current circulation of the North Pacific.

This requires no explanation of the circulatory system.

If you underline on the paper the command word and the subject requested, you will be more likely to stick to the point.

Frequently, candidates have misunderstood a question because they were unfamiliar with the vocabulary used. Here are some words, not confined to geography, which seem to give trouble:

Economic: to do with the production and distribution of wealth.

Economic factors: power, raw materials, mechanization, finance, labour, transport and demand are the economic factors considered in geography.

Environment: the surroundings; landscape. This may be the physical or the human landscape, but more usually refers to the former.

Evolution: development and change through time.

Geographically: in terms of the physical and human landscape, e.g.:

Q. 40. Discuss the view that the Mediterranean has many islands, but geographically all are indisputably part of the lands fringing the sea.   [NI]

Inter-dependent: dependent upon, i.e. subject to, each other.

Inter-related: connected with each other.

Limitations: weaknesses in some areas, as in:

Q. 41. What are the limitations of . . . A. Weber's model of industrial location?   [OXF]

Periphery: outer region, furthest parts from centre.

Physical: aspects of geography concerned with the natural environment.

Social: concerned with human beings.

Spatial: in terms of extent or area – *not outer space*.

Specific examples: named, real-world examples.

Structural: concerned with the make-up, or component parts, thus:

Q. 42. In which ways do Third World cities differ from those in Western countries in structural and social terms?   [NI; part]

Technological: usually, in geography, to do with machinery and practical engineering.

C. Writing an essay

1. What are the characteristics of a good essay?

According to the Associated Examining Board,* a good essay 'has relevant ideas presented in an interesting way . . . making . . . use of a wide vocabulary. The composition is arranged so that the arguments are cogently presented . . . The essential detail stands out . . . sentences are correctly structured . . . the work is correctly paragraphed, with linking between the paragraphs . . . [and] with few mechanical errors' (i.e. spelling, punctuation).

2. Some hints on essay-writing†

Planning
(a) Question the question to find exactly what it means, by defining every word.
(b) Find out the basic aim of the question.
(c) Jot down, in a circle, any items which may be relevant at a general level.
(d) From these items, work out a structure.
(e) Add examples wherever possible, making one or two really detailed.
(f) Decide which diagrams would be helpful. Number them.

---

* Associated Examining Board, *How AEB Examinations Are Set and Marked*, 1981.
† This section owes much to H. Prudden's 'Essay writing at A-level', in *Teaching Geography*.

Writing

(g) Start with definitions and an outline of your intentions.

(h) Keep using the words of the question to keep being relevant.

(i) Never mis-spell geographical terms and place-names.

(j) Refer to your diagrams, by number, in the text.

(k) Make a conclusion *only* when necessary in answering the question.

D. Data-response questions

In this type of question, you are provided with information which you are required to use in your answer. Some Boards have an entire data-response paper; others combine data-response questions and essay questions. The nature of the data varies greatly.

1. Statistics

Refer to these in your answers, wherever relevant. Calculate proportions and percentages. For example, from Table 28:

Table 28.

	Cuba		Dominican Republic	
National income per person (in £s)		240		240
Electricity consumption per person (in kWh)		531		302
Exports by value (in £m)		1,145		272
Exports by percentage of total	Sugar	86	Sugar	51
	Nickel and		Cocoa	8
	copper	6	Coffee	7
	Tobacco		Tobacco	6
	products	2	Bauxite	3

'Although per capita income is the same in both countries, Dominica's consumption of energy per capita is only 57% (302/531 × 100) of Cuba's', or 'Cuba's sugar exports are worth £984.7 million (£1,145 × 86/100)'. Deductions like these assist greatly in answering questions.

2. Line graphs

Q. 43. Describe the relationship in Fig. 43a. [2 marks] [LON]

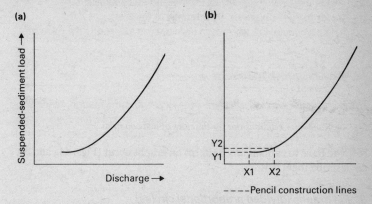

Fig. 43 *Idealized relationship between river discharge and load*

This is easily answered by considering each end of the line in turn and reading back the co-ordinates. Thus: 'When discharge is low, suspended-sediment load is low; when discharge is high, suspended sediment is high.' Having noted this in rough, turn it into a more elegant form: 'As discharge rises, so does suspended-sediment load.' Note the mark allocation of 2 – clearly no more is required.

In more detailed analyses, the slope of the graph may be interpreted. On normal graph paper a straight line indicates a constant *amount* of change – the steeper the slope, the faster the amount of change. A curve indicates variations in the amount of change. (Do not stray into discussing very confusing *rates* of change.)

Should you be required to extract from, or insert data on to, a graph with a scale, use a set square for accuracy. Where no scale is given, you can use proportions. Thus, with reference to Fig. 43b, when discharge has doubled (point X2), load has increased by less than one-third:

$$\left(\frac{\text{distance Y2}}{\text{distance Y2} - \text{Y1}} \right)$$

Be especially watchful for graphs drawn on logarithmic scales. You cannot use proportion here. Remember that the values increase very rapidly along the axes on these graphs.

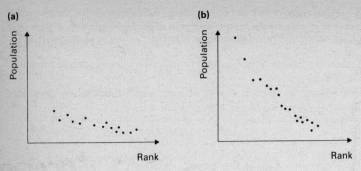

Fig. 44 *Rank–size relationships for the cities of two countries*

If you have to explain why patterns on graphs occur (Figs. 44a and b), do describe them first.

3. Pie graphs (divided proportional circles)

Learn to calculate proportions and percentages from these – *you will need a protractor*:
1) measure angle subtended by arc: a
2) calculate a/360 × 100 to produce percentage.

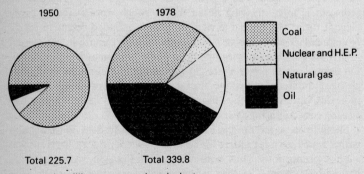

Totals are in million tonnes coal equivalent

Fig. 45 *Primary fuel consumption for a developed country*

In Fig. 45 natural-gas consumption in 1950 was 21/360 × 100 = 5.8% of 225.7 = 13.16 million tonnes coal equivalent.

In 1978 it was 60/360 × 100 = 16.6% of 339.8 = 56.63, i.e. a four-fold increase. Incorporate detail like this in answering Question 44.

Q. 44. With reference to Fig. 45, describe and account for the changing patterns of primary fuel consumption in a developed country of your own choice.   **[12 marks] [SCO. A]**

Only make calculations like these if you have a calculator and can work quickly.

Comparisons like these may be more easily made when the information is presented on bar graphs and flow lines.

4. Diagrams

Fig. 46 shows some survey results. You can use the map scale to determine the section scales both horizontal and vertical, and hence the enlarged section scale. Thus, on the map 1 cm represents 20 m; on the

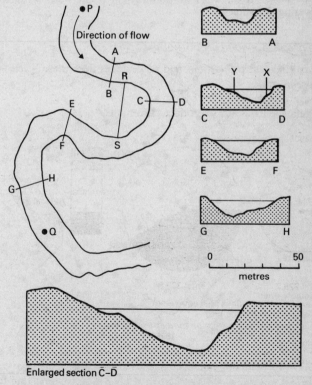

Fig. 46 *Map and sections derived from river survey*

sections horizontally 1 cm represents 10 m; vertically 1 cm represents about 6.6 m; on the enlarged section horizontally 1 cm represents:

$$\frac{\text{length section CD}}{\text{length enlarged section CD}} = \frac{2.3}{7.6} = 0.3 \times 10\,\text{m} = 3\,\text{m}.$$

Now you can use measurements in answering:

Q.45. Comment on the changes in the cross-section of the river in Fig. 46.

In Fig. 47, you should calculate the numbers of collieries closed since 1951 and the percentages of closures since 1951, i.e.

$$\left(\frac{\text{collieries closed since 1951}}{\text{collieries open} + \text{collieries closed since 1951}}\right) \times 100,$$

in answering Question 46.

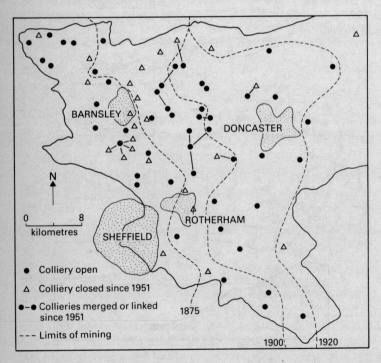

Fig. 47 *Yorkshire collieries*

Q. 46. Examine Fig. 47 giving selected information on the Southern Yorkshire Coalfield. Describe and suggest reasons for the changes which have taken place there since 1951. [SCO. A]

5. Photographs

You can use the height of a person – around 5 ft 8 in. or 1.7 m – to estimate the dimensions of a landform (allow for perspective), should they both appear in one photograph, as below.

If no reference point is available, proportions may be used. Thus, with reference to the photograph, 'The horizontal jointing at the top of the face is up to seven times more widely spaced than that at the foot.' You may mark the photograph with reference numbers and hand it in, if you wish. Don't forget to name and number the photograph with your personal details, if you do.

Q. 47. The photograph shows enclosed depressions in an area of massive limestone in southern Spain. The soil depth is up to one metre. Describe the landforms shown and provide a reasoned account of how they may have been formed. [OXF]

The only way to recognize a landform from a photograph is to have looked at landforms in photographs* and in the field.

6. Weather maps

You cannot explain weather maps without a thorough knowledge of (a) weather symbols and (b) meteorology (Chapter 10). You can improve your answer by referring to different parts of Great Britain by name.

All the techniques used in this chapter will 'sharpen up' your answers. Only *you* can decide whether (i) you have time to use them; (ii) the mark allocation indicates that it is worth taking the time to use them.

---

* The photographs in Holmes, A., *Principles of Physical Geology*, 3rd edn, Nelson, 1978, are excellent.

8. Projects – local studies – 'geographical essays'*

> No profit grows where is no pleasure ta'en;
> In brief, sir, study what you most affect [enjoy].
> (Shakespeare, *The Taming of the Shrew*)

Examiners increasingly require evidence of fieldwork. In addition to quoting fieldwork experience in answering examination questions, many candidates are obliged to submit reports on projects. Other Boards allow the project to be offered in addition to a practical examination paper and take the higher mark of the two.

There is an enormous variety in the place of the individual investigation within the overall mark structure – from 10% of the marks in Northern Ireland to 25% in the Scottish Higher Alternative syllabus, at the time of writing. Similarly the maximum number of words varies from 1,000 (SCO.A) to 5,000 (AEB). In the light of this variety, it is essential that you check:

(i) whether study 'titles' have to be submitted for approval and, if so, by what date
(ii) the closing date for entries
(iii) the size of paper: usually A4
(iv) the word limit
(v) whether there is an oral examination on the report of the investigation. If so, you are strongly advised to make a photocopy of your report so that you can revise from it and answer questions on it with confidence
(vi) whether there are any restrictions on your choice of study.

The answers to points (i)–(v) will be found in the copy of *Regulations and Syllabuses* for the appropriate Board. Make sure your copy applies to the year in which you are sitting A-level – many geography syllabuses have recently changed, or are about to.

Some Boards issue notes for the guidance of candidates undertaking individual research. At present these may be obtained from the Chief Examiner, Geography, Northern Ireland, and the Cambridge Secretary of the Oxford and Cambridge Board. (See point 2, p. 9.) Basically, however, the examiners are looking for the same things in a project.

* Required by the Scottish Higher Alternative syllabus.

135

A guide to individual investigations

1. The topic

A report based on a fieldwork exercise carried out by a whole class will not be acceptable. The best individual investigations are based on hypothesis testing, i.e. a careful study to determine whether a geographical idea holds good in real life. Thus,* instead of a vague title like 'An analysis of social segregation in West Belfast', you could single out one line of study on one theory to test. Possible options to the title above are:

   (i) How have patterns of social segregation changed in West Belfast between 1951 and 1981?
  (ii) How far do the patterns of social segregation in West Belfast run counter to the theories of Hoyt?
 (iii) Is class more important than religion in determining social segregation in West Belfast?

Keep your topic to a size you can investigate properly, with the apparatus available to you, and in the time available.

   Should your submitted title be rejected (referred) you should have an alternative in mind. The best thing to do is to submit more than one title, in case the first choice is referred. (8% of titles were rejected by the Northern Ireland examiner in 1981.†)

2. Aim

You should begin your investigation with a clear idea of the objective of the work. Your aim should be narrowly defined, and clearly stated when you write your report.

3. Data collection

After consulting background (**secondary**) sources, decide what data you are going to collect, the sampling methods, where relevant, and the techniques. Give yourself enough time to collect all the necessary information: lack of time is not an acceptable excuse for any shortcomings in your report. Do not rely too heavily on one technique: it may fail you. (This applies particularly to questionnaires.)

---

   * These suggestions are from *The Report of the Chief Examiner*, Northern Ireland Examining Board, 1981.
   † Northern Ireland Examining Board, op. cit.

4. Data analysis

If you are using statistical tests confine yourself to those (a) which are appropriate, and (b) which you understand. Table 29 may be helpful here.

Table 29. Statistical techniques

Statistical technique	Use	Comment
Calculation of mean value	Gives a representative figure	Calculate standard deviation to indicate how typical the mean is
Calculation of median	Gives a representative figure	Calculate interquartile range to indicate how typical the median is. Less valuable than mean
Calculation of standard error	Necessary to estimate how representative sample is	—
Chi-squared (χ^2) test	To establish whether causal factors are involved in a distribution*	Difficult to apply
Spearman's rank correlation	Tests for correlation by comparing ranks	Quick; simple; not very accurate
Pearson's coefficient	Tests degree of correlation	Longer, more complex, but more accurate than Spearman's coefficient

* i.e. whether some factor has caused the distribution of the phenomenon you are studying or whether it's just chance.

Writing the report

(a) State the aim of your investigation.
(b) By means of a map, locate the site(s) of your investigation.
(c) *Briefly* sketch in the geographical background to your study area, i.e. place it in its geographical context.
(d) Outline your plan of research, explaining the thinking behind it.
(e) Explain clearly the field-study techniques employed. Use diagrams wherever helpful, but don't sketch objects with which the examiner is familiar.

(f) Summarize your data. Full details can be given in tables at the end (**appendices**).

(g) Acknowledge any source other than your own fieldwork by means of footnotes, at the base of the page on which the information appears. Give the author's name first; then the title of the work, underlined; the name of the publisher; and the date of publication.

(h) Apply any necessary statistical analysis. You need only show the full method and working for any test on the first occasion of its use.

(i) Use a variety of cartographic methods to present your data. Number all maps and diagrams and refer to them by number in the text. Examiners frequently complain of the low standard of cartography – do take pains over your presentation.

(j) Interpret your findings. Support any statement you make with relevant evidence.

(k) In your conclusion, state what can be deduced and what cannot.

(l) Evaluate your study, showing an awareness of its weaknesses. Indicate how these might be overcome if you had access to all the facilities needed.

Some hints

Extra marks are given for originality and initiative. These are things that cannot be taught, but it might be helpful to know that urban studies predominate in each year's projects and that investigations into agriculture and geomorphology are rare. It is possible to undertake a library-based study for some Boards. One candidate impressed the examiners by making an explanatory comparison of the English and German motorway networks, using published sources.*

Finally, do try to find a topic which genuinely interests you (see Shakespeare, p. 135).

* Northern Ireland Examining Board, op. cit.

Part Two: Subject matter

9. Geomorphology

Geographers have their limitations.
(Salman Rushdie, *Shame*)

1. *Introduction*

Geomorphology is full of uncertainty. It is almost impossible to assess all the factors involved in landscape evolution and 'there is no prospect of proof in the absolute sense as in mathematics'.* In your writing, therefore, use terms like 'may' and 'is thought to be'.

The wording of the question is vital. Re-read pp. 120–27, and note also the following:

Give an example: simply naming one is insufficient; locate your example in its geographical context.

Process: the mechanism(s) creating the landform.

Landform: distinctive feature of crust's surface (also **landscape feature**).

Landscape evidence: aspects of landforms which support a theory.

Lithosphere: crust and upper mantle of the earth.

Describe (for landform): give shape, dimensions, locations
          (for process(es)): give a chronological explanatory account of
          the mechanism(s).

A. *Hints*

1) Allocate your time according to the mark allowance.
2) Answer the specified number of questions; only give the correct proportion of time to any question.
3) If you are given data, *use them* to comment and make deductions (see pp. 128–33).
4) For every landform, you should know: its appearance in the field and on O.S. maps; scale; the processes involved; and an example. Examples are given throughout this chapter, but it is much better for you to find your own.

* Pitty, A. F., *Introduction to Geomorphology*, Methuen, 1971.

5) *Spell geomorphological terms correctly.*
6) Study the type of question your Board asks. At present, JMB tends to set questions which encompass a range of topics, and JMB candidates are advised to learn *all* their geomorphology to cope with this question type. AEB favours questions which link landforms and human geography:

Q. 1. For two rock types, outline the influence which they have on man's activities. [AEB; part]

B. Some themes in geomorphology

(i) Dynamic equilibrium
This theory suggests that all forces in an environment will interact to produce a landform, and that when a delicate balance of forces (e.g. between erosion and deposition) has been achieved, the landform will retain its shape and dimensions (although it may change location). No landscape evolution will occur thereafter. The landform is self-adjusting to absorb changes. In this way a slope will adjust to prevailing conditions until height and angle are 'correct' – a state of equilibrium. If conditions change, the slope will change in height and angle until equilibrium is again achieved. This element of change is implied in the word 'dynamic'.

This theory is hotly contested. It does not take past processes – now not operating – into account. B. W. Sparks* tries to resolve the controversy by using as analogies two aspects of urban geography:
1) the town as a reflection of its history up to the present day
2) present-day patterns of activity in the town.
Both are equally important, but different, themes. In geomorphology the equivalents to the urban analogy are:
1) the landscape as a reflection of processes and conditions from past to present
2) present-day balances of factors: equilibrium.
   Dynamic equilibrium will be referred to again in connection with slopes, rivers and coastal geomorphology.

(ii) Convergence of form
i.e. can different processes form similar features? Mudflow deposits are very like boulder clay, for example.

* Sparks, B. W., *Geomorphology*, Longman, 1972.

Q. 2. 'Landforms of apparently similar shape may have been formed by different processes.' Discuss. [OXF]

Further examples are the 'steps' in the long profiles of some river valleys, caused either by glaciation or rejuvenation (pp. 170–72). Since shape, not size, is stressed you may also include weathering pits, about 20 cm across (p. 155), and nivation hollows, 10–60 m wide (p. 185).

(iii) Climatic geomorphology
Do differing climatic zones each have distinct landforms?

(iv) Are slow, small-scale processes more important than rare, but violent events, e.g. soil creep versus landslides?

2. Crustal movements

In 1915, WEGENER suggested that the continents, once joined, have drifted apart (**continental drift**). Supporting evidence came later:
  (i) The outlines of the continental shelves at the 500-m depth have a jigsaw 'fit' along most of their length.
 (ii) The geology and structure of eastern Latin America and West Africa, and eastern India and Western Australia, are strongly similar (Du Toit, 1937).
(iii) The magnetic orientation of continental rocks has changed (Creer, 1973).
Expansion of points (i)–(iii) through further reading* is necessary for most Boards.

A. Plate tectonics

Since 1965, Wegener's ideas have been developed into the theory of **plate tectonics** (**tectonic** = relating to the deformation of the earth's crust).

The crust is divided into sections, called **plates**; continental plates are up to 35 km deep, oceanic plates up to 5 km. Three types of plate **margin** (edge) are recognized (see Fig. 48):
  (i) **constructive** (**accreting**) margins, found at mid-oceanic ridges and, perhaps, rift valleys. Here, the crust splits and divides

* Tarling, D. H. and M. P., *Continental Drift*, Penguin, 1977.

(ii) **destructive (consuming)** margins, where the crust is 'narrowed' because

    (a) oceanic crust plunges into the mantle (**aesthenosphere**), forming **trenches** (or **ocean deeps**)

    (b) one continental plate underthrusts another. Where the Indian plate underthrusts the Eurasian the latter is compressed, forming the Himalayan fold-mountain range

(iii) **conservative (shear)** margins, which resemble transform faults.

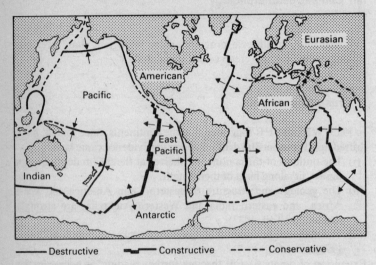

Fig. 48 *The distribution of plate margin types*

Plate tectonic theory can be used to account for:

1) volcanoes: located near mid-oceanic ridges, rift valleys, and destructive margins, where the submerged material metamorphoses (in the **subduction zone**) and rises (Fig. 49); *but* some volcanic exceptions are in the Eifel and Verkhoyansk Mountains (extinct in the first case and active in the second)

2) fold mountains (see pp. 146–7); *but* the Urals are not at a plate margin

3) island arcs, evolving where two oceanic plates collide

4) rift valleys (above). The Red Sea is at a constructive margin. The East African rift valley may be, *but* African volcanic material differs from that at oceanic ridges

5) ocean trenches (see above and Fig. 49).

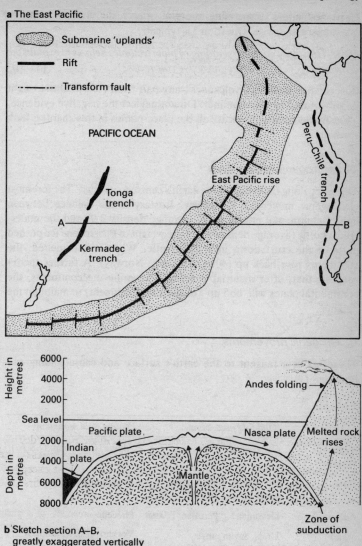

a The East Pacific

Submarine 'uplands'

Rift

Transform fault

PACIFIC OCEAN

Tonga trench

Kermadec trench

East Pacific rise

Peru–Chile trench

A — B

b Sketch section A–B, greatly exaggerated vertically

Height in metres — 6000, 4000, 2000

Sea level

Depth in metres — 2000, 4000, 6000, 8000

Andes folding

Pacific plate

Nasca plate

Melted rock rises

Indian plate

Mantle

Zone of subduction

Fig. 49 *Part of the Pacific, with explanatory cross-section*

Learn the nature of the plate margins, often tested by data-response questions. Otherwise, Question 3 is typical:

Q. 3. How does an understanding of plate tectonics help us to explain the distribution of earthquakes and active volcanoes? [SUJB]

For 'earthquakes' and 'volcanoes', any pair from (1)–(5) above might be substituted by the examiner. Do not neglect the negative evidence. You should be able to locate all the place-names in this chapter; look them up.

B. Epeirogenic movements

These act along the radius of the earth's centre to its crust. The foremost epeirogenic movement is **isostasy**. Isostasy is the balance between lighter continental crustal rocks (average density 2.9) and the underlying mantle (average density 3.3). The weight of Pleistocene ice pushed parts of the crust down into the mantle. When it had melted, the continents rose back up (40 m in Narvik, Norway). A further theory suggests that, after material is eroded, lowering the continents, the continental plates will 'bob up' (**isostatic readjustment**) to maintain the balance.

C. Orogenic movements

These act at a tangent to the earth's surface and cause folding and faulting:

Table 30.

	'Old' fold mountains		'Young' fold mountains
Name of orogeny	Caledonian	Hercynian	Alpine (Cascadian: U.S.A.)
Date	395 million yrs B.P.*	225 million yrs B.P.	65 million yrs B.P.
Era	Devonian	Permian/Triassic	Pliocene
Major locations	Urals, Sayan range (U.S.S.R.); Scandinavian mountains; Vosges; Grampians; Appalachians (U.S.A.); Great Divide (Australia)		Verkhoyansk Mountains Caucasus (U.S.S.R.); Himalayas; Zagros, Elburz (Iran); Carpathians (Romania); Dinaric Alps (Yugoslavia); Alps,

	'Old' fold mountains	'Young' fold mountains
		Apennines (Italy); Pyrenees; Alaska, Cascade, Sierra Nevada (U.S.A.); Andes
Characteristics	Only bases remain after prolonged erosion. Rarely rise over 1,000 m. Intensely deformed and metamorphosed	Curve-shaped ranges, narrow zones, along continental margins. Elevations 1,000–10,000 m. Intense folding; overfolds and overthrust faults
Landforms	Long, narrow ridges, lakes in lowlands. Old volcanic landforms	Ridge and valley topography. Features of glacial erosion because high enough to be permanently above snowline during Pleistocene. Active volcanoes

* Before the present.

You should be able to plot the young and old fold mountains on a world map:

Q. 4. Using a world map to illustrate your answer, describe and explain the distribution of the principal young fold-mountain systems.   [OXF]

The link between folding and plate tectonics is as follows:

1) colliding continental plates cause depression of the land. A slowly subsiding shallow sea (**geosyncline**) forms
2) thousands of metres of sediments accumulate as the geosyncline continues to sink
3) with further collision of the plates, these sediments are intensely folded, forming mountains. The sea drains away
4) faulting occurs
5) igneous activity exploits the faults. Batholiths, volcanoes and lava plateaux form. The latter are eroded to make **intermontane** (between mountains) plateaux.

Make up and practise diagrams to illustrate stages (1)–(5).

D. Faulting

You should be aware of the terminology of, and features produced by, faulting.

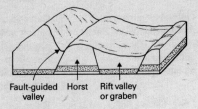

Fault-guided   Horst   Rift valley
valley   or graben

Fig. 50 *Some features of faulting*

Questions tend to concentrate on the effects of faulting:

Q. 5. Discuss the landscape evidence for faulting.   [LON; adapted]

In addition to conspicuous landscape features like **horsts** and **graben** (Fig. 50), you should note the formation of **fault scarps** produced where a weak rock and a strong one are brought together after faulting. The weaker rock is eroded more rapidly, leaving the resistant rock as a scarp. If you suspect a feature is a fault scarp, look for evidence of differing geology facing the scarp. **Breccia** – a shattered rock – is evidence of faulting. It is weak and therefore often exploited by rivers (**fault-guided valleys**). *But remember*: many faults exist without showing any trace in the landforms.

Resource aspects of faults include ore deposits, resulting from the upwelling of mineralizing fluids along the fault, and hot and cold springs utilizing the same route. You should find examples of all these from your regional studies.

3. Endogenetic landforms

The term **endogenetic** applies to processes and materials originating within the earth, notably earthquakes and **igneous activity**, i.e. upwelling of magma. **Intrusive** igneous activity is confined below the earth's crust; **extrusive** igneous activity is when magma – now termed **lava** – flows over the surface.

Most questions on igneous activity are concerned with landscape

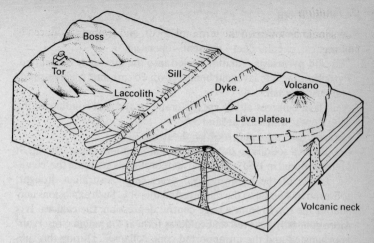

Fig. 51 *Possible relationship between igneous rocks and relief (after Sparks)*

appearance of igneous rocks (Fig. 51). Question 6 is a good basis for revision if you need to develop this topic.

Q. 6. (a) Define the term 'endogenetic process'.

(b) With reference to an area of between 20 km² and 200 km² which you have studied in the field or in class, describe the main endogenetic processes which operate and assess their importance in the development of landforms in the selected area. [WEL]

You might choose the granite intrusions of Devon or Cornwall, or the volcanic rocks in North Wales, the Lake District, or the Border Country. The detail you need is readily available in A. E. Trueman's *Geology and Scenery in England and Wales*, revised edition (Penguin, 1972).

Check your syllabus to see if you are required to study volcanoes, a summary of which follows.

Volcanoes

Whereas **volcanism (vulcanism, vulcanicity)** refers to *all* igneous activity, a **volcano** is the point at which igneous material erupts through the crust, and **volcanic** features are limited to those formed by volcanoes.

(i) Development

(a) COMPOSITE VOLCANOES

1) A vertical, circular duct – the **vent** – opens up.
2) Gas and **pyroclasts** – matter hurled into the air – may be emitted. Pyroclasts include lava and **bombs** (over 20 cm), **tuff** (pebble-sized) and dust-fine **ash**.
3) Acid lava emerges either via the crater or through conduits in the ashy slopes, which are around 30°.
4) Parasitic ash cones may form on the flanks.
5) Should lava solidify in the neck, violent eruptions occur. Mount St Helen erupted in 1981, and some meteorologists attribute the 'climatic' freaks of the following two years (e.g. Australian drought, followed by floods) to the dust ejected thereby. Such explosions may shatter the top to form a large central depression: the **caldera**. It is more generally believed that calderas form as the magma 'reservoir' is exhausted and the unsupported cone collapses. During this subsidence, concentric fissures may develop around the crater. Lava welling up into them solidifies to form **ring dykes**.

(b) SHIELD VOLCANOES

Basic, highly fluid lava spreads out widely from a central vent and from fissures on the gentle (3–4°) slopes.

(ii) Landscape features

Volcano slopes vary according to the nature of the lava (see above). Erosion modifies them. Ash absorbs rain; there is no erosion until overland water flow can occur. This will happen when weathering processes develop soil.

Drainage develops radially in humid climates. Harder volcanic rock resists water erosion, leaving the neck and dykes as pronounced features. Acid lava with **vesicles** (bubbles like those found in 'Aero' chocolate bars) forms rough terrain as in the 'malpais' or badlands of the south-western U.S.A.

In *hot* arid areas, running water acts rarely (p. 186); alternate heating and cooling may cause shattering (but see p. 190) and a debris-covered surface. In *cold* arid areas, frost shattering is important.

Q. 7. (a) *Describe the different types of volcanic features which may be formed on the earth's surface and within the earth's crust. Give named examples where appropriate.*

(b) *Discuss the ways in which volcanic activity can have both destructive and constructive influences on man's activities.*

[SCO.T]

4. Lithology and landscape

Lithology refers to the physical and chemical characteristics of rocks. In Chapter 1 (p. 26) we saw something of landforms associated with sedimentary rocks. You can use the details of the Corfe area given in Chapter 1 to answer Question 8.

Q. 8. Choose any two rock types:
(a) examine the relationships between lithology and landform develop-
    ment;
(b) for the rock types which you have selected, outline the influence
    which they have on man's activities.   [AEB]

Choose two contrasting types – for example the chalk and the sandstone. Enlarge the relevant section of the traverse (p. 18) to illustrate your points.

Equilibrium and lithology

HACK, an initiator of the 'dynamic equilibrium' concept, claimed that to transport weathered material on quartzite at the same rate as shale, 'greater energy, and therefore greater relief and steeper slopes are required', i.e. the slope develops to the required angle (different in each case) and then stops.

Some examples of lithological control of landforms

(i) Karst scenery – a summary

1) NECESSARY PRECONDITIONS

Area: large enough for some part to be free from influences of other lithologies.

Thickness: deep enough – as above.

Limestone type: (a) crystalline, therefore hard: karst features are not
                        eroded from soft limestones
                  (b) well **bedded** – layered – and **jointed** – divided into
                        blocks by cracks. Beds and joints guide the under-
                        ground drainage.

Elevation: well above sea level for underground water circulation to develop.

Rainfall: over 500 m for sufficient water provision.

2) PROCESSES

(a) The solution of limestone along joints and bedding planes by slightly acid rainwater (carbonic acid).*

(b) The re-deposition of limestone on evaporation of water in (a).

(c) The subsidence of areas weakened by underground solution.

Fig. 52 shows the main karst features, labelled (a), (b) and (c) to indicate the above-described processes.

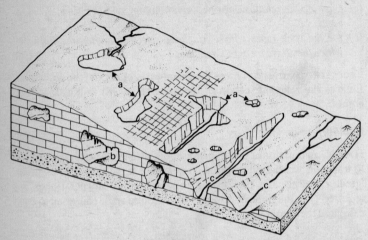

Fig. 52 *Processes in karst landform development (after Sparks)*

3) PROBLEMS†

(a) Do solution holes result from ground-level processes or underground solution and collapse?

(b) Is climate or lithology more important in karst formation?

(ii) Chalk scenery

The characteristics of chalk scenery are noted in Table 3, p. 26. A **dry valley** occurs chiefly in chalk and limestone areas. Several explanations have been advanced for their formation:

1) as the water table fell, so the streams 'dried up', leaving a valley

2) river capture diverted the valley-forming stream

3) the valley was cut by mud glaciers in periglacial conditions

4) surface streams flowed over partially frozen ground in periglacial

---

* Sometimes called carbon dioxide weathering.

† For a full discussion, see Sparks, op. cit., pp. 200–201.

conditions. The lowered sea level at this time contributed to the steep downcutting.

(iii) Igneous landforms

Table 31.

Rock	Formation	Landscape effect	Example
Granite	**Batholith**: large intrusive dome	Extensive uplands	Henry Mountains, Utah; Dartmoor
	Boss: circular intrusion <25 km	Steep-sided upland	St Austell Moor
	Tors: small outcrops weathered along joints	Rectangular blocks	Yes Tor, Dartmoor
Dolerite	**Sills**: concordant with bedding	Linear ridges, ledges	Great Whin Sill, Northumberland
	Dykes: cut across bedding		
Basalt	**Lava**: plateau	Elevated flat land, edges abrupt and often jointed polygonally	Antrim plateau

PROBLEMS

Are tors formed by underground weathering and subsequently exhumed? Do tors form only where chemical weathering is very active? Are they the result of periglacial processes?*

Remember that all rocks have variations of composition and structure.

Relationships between lithology and landforms are not constant and predictable.

On a smaller scale, lithology has a great effect on the nature of weathering in the landscape.

* For the periglacial theory of Palmer and Neilson, see Small, R. J., *The Study of Landforms*, Cambridge University Press, 1978, pp. 133–5.

5. Weathering

Be absolutely clear: **weathering** breaks down rocks *in situ* (on the spot); **erosion** is the breakdown *and transport* of rock by a moving force. Pitty* maintains that 'all weathering reactions involve water' and that 'the crucial factor is the ease with which water enters the rock'. Not everyone would agree: see 'Desert landforms' (p. 189).

Table 32 gives a basis for answering Question 9. You can improve your answer by giving full explanations and examples.†

Q. 9.   (a) *What is understood by the terms:*
          (i) erosion and (ii) **weathering***?*
     (b) *Discuss the weathering processes important in TWO of the following landscapes:*
          (i) arid deserts;
          (ii) alpine mountain summits;
          (iii) coastlines;
          (iv) karst.   [NI]

Note the inclusion of coastlines in this question. Weathering is a factor in coastal geomorphology which most candidates ignore.

Factors affecting weathering rates in rocks

(a) MINERAL CONTENT:
Lighter minerals (e.g. quartz) are generally more resistant than dark (e.g. mica). A **micaceous** band can be a source of weakness in a resistant rock.

(b) CRYSTAL SIZE (texture):
Coarse-grained rock (e.g. granite) should weather more rapidly than finer-grained counterpart (i.e. rhyolite).

(c) JOINTING:
Weathering along joints leaves unaltered blocks between: **spheroidal weathering**.

N.B.: Note these sources of weakness in resistant rocks.

(d) CLIMATE:
See Fig. 53.

(e) TIME.

* op. cit.
† Sparks, op. cit., pp. 22–32.

Two themes recur in 'weathering' questions:
1) The role of weathering in landscape development. Revise for this by choosing two named examples of contrasting landscapes, e.g. clay vale, granite upland. For each, in turn, explain the weathering types involved. Then comment on other relevant factors from: lithology, structure, agents of erosion (ice and water: discussed later).
2) The relative importance of mechanical (physical) and chemical weathering in different climatic environments.

Q. 10. 'Although stress is often laid on mechanical weathering in certain environments and on chemical weathering in others, this merely indicates their relative importance.' Amplify this statement. [OXF]

Fig. 53 sums up the variations in weathering type with climate. Do not learn it: make notes from it. Supplement it with information from Table 32 (overleaf).

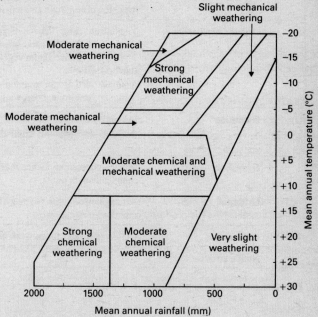

Fig. 53 *Weathering, temperature and rainfall (source:* Annals of American Geographers*)*

Weathering pits are hollows found in rock outcrops in all latitudes. Salt and evaporation seem to be important in their formation.

155

Table 32.   Major weathering processes

	Weathering process	Summary
MECHANICAL	**Pressure release**	As erosion exhumes landforms, rocks expand, cracking: (i) along the joints (ii) parallel with surface: **sheeting**
	Crystal growth	1) Ice. Water expands by 9% on freezing: (i) **frost shattering**: atmospheric moisture on rock (ii) **freeze–thaw**: water infiltrates rock 2) Salt crystals
	Thermal expansion	Heating expands and cooling contracts rock. Resulting strain shatters rock
	Organic weathering	Vegetation: fungi, lichens, tree roots fracture rock; **humic acid** derived from vegetation Bacteria: vital Animals: bird droppings (guano) attack limestone; burrowing animals
CHEMICAL	**Hydration***	Minerals expand as they absorb water. Alternate wetting and drying causes cracks
	Hydrolysis*	Minerals decompose when reacting chemically with water
	Oxidation	Atmospheric oxygen reacts with rock: less resistant oxides formed
	Carbonation	CO_2 in rainwater forms weak **carbonic acid**
	Humic acids (above)	

* Not to be confused; remember: the A in HydrAtion = Absorption.

Comments	Where found / landform
Confirmation: in igneous rocks, joints rarely extend below 10-m depth	Granite
Leads to **exfoliation**: splitting of outer rock surface	Exfoliation zone
Restricted to rocks permeable because of pores or joints	Greatly affects saturated chalk
Dependent on occasional rainfall; high evaporation rates	Hot deserts
Questioned by Grigg (p. 190)	Hot deserts
Mechanical and chemical process inter-related	Wherever life-forms exist
Organic weathering GROSSLY NEGLECTED BY CANDIDATES	
Clays can expand by >35% during hydration	Polygonal cracks in mudflats, deserts
Hydration alone fragments shales	
Usually found in conjunction with hydration	Igneous rocks susceptible in humid environments
Affects iron compounds in rocks: colour-changes are common	Temperate and tropical, humid; sedimentary rocks, notably clays
Often supplemented by humic acids	Limestones, dolomites
Can form pits 3–12 m in diameter	S. Piedmont, U.S.A.

6. Mass movement

This term, synonymous with **mass wasting**, gives candidates unnecessary difficulty. It is simply the downslope movement of material, influenced by gravity and lubricated by water.

Types of mass movement

SHARPE suggested this series:
1) **slopewash**: rainwater; a little fine debris
2) **sheetflow**: rainwater; fine debris
3) **mudflow**: saturated, viscous, fine debris
4) **soil creep**: saturated debris and soil
5) **debris avalanche**: rock particles, little water
6) **landslide**: abundant debris, very little water.

The ratio of water to debris decreases down the series. The debris either **flows** (1)–(4) or **slides** (5)–(6). Fig. 54 shows the difference.

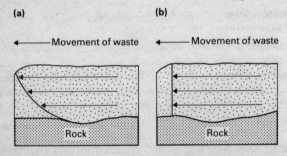

Fig. 54 Velocity distribution in (a) a flow and (b) a slide (after Sparks)

The slope angle needed to trigger off each type rises down the series. **Soil creep** is the most frequently occurring form of mass movement in Britain.

Evidence for soil creep includes:
(a) fences and telegraph posts leaning downhill
(b) walls bulging under the weight of soil
(c) turf rolls
(d) particles found downslope from higher outcrop.

Causes of soil creep include raindrop impact, rainwash, and the lifting of particles by the growth beneath them of ice crystals: **frost heaving**.

Rates of soil creep can be measured by digging **Young pits**. A hole is dug with sides parallel to the direction of maximum slope. Wires are set in vertically. The pit is filled in. When re-excavated, any downslope movement of the wires can be checked against a plumbline.

Landslips usually occur when a resistant, permeable rock is underlain by a weak impermeable clay. They can produce scarps 30–60 m high and up to 3 km long. *Slipping* should be easily distinguishable from *faulting* because the dip angles are the same in faulting. However, faults don't show up well in clay, and later debris accumulations obscure faults.

Examiners are distressed because candidates do not seem to have seen any weathering and mass wasting (sometimes also called **sub-aerial processes**) – and yet these operate on every slope in Britain. Go outside: observe; measure; note down.

7. Slope development

The morphology (form) of a slope has been attributed to:

(i) Lithology, e.g. lower slopes (**pediments**) in Australia are 3° on granite, 5.8° on gneiss.

(ii) Structure: 'it cannot be too strongly emphasized that structure is the most important factor determining the morphology of slopes' (C. R. Twidale).*

(iii) Past processes, e.g. glacial erosion (pp. 180–81), periglacial processes (pp. 183–6), vulcanicity.

(iv) Present processes:

(a) WEATHERING. Weathered material from upslope accumulates as scree downslope (Fig. 55a (WOOD)).

(b) WATER EROSION. Rainwash, spread thinly (unconcentrated) upslope, increases in volume downslope. Gullies form, erosion and, therefore, slope angle increase (Fig. 55b (FENNEMAN, LAWSON, HORTON)).

* Quoted in Pitty, op. cit.

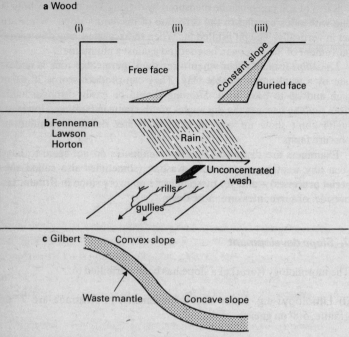

Fig. 55 *Some models of slope development*

(c) SOIL CREEP. As the volume of material increases downslope, the slope steepens to transport the soil (Fig. 55c (GILBERT)). This utilizes the dynamic-equilibrium concept discussed above (pp. 142 and 151).

(d) MASS MOVEMENTS including soil creep, and finally:

(e) PARALLEL RETREAT (slope angle is constant as hillside is cut back):

Arguments against	*Arguments for*
1) Debris accumulation would prevent erosion over whole face	1) (a) Powerful, undercutting rivers will remove debris (b) Scree destroyed by further weathering in Colorado sandstones (SCHUMM; CHORLEY)
2) Some valleys in homogeneous rocks have asymmetrical	

160

Arguments against	Arguments for
cross-sections (at different angles)	
3) Laboratory experiments show that slope angles change with continued water erosion	3) Experiments cannot replicate actual conditions
	4) Solifluxion (p. 185) could 'skin' a slope rapidly

The notion that slope angles decline (angles get lower, thus changing) is at variance with the concept of parallel retreat. Most probably, both slope-angle lowering and parallel retreat occur, the latter dominating where the debris is removed efficiently.

If you are now 'confused, and suspect that there are . . . contradictions in the various ideas . . . rest assured that this is a reflection of the state of slope study'.* Make this clear in answering slope questions:

Q. 11. Explain, with the aid of models, the main theories which have been advanced for the evolution of slopes. [WEL; part]

Dynamic equilibrium and slopes

Q. 12. How does the concept of dynamic equilibrium add to our ideas of slope development? [LON]

First, re-read the outline of the dynamic-equilibrium concept (p. 142). Secondly, show some of the forces acting on a slope, as in Fig. 56.

The concept is useful because it stresses the importance and interaction of forces peculiar to *each* slope – in strong contrast to the ideas of W. M. DAVIES who thought that, for example, all humid landscapes would develop in the same way, given time. Thus, lithology, structure, river erosion and debris accumulation help to determine the slope angle; rates of weathering and the effects of vegetation influence soil depth; climate and soil properties are reflected in the amount of soil water, which is itself an important factor in mass movement and hence slope form.

The theory has also been invoked in Gilbert's soil-creep hypothesis (pp. 160–61). Furthermore, it may contribute to the discussion of one of the controversies on p. 143: the relative importance of slow small-scale

* Sparks, op. cit.

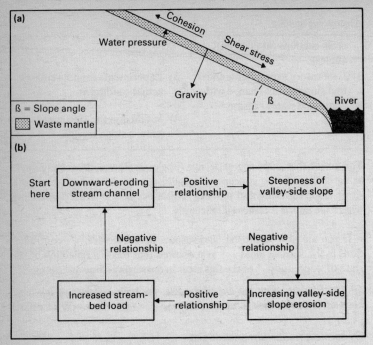

Fig. 56 *Some balances of forces on a slope*

movements and short but violent ones. Equilibrium has been attained through the long-term effects of weathering, lithology and structure, soil creep, etc. If the balance is lost, we may see a violent reaction occurring, like a landslide, to re-establish an equilibrium.

8. Hydrology

Hydrology is the study of water on earth. **Geographical hydrology** is mostly concerned with the movement of water between the atmosphere, land and sea. Fig. 57 shows something of how water circulates between these environments in the **hydrological cycle**.

Hydrologists are particularly concerned with the processes whereby water reaches a river; some precipitation will be in the form of snow and may therefore remain static until the snow melts. Rain, fog and dew may be **intercepted** (absorbed) by vegetation: 50% or more in tropical

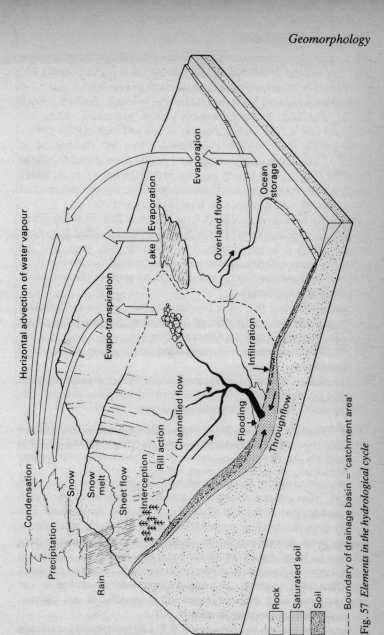

--- = Boundary of drainage basin = 'catchment area'

Fig. 57 *Elements in the hydrological cycle*

Rock

Saturated soil

Soil

rain forests. Some of the remaining water will **infiltrate** (seep into) the soil. The amount of infiltration depends on: the soil – its porosity and water content; the precipitation – particularly its intensity.

Infiltration capacity is the maximum rate, in mm/h, at which rainfall can be absorbed. If the underlying rock is permeable, water will percolate into it. The **storage capacity** of soil and rock may be filled – more quickly if the rock is **impermeable** (does not allow water to infiltrate) – and the level of underground water – the **water table** – rise to meet the surface. This usually happens first at the bottom of the valley which is also receiving water via **throughflow** from lateral movement of water through the soil, above the level of the water table.

When the capacity is exceeded, water moves in films or sheets across the ground: **overland flow**. (This differs from the **channelled flow** of the streams which is usually confined between the river banks.) If the volume of water entering streams and rivers (**run-off**) is too great to be held in the channel, and/or the storage capacity of the catchment area is exceeded, flooding occurs.

It should be clear that there is a time-lag between the precipitation falling and any rise in the volume of the river. See the hydrograph, Fig. 23b, p. 56. This time-lag varies according to:

(a) the amount of interception (depending on the nature and extent of vegetation)

(b) the storage capacity of the catchment area; in turn dependent on soil type and depth, rock type, and pre-existing soil water content

(c) the gradients of the catchment-area slopes.

Q. 13. What conditions are likely to cause flooding along a British river and what steps might be adopted to control flood-water discharge and to limit damage to land and property? [SUJB]

The construction of buildings and roads radically affects infiltration capacity. Tiles, slates and tarmac do not absorb much water: there is so little storage that drains and storm sewers must be constructed. This usually stops the flooding that would otherwise inevitably occur but, of course, areas downstream of the buildings will rapidly receive large volumes of 'town' water. Not all the water runs to the sea. Plants emit water vapour by transpiration; evaporation occurs. These two processes are considered together as **evapo-transpiration**. Hydrologists can measure how much evapo-transpiration is possible in any climate. This is **potential evapo-transpiration (P.E.T.)**.

Some aspects of the interaction of P.E.T. and precipitation are shown in Fig. 58, taken from a London data-response question:

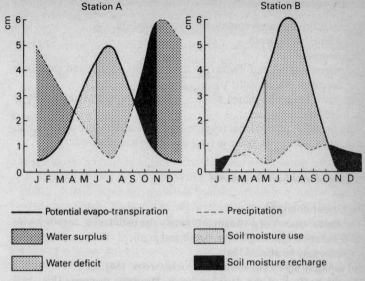

Fig. 58 *Soil moisture budgets*

Q. 14 (a) **From the graphs** *derive a definition for each of the following terms used:*
  (i) soil moisture use;
  (ii) soil moisture recharge.
  (b) Account for the differences in the soil moisture budgets of A and B. [LON; adapted]

9. Rivers

Rivers erode by **hydraulic action, **corrasion** and **solution** (corrosion). They transport their load in three forms: **dissolved load**, **suspended load**, **bed load**. Their capacity to hold the load depends on:
  (i) **discharge**: amount of flow in cubic metres per second (**cumecs**)
 (ii) **velocity**: often determined by gradient; checked by lakes and seas**
(iii) cross-section: see hydraulic radius (p. 56).

  – ** You should know the section between asterisks, and much more about rivers, from O-level. To revise this, see Mayhew, S., *Penguin Passnotes: Geography*, Penguin, 1984, pp. 56–65.

Stream-course analysis

The relationships most commonly investigated are:
 (i) radius* with depth
 (ii) sinuosity
(iii) wave length* and discharge: investigators have found that wave
      length ∝ (varies with) √bankfull discharge
(iv) wave length:* channel width – normally found to show a ratio of
      10:1.

If, in the field, you find that relationships (iii) and (iv) do not hold good,
you might assume a change in river discharge has occurred.

Changes in the river channel

(i) Linear changes

The **linear** aspects of a stream are simply the path taken, together with
its tributaries, ignoring width, depth and gradient. The course taken by
a stream may be affected by:

(a) small structures in underlying rocks (see p. 154)
(b) the geology of the drainage basin. **Dendritic drainage** (Fig. 59a)
    develops on homogeneous (all of the same kind) rocks, especially
    when the rock is clay. **Trellised drainage** (Fig. 59b) is often associ-
    ated with areas of gently dipping beds; on domes a **radial** and
    concentric pattern may develop (Fig. 59c)

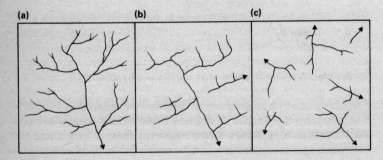

(a)   **(b)**   **(c)**

Fig. 59 *Drainage patterns*

---

* See Fig. 23d (p. 56) for explanations of these terms.

(c) glacial diversion (p. 183)

(d) **stream capture**: **subsequent** streams (those following lines of geological weakness) cut down rapidly. They also erode back from their springs (**spring sapping**). If, by this process, a subsequent stream reaches another river which is either flowing more slowly and circuitously and/or has most of its course at a higher level, it may divert part of that stream into its own course: stream capture. See also pp. 27–9

(e) **superimposed drainage patterns**,* i.e. drainage developed in response to rocks of different structure which have now been completely removed by erosion. The pattern has persisted, although the geology is now different

(f) **antecedence**: a stream continues to cut through a fold rising in its path.

Points (a), (b) and (d) would support the contention that drainage patterns are related to geological structure and point (e) indicates the influence of past geologies. Points (c) and (f) indicate that other factors influence drainage patterns. Use the Corfe extract and geology map to provide examples.

(ii) Cross-sectional changes

Q. 15. Using illustrations, describe and discuss the reasons for changes in river-channel cross-section which occur along a river as it moves from its inception in the uplands to the flat valley plain. [NI]

Question 15 seems to indicate that there is an orderly development of channel cross-sections from start to finish. This is suspiciously like W. M. Davies's ideas of Youth, Maturity and Old Age, to which you should *not* refer unless directly asked to.

The following will affect the shape of the cross-section:

(a) STRUCTURE: streams exploiting faults will find vertical erosion easier.

(b) COMPOSITION OF BANK: **lateral erosion** (sideways broadening of channel) is easier in weak rocks, e.g. tropical river banks where chemical weathering has been very active; unconsolidated fluvio-glacial sands and gravels. Meanders occur most in clay; braiding in sand.

(c) NATURE OF LOAD: a river carrying coarse sediment tends to have a wider, shallow channel.

* See Sparks, op. cit., pp. 150–55, for superimposed drainage. Pick *one* example.

(d) DISCHARGE (i.e. volume of flow per second): given a sudden increase in discharge (perhaps as a tributary enters), a meandering river will start braiding.

(e) PROCESSES:
 (i) *Meandering*. Every physical geography text will show the asymmetrical cross-section of a meander. Note here that meandering:
   – does *not* occur because 'the river cannot downcut further'
   – is *not* caused by obstacles
   – is *not* restricted to any 'stage' of stream development.
 (ii) *Erosion*. A stream can erode vertically and/or laterally. Why lateral erosion should sometimes dominate is unclear, but it is lateral erosion that is responsible for cutting the flood-plain (primarily an erosional feature, often overlain by later sedimentation).
 (iii) **Deposition** occurs when velocity slackens. Do not think of deposition as quite separate from erosion: they occur simultaneously across a meander belt. Scouring will occur as a river rises, in flood, to be followed by deposition as it subsides. One feature caused by deposition is . . .
 (iv) **Braiding**, i.e. the dividing and reuniting of the stream. We have seen above how braiding is related to gradient and load.
 (v) **Pool and riffle development**. Rivers develop deeper sections – pools – and ridges of sediments causing shallow water – riffles (or **shoals**). Riffles occur regularly in rivers, at distances five to seven times the river's width. The reason for this is not fully understood.
 (vi) **Rejuvenation**. After uplift of the land, streams are given greater power to erode vertically (p. 170).

Equilibrium states and rivers

MACKIN developed the idea that streams reach a state 'in which slope is delicately adjusted to provide just the velocity required for the transportation of all the load'. This state he termed **grade**: beyond which a river would not change.

Some writers have attempted to explain meander development in terms of self-adjustment of a stream. Velocity is high as the stream emerges from the uplands, so meanders develop to absorb excess energy.

Drainage (fluvial) morphometry

Morphometry is the precise and objective measurement of landforms. In fluvial morphometry, the emphasis has been on the geometric properties of rivers and their basins.

Stream orders

STRAHLER developed the idea of ranking streams from Horton. At their initiation, all streams are **first-order streams** with no tributaries. When two first-order streams meet, a **second-order stream** forms. Two second-order streams meet to make a **third-order stream**, and so on. If a stream of lower order meets any stream, there is no change in rank.

The 'law'* of stream numbers is that the number of streams decreases as you go up the order: there are more first-order streams in a drainage basin, fewer second-order, and so on. The **bifurcation ratio** is the ratio of the number of streams of one order to the number in the rank above. Furthermore, stream length increases as order increases, and drainage-basin area increases as order increases.

Drainage density is calculated as:

$$\frac{\text{total length of channels in basin}}{\text{area of basin}}.$$

Q. 16. (a) *Explain the meaning of the following hydrological terms: 'stream order', 'bifurcation ratio', 'drainage density', and 'area of catchment'.*
   (b) *Discuss the relationships which are considered to exist between them, illustrating your answer with a named example.*
                                                                 [WEL]

You can best revise this by studying any drainage basin on an O.S. map. Trace off the drainage network, order the streams, count the number in each order to work out bifurcation ratios and, using dividers, calculate the mean length of streams in each order. Note the word 'considered' in part (b). You will be able to say whether these relationships do, in fact, exist in an area you have studied.

Drainage density

The greater the drainage density, the faster the run-off (because water moves faster in channels than through the soil). Thus flooding, for a given quantity of rainfall, is more likely in a region with a high drainage density.

* Not a true law; simply a statistical probability in *any* branching system.

Drainage density in an area is affected by:

(a) LITHOLOGY: note these observations:

Rock	Drainage density
Southern England: chalk	1.8–2
Eastern U.S.A.: sandstone	4
U.S.A.: deeply weathered, metamorphic	10–20
U.S.A.: soft, Pleistocene sediments	20–30

(b) Clearly WEATHERING has a part to play.

(c) MEAN ANNUAL FLOOD: Smith and Stopp show clear relationships between mean annual flood in cumecs and drainage density in Wales, Wisconsin and north-eastern U.S.A.*

(d) RAINFALL INTENSITY: the higher the rainfall intensity (in mm/min), the greater the drainage density.

(e) VEGETATION COVER is thought to lower drainage density.

10. Changes in sea level

A positive change in base level involves a rise in sea level; **a negative change in base level** occurs when sea level falls.

These changes may be due to movements in the land. An isostatic change is an upward movement of the crust to maintain the crust/mantle balance (p. 146). **Eustastic** change occurs when:
 (i) the volume of sea water changes and/or
(ii) the capacity of the ocean basins changes through tectonic movements.

Rivers and sea-level change

In a negative change, sea level and hence **base level** (the lowest level to which a river can erode) fall. The river is now higher in relation to base level than formerly and hence has more energy, i.e. the river is **rejuvenated** (mnemonic: Negative = Base Lower = Rejuvenation (NoBLeR)).

Possible consequences of rejuvenation are:

* Smith, D. I., and P. Stopp, *The River Basin*, Cambridge University Press, 1978.

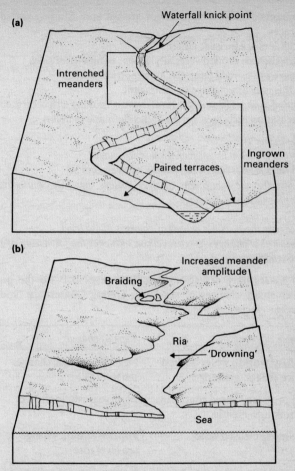

(a)

Waterfall knick point

Intrenched meanders

Ingrown meanders

Paired terraces

(b)

Increased meander amplitude

Braiding

Ria

'Drowning'

Sea

Fig. 60 *Some effects of base-level change on rivers*

1) the extension of the river course from the old to the new shoreline
2) renewed erosion starting from the mouth to form a steeper section which may recede upstream (**headward erosion**)
3) where the new profile meets the old, a break of slope or **knick point** (often marked by a waterfall) may occur. The presence of several knick points on a river (showing as steps in the long profile) indicates a number of base-level changes

4) remnants of the old valley floor are cut into, forming **paired** river terraces*
5) meanders are **incised**: either
   - **intrenched**: eroded vertically: steep, symmetrical sides
   - **ingrown**: eroded laterally: asymmetrical sides.

All of this may affect slope development.

Positive changes (rise in sea level) have a 'braking' effect on the rivers. Sedimentation increases, on the valley floor and in deltas.

Q. 17. Either (a)
 (i) *What is meant by rejuvenation of drainage?*
 (ii) *What theories have been advanced to explain it?*
 (iii) *Describe the landforms of river valleys that can be attributed to rejuvenation of drainage.*

Or (b)
 (i) *Review the possible causes of changes in sea level.*
 (ii) *Show that changes in sea level can influence the formation of certain coastal features.* [NI]

The Quaternary era (from 2 million years B.P. to the present) has seen many changes of sea level. During Quaternary times, the **Pleistocene** glaciations occurred.

Sequence of events	Type of change
1) 30% of world's water 'locked' in ice sheets, glaciers	Negative eustatic change: sea level fell
2) Ice pressure caused continents to sink into mantle	Positive isostatic change
3) Ice melt released water	Positive eustatic change: sea level rose
4) Ice pressure no longer on continents: they rose from mantle	Negative isostatic change: sea level fell as land rose

This sequence occurred entirely, or in part, several times. Fig. 61 shows how these fluctuations might have affected coastal landforms.

* Terraces can also be formed in fluvio- and periglacial conditions, where large quantities of material overload streams. **Aggradation** (building up a surface by deposition) occurs. Climatic change leads to reduced debris supply and the incision by rivers into these deposits, hence terrace creation.

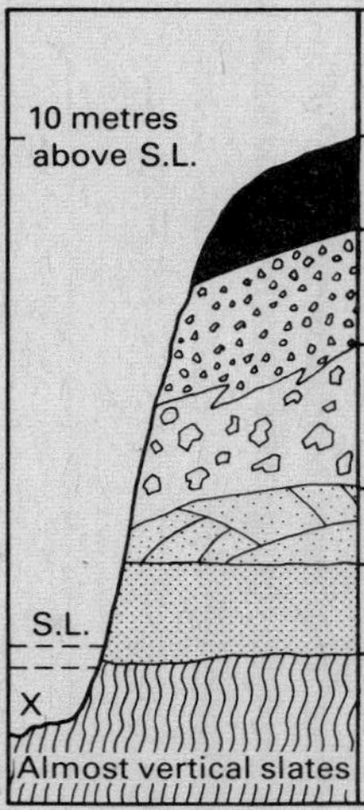

Deposit	Sea level in relationship to present day	Comments
Soil	Same	Weathering and sub-aerial erosion
SOLIFLUXION DEPOSITS: Medium-grade angular debris	Lower	Solifluxion at end of Quaternary
SOLIFLUXION DEPOSITS: Coarse-grade angular fragments Fossil ice wedges	Lower	Periglacial process during Quaternary
Dune sands Dune bedded	Higher	Dune bedding
Marine sands and shelly fossils	Higher	Beach deposits, 2 m thick, now 1 m above sea level
	Lower	Note wave-cut platform at X

10 metres above S.L.

S.L.

X

Almost vertical slates

S.L. = Sea level

Fig. 61 *Sea-level changes and coastal scenery (source: JMB Paper I, 1981)*

173

Fig. 61 is on a small scale, but a detailed example like this will suffice for the first option in Question 18.

Q. 18. 'Positive and negative changes in base level have had a profound effect on coastal landforms.' Discuss and illustrate this statement with reference to either one detailed coastal example or a range of less detailed examples. [LON]

Your answer must begin with definitions. Should you choose a 'range of examples', you should mention:

(a) **'drowned' coastlines (coastlines of submergence)**. Atlantic and Pacific coastlines; rias; fjords. In sheltered, recently 'drowned' areas, the typical features of coastal erosion (p. 178) may be absent, and weathering and mass movement will dominate the landforming processes

(b) **coastlines of emergence**. The resulting offshore gradient may be very gently sloping so that shoreline sedimentation, resulting in offshore bars, banks, sand-dunes and salt marshes, will dominate.

However, 'there are serious dangers in generalizing about coastal features produced by sea-level changes. So much will depend on other factors.'*

Raised beaches certainly are a result of a fall in base level; whether or not they are accompanied by **dead cliffs** depends on the former coastline.

In Britain, there has been post-glacial **marine transgression** ('drowning') and isostatic recovery, particularly in northern England and Scotland. The '8-m beach' is the result of the latter. It shows up in the form of shingle deposits, marine clays, spits and, in places, cliffs and a wave-cut platform, all between 1 and 12 m O.D. (above sea level). In western Scotland, a series of raised beaches occurs.

Remember that sea-level changes have not affected the whole world in the same way, as Fig. 62 indicates:

---

* See Small, op. cit., p. 434, where the 'other factors' are discussed.

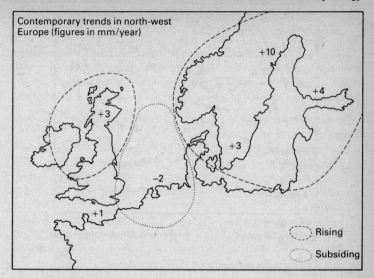

Fig. 62 *Present-day trends of sea-level change in north-west Europe*

11. Other coastal landforms

Dynamic equilibrium and coasts

It is in coastal geomorphology that equilibrium states seem to be found most often; for example, a spit forming across an estuary will narrow the course of the river, thereby increasing river velocity until no more deposition is possible. This is the point of equilibrium. Beaches also represent the changing balance of cliff composition, beach material, wave action, tides, currents and weather, and may produce lasting profiles.

Q. 19. Consider and exemplify the view that the coast may be regarded as an equilibrium system (i.e. that it represents a balance between constructive and destructive processes). [LON]

Any answer must be based on actual examples ('exemplify'), preferably from fieldwork. A small bay on a steep rocky coast is often an independent system, analysis of its beach material showing that it is derived from the cliffs behind. Fig. 63 shows some of the features you might be looking for:

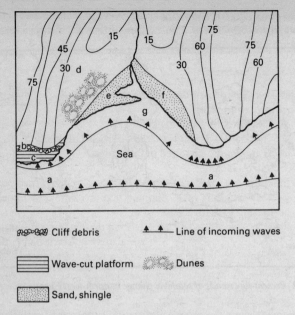

Fig. 63 *Balance of constructive and destructive forces on a coastline*

Wave refraction (a) is the process whereby waves are 'turned' to concentrate their erosive power on headlands (**forelands**). This has been attributed to:

(i) friction from the sea floor, or

(ii) changes in the flow pattern of the waves enforced as the water shallows. Wave refraction could smooth an indented coastline *if it is of one rock type.*

Material eroded from the cliff face may form a protective layer against further erosion at the cliff base (b) or part of a wave-built platform (c), which will lessen the impact of the waves on the cliff. The cliff headland itself may provide sufficient shelter for dunes (d) to form on land, or sedimentation (e) to occur in the bay. Beach gradients (f) are affected by waves: steep (destructive) waves move sediment downbeach, 'flattening' the beach and reducing wave steepness. Flatter waves build the beach up until its steepness affects the waves, making them destructive again. Bay mouth bars (g) retain their form, being attacked on the seaward side and depositing on the landward side.

However, Fig. 61 shows that *past processes and conditions* have also affected coastal scenery. Coastal form is thus not always a reflection of the balance of present conditions.

Cliff-form: controls

A **cliff** is any steep slope descending to the shore.

Structural controls include:
(a) *dip*: seaward dip – sloping cliff likely
    horizontal or landward dip – vertical cliff likely
(b) *joints and faults*: exploited to form inlets.

Other controls include:
(c) lithology: e.g. **badland** – deeply dissected – cliffs form in **incoherent** (loosely bonded) rock. Slipping occurs where clay underlies impermeable rock (p. 159)
(d) *process*: **live cliffs** – still experiencing marine erosion – usually have a free rock-face section. Sub-aerial denudation also operates. **Dead cliffs** slope gently, or are convex as a result of weathering and mass wasting
(e) *past processes*: periglacial areas experienced frost weathering – gentle debris slopes result.

Some cliffs show the effects of different processes at different points. You will need to find examples. Small* will be helpful; your own fieldwork would be better.

Processes of marine erosion

These include:
(a) **corrosion** (chemical action), notably in limestone cliffs and wave-cut platforms
(b) **hydraulic action** (impact of water) ⎫ exploits joints,
(c) **pneumatic action** (impact of trapped air) ⎭ faults, etc.
(d) **corrasive scour** (impact of trapped debris) – a major factor.

The *size of waves* – determined by the time the wind has been blowing, and the **fetch** (distance over which the waves have built up) – may not be as important as their **frequency**. LEWIS contended that steep, plunging, **destructive** waves come in at high frequency (13–15/min) and that long, low, **constructive** waves occur at lower (6–8/min) frequencies. This has been contested (Guilcher). The nature of the wave seems to determine whether erosion or deposition dominates, particularly on beaches.

* op. cit., pp. 456–61.

MAJOR EROSIONAL FEATURES are cliffs (see above), wave-cut platforms, caves, arches, stacks. Questions on the topic are rarely as easy as Question 20, included here because it highlights again the need for examples and diagrams.

Q. 20. (a) *Describe the ways in which sea action erodes rocks and deposits the eroded material.*

  (b) *Describe and explain the main landforms produced in the process of coastal erosion. Refer to specific examples and use annotated diagrams.*

  (c) *Discuss ways in which man may prevent coastal erosion.*

[SCO.T]

Beaches

Fig. 64 shows the features you should know:

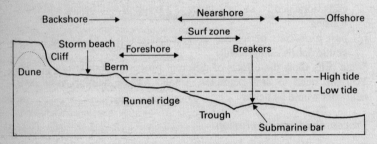

Fig. 64 *Beach profile, showing terminology (after King)*

The **storm beach** is above the level of the highest spring tides,* and **berms** are ridges just below that level, but above normal tides. Large destructive waves fling shingle up, while at the same time the mass of breaking water crashes directly downwards. The small proportion of water which moves up the beach (**swash**) encounters the **backwash** from the wave before and is checked. This type of wave thus combs material downslope (seawards). You would therefore expect increases in the height of the storm beach and changes in the berms above normal tide level, and erosion below it, in answer to Question 21.

---

* These occur twice a month – around the times of new and full moon – not only during the spring season.

Q. 21. (a) *What physical changes would you expect to see in the morphology of a shingle beach in the course of a stormy winter?*
(b) *What processes would cause the changes?*
(c) *How would you measure and record the changes?* [SUJB]

Surveying techniques are outlined on p. 57. Obviously you could not
know whether change had occurred unless you had surveyed the beach
before the winter.

SPITS, BARS AND TOMBOLOS are regarded as secondary beach forms.
These features reflect the presence of **longshore drift**, effected by the
difference between the direction of the incoming swash and the down-
draining backwash.

Evidence for longshore drift includes:
(a) the accumulation of shingle against one side of jetties and groynes
(b) 'planting' coloured pebbles and noting their movement over
time
(c) introducing a patch of coloured dye (or an orange on a rope) into the
sea water and observing its movements,

in addition to the natural features noted above. It has been suggested
that sea-bed drift occurs in the opposite direction to longshore drift and
that this acts as a counter-balance to erosion.

Q. 22. (a) *What is longshore drift and under what circumstances does it
operate?*
(b) *Describe the techniques you would use to determine the rate
of movement of water and sediments by longshore drift.* [NI]

Base your answer to Question 22 on the information outlined above.
Add to it by drawing diagrams for part (a), and by considering exactly
how you would apply the techniques using coloured pebbles and dyes,
i.e. equipment needed, timing of measurements, likely snags (standing
in the breaker zone can be dangerous!), and so on. In addition, you
should make a study of one named shingle-spit, one named sand-spit
and one named bar.*

12. Glaciation

An **ice sheet** is a continuous, thick (Antarctic ice is estimated at 3,000 m),
almost flat mass of ice and snow. During the Pleistocene glaciation, ice
sheets covered huge areas, such as Canada and much of the U.S.A. Ice

* Sparks, op. cit., is useful here.

sheets are **cold glaciers**: their bases are frozen to the bedrock. Movement is therefore slow, especially in lowland areas. Erosion was limited – perhaps only a 10-m depth of material was removed from the surface of the Laurentian (Canadian) Shield. After ice melt this left a landscape of rocky basins, often lake-filled, and bog. As the ice wasted and the ice terminus retreated (N.B.: *ice did not move backwards*), huge **terminal moraines** were deposited.

A **warm glacier**, e.g. many valley glaciers, is not frozen to its bed. Consequently movement is easier and erosion (and hence deposition) greatly facilitated.

You may be asked to comment on a statement, e.g. 'Glaciers erode, ice sheets deposit.' From the above, you can see that ice sheets do both. Use your textbooks to provide examples of glacial erosion – corries, arêtes, horns (pyramidal peaks), U-shaped valleys, truncated spurs, ribbon lakes, crag-and-tail, roches moutonnées; and glacial deposition – moraines (ground, terminal, lateral and medial), drumlins, eskers, kames, kettleholes.

A similar generalization is that erosion is found in uplands; deposition in lowlands. It is true that the 'best' glacial erosion features are found in resistant rock – *perhaps because*:

(a) the hardest rocks formed the highest pre-glacial relief and were therefore centres of ice accumulation and had steep gradients to increase ice-flow rates

(b) glacial features are best preserved in resistant rocks, which are less readily altered by post-glacial erosion

(c) resistant rocks often have well-developed jointing which may aid plucking (below).

Thus there is a link between resistant rock, and hence uplands, and a seeming predominance of glacial erosion. Look up the geology of the classic areas of glacial erosion in Britain.

Glacially eroded lowlands do exist, however, as in the Lochinver area (north-west Scotland). Hills are low (mainly below 200 m), bare of soil, rounded. Erratics are common. Lakes and tarns, linked by winding streams, are numerous.

Erosional processes

No one knows exactly how glaciers erode. The processes of erosion are thought to include:

(a) the removal of the weathered layer created in temperate latitudes during the warmer, wetter Tertiary era

(b) **abrasion**: the grinding away of bedrock by fragments of bedrock incorporated in the ice. Evidence of abrasion includes: polished rock surfaces; deep grooves in soft rock and fine striations in resistant rock; **rock flour** (finely ground rock material).

Problems: CAROL noted that below 22 m ice moved with plastic flow and could no longer hold particles firmly. Perhaps abrasion is only important in weak rocks – hard, widely jointed rocks being unaffected

(c) **plucking** (**quarrying**) is said to occur when ice freezes to pre-shattered rock and carries it away as the glacier moves downslope. Since ice has a low tensile strength (resistance to breaking under strain), the rocks must first be broken by freeze–thaw action or pressure release (below). Quarrying is thought by many to be the predominant process of glacial erosion

(d) **pressure release**: Lewis considered that rocks were consolidated under the weight of overlying strata. When the glaciers removed these strata, and then melted, the rocks 'burst upwards', cracking and shattering, forming a loosened layer easily removed by later re-glaciation.

Transport occurs:

 (i) on the surface of the glacier – probably the transport mechanism of erratics

 (ii) within the ice

(iii) at the base – but see Carol, above.

Glacial deposition (drift)

Textbooks usually consider (i) direct deposition beneath the ice; (ii) deposition from meltwater (**fluvio-glacial action**). Ice cannot deposit without first melting; thus the two processes are not completely distinct. However, the nature of the deposits varies (see Table 33) and is of considerable importance in recognizing the various depositional forms in the field. Question 23 is typical of those on glacial deposition.

Q. 23. (a) *Examine the landscape features found in lowlands which would indicate the direction of movement of an ice sheet.*

 (b) *Explain the formation of TWO lowland geomorphological features resulting from the ablation and retreat of an ice sheet.*

[NI]

Alternatively, two or three features may be specified. SUJB seems to prefer this.

Table 33. Landforms of glacial deposition

	Feature	Formation	Appearance	Sediment characteristics
GLACIAL	Moraines: Ground moraine	Compressed during transport. Deposition by surface and bottom melt	Gently undulating. Kettleholes	Lithology ∝ rocks over which ice moved. Jagged fragments in fine clay. **Unstratified** – not sorted into layers
	Terminal moraine	Deposited against snout	Cross-valley, often semi-circular, ridge	Varies: fine clay to coarse boulders. Some stratification
	Lateral moraine	Chiefly formed from material fallen from valley sides	Valley-side ridges	Angular, rocky debris
	Push moraine	Pushed up by advancing glacier	Cross-valley ridge	Very mixed, includes soil
	Drumlin	? Irregular till deposits moulded by ice re-advance	Elongated, streamlined hills of boulder clay. **Stoss** slope (steeper) faces ice direction	Varies: pure rock drumlins veneers of drift over rock drift drumlins
FLUVIO-GLACIAL	Lake clays	Meltwater-borne sediments settle in **pro-glacial** (between end moraine and snout) lakes	Even layer, covering, but not disguising, irregularities	Often **varved**: alternating coarse and fine deposits
	Kames	Ice contact features, developing in surface water on ice or deltas	Kame terraces – valley-side mounds, flat topped	Originally stratified, now slumped, detail blurred by later weathering
	Eskers	Unsure. Perhaps from meltwater streams flowing in tunnels	Winding ridges, originally steep-sided, superimposed on present relief	Gravel
	Outwash sands and gravels	From meltwater streams, found beyond glacier limit	Flat plains	Sorted: coarser material near terminus, fine material further away

Glacial diversion of drainage

Rivers may be dammed and lakes form between glaciers and rock walls. The lake level will rise until the water can escape over the lowest available col, cutting an overflow channel. After glaciation, the drainage may take the new course cut by the overflow (of water, or of ice). Evidence of changed drainage includes:

1) reconstruction of the old pattern by boring through lake clays to the pre-glacial surface
2) the sinuous gorges of overflow channels, now occupied by dispro-portionately small (misfit) streams
3) old lake terraces and deltas.

Question 24 shows the inclination of JMB examiners to get you to think across any divisions within topics. You will have to learn your material well enough to sort through it during the examination and pick out a theme:

Q. 24.   (a) *Explain the various ways in which glacial action may result in the formation of lakes.*

       (b) *Discuss the processes which lead to the eventual disappearance of lakes. Illustrate your answer by referring to lakes in different environments and of different modes of origin.*

[JMB]

Note the word 'processes': make sure you know *how* changes occur.

London examiners often select an area of controversy and ask you to evaluate different theories. In glaciation, contested topics include: formation of corries; over-deepening in corries and fjords; an explanation of the 'steps' in the long profile of glacial troughs. B. W. Sparks* writes fully about geomorphological controversies.

13. Periglacial activity

Q. 25. *'Few landforms in the British Isles do not show the effects of the Ice Ages.' Discuss.*   [OXF]

Too many candidates read the words 'Ice Ages' and think only of direct glacial action: erosion and deposition. Other effects include: eustatic changes in sea level, notably post-glacial 'drowning' (pp. 171 and 174);

* op. cit.

isostatic depression and recovery (p. 146); and the displacement of climatic belts creating:

PERIGLACIAL CONDITIONS: These are found in cold regions bordering on glaciers (e.g. southern Britain during the Pleistocene) and in high mountains.

– *Winters*: long, bitterly cold. Ground and surface water frozen. Almost no **denudation** (i.e. weathering, mass movement, erosion).
– *Summers*: mild. Ground thaws, though lower layers may be permanently frozen (**permafrost**).

The times between summer and winter are the most important because:

(a) nightly freeze and daytime thaw cause rock disintegration (**congelifraction**)
(b) during snow melt, ground water is abundant, lubricating weathered material and soil which 'flow' downhill: solifluxion
(c) 'springtime' sees the development of meltwater streams which, though short-lived, erode laterally and vertically, and remove weathered material.

The nature of the landforms will depend on: (i) the processes; (ii) the relative position of the landform.

Processes

(a) EFFECTS OF PERMAFROST: Permafrost is impermeable: surface run-off increases; lakes, swamps and bogs form in lower areas; solifluxion is enhanced.

(b) EXPANSION OF FREEZING GROUND WATER: **Frost heaving** moves material upwards, distorting horizontally layered sediments. Patches of ground water may remain between frozen ground. As they, in turn, freeze and expand, the ground may be mounded up into **pingoes**, which later collapse with warmer conditions. The irregular ground surface looks like that found in Carboniferous limestones, such that the word **thermokarst** (or **cryokarst**) is used to describe the collapsed surfaces of periglacial landscapes.

Depressions also occur in association with **ice wedges**. As unconsolidated clays and silts freeze, first they expand, then contract with temperature falls of around $-20°C$. The deposits split on contraction, like cooling basalt. In the wedge-shaped cracks ice accumulates. When closely spaced wedges melt, the intervening ridges may collapse. Large **alas** depressions result.

Fossil pingoes and irregular ground are found in East Anglia. Fossil wedges, now stone filled, occur in south-east England.

(c) SOLIFLUXION is often initiated when a late-lying patch of snow melts. The thick mud flows easily over the permafrost below, forming bulges – **solifluxion lobes** – and terraces.

(d) NIVATION: Snow in hollows seems to 'erode back' into the hillside: no one quite knows how. **Nivation hollows** are common on the South Downs.

(e) WIND ACTION: Frost shattering will reduce rock to debris so fine that it is picked up by the wind: especially since the atmosphere is so dry – all water being frozen. Wind-blown sediments have formed belts of fine **loess** soil and wind-swept pebble pavements in past periglacial environments.

Position

Frost heaving and wedging appears to force stones to the surface. The pattern these make depends greatly on slope angle (Fig. 65).

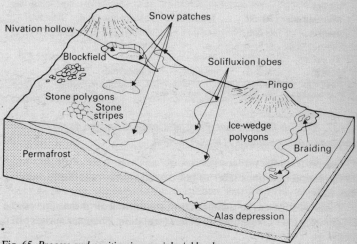

Fig. 65 *Process and position in a periglacial landscape*

Since relatively finer material tends to be transported during solifluxion, the large fragments remain at the top of slopes. These areas of stone blocks are called **blockfields (felsenmeer)**. In southern England, weathered material, brought to the valley floor by solifluxion, has filled dry valleys with chalk fragments and broken flints: **coombe rock**. Question 26 reminds you of the need to find detailed examples:

185

Q. 26. Describe and comment on the effects of frost and thaw action on the landscapes of Britain during and immediately after the last Pleistocene glaciation. [SUJB]

14. Arid environments

Three types of deserts are recognized:

Table 34. A summary of desert types

Name	Latitudes	Continental location	Prevailing air mass	Annual precipitation in mm
1) Arctic and polar, including tundra	60–90° N & S	All	Polar continental, arctic	Under 300
2) Mid-latitude deserts	30–50° N & S	Interiors	Polar continental, tropical continental	100–500
3) Tropical deserts	10–35° N & S	West coast, interior	Tropical continental	Under 250

Source: Strahler, A. N., *Physical Geography*, Wiley, 1975.

Q. 27. Discuss the view that many landforms in present-day deserts were formed under conditions of higher rainfall. [SUJB]

Question 27 does not restrict you to any one type of desert. Most examination questions refer to hot deserts; always check the wording carefully.

Table 34 stresses the significance of **continental air masses**, i.e. those originating over a continent, in desert formation. These air masses often develop:

(i) *cold anticyclones*: these form both during the long polar night, and above mid-latitude deserts (Turkestan, Gobi, and Great Basin deserts). The chance of precipitation with very high pressure is slight

(ii) *outward-blowing arid winds* which create desert conditions as in the west-coast deserts: Atacama, Namibia, Lower California, south-west Australia.

Other factors in desert formation include:

(a) CONTINENTALITY: deserts in continental interiors are far from oceanic sources of moisture.

(b) MOUNTAINS: deserts often form in the lee of mountain ranges. As the air descends, it is warmed **adiabatically** (p. 197) and can easily hold the vapour it carries.

(c) OCEAN CURRENTS: many west-coast deserts are associated with cold currents which may cool the winds, reducing their capacity to hold vapour. As the winds move inland, they are warmed and can easily retain what little vapour they absorbed over the sea.

(d) PREVAILING WIND DIRECTION: the mid-latitude deserts are in the westerly wind belt. The wind has travelled great distances before it reaches them. Moisture sources are often nearer, to the east, but the wind direction is wrong.

(e) HIGH TEMPERATURES: in the hot deserts temperatures are so high (30°C+) that P.E.T. rapidly disposes of most of the water.

(f) MAN: **desertification** is the 'impoverishment of arid and semi-arid areas by the combined impact of man's activities and drought'.

The Sahelian zone – to the south of the Sahara – saw an influx of people in the wetter 1950s. Cattle numbers rose, helped by vaccination schemes. Wells were sunk. When the droughts recurred around 1971, the vegetation cover was destroyed by grazing animals. The pumping schemes increased the **salinity** (salt content of the soil). The edge of the Sahel began to turn into desert.

The prospect of desertification threatens 30% of the earth's land surface and one-sixth of its people.

Remedies for desertification

A United Nations Conference has proposed:
1) the establishment of belts of trees along the rim of the Sahara
2) careful management of livestock in the Sahel
3) exploitation of aquifers in north-east Africa.

Indications that a desert is expanding include:

1) the extension of typical desert features: active dune systems; **reg** – sheets of angular pebbles; **hamada** – bare rock, swept clear of sand and dust by the wind

187

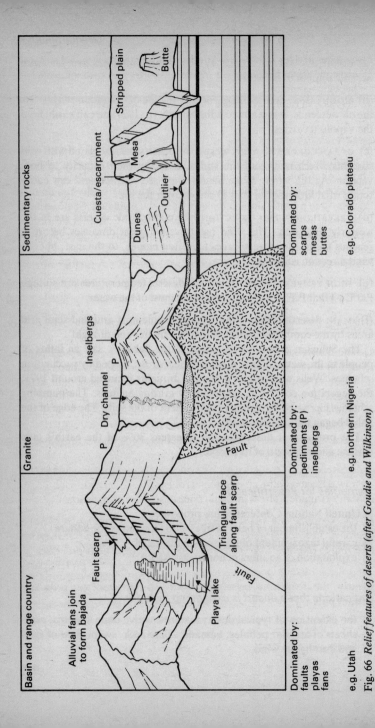

Fig. 66 *Relief features of deserts (after Goudie and Wilkinson)*

| Basin and range country | Granite | Sedimentary rocks |

Alluvial fans join to form bajada

Fault scarp

Triangular face along fault scarp

Fault

Playa lake

Inselbergs

Dry channel

P

P

P

Dunes

Cuesta/escarpment

Mesa

Outlier

Stripped plain

Butte

Fault

Dominated by:
faults
playas
fans

e.g. Utah

Dominated by:
pediments (P)
inselbergs

e.g. northern Nigeria

Dominated by:
scarps
mesas
buttes

e.g. Colorado plateau

2) changes in river response to floods; with vegetation removal and soil erosion, **flash flooding** – a sudden, short-lived rush of water – becomes common
3) decrease in rainfall, increase in P.E.T., in border areas.

Desert landforms

In addition to reg and hamada (above), sandy deserts – **erg** – occur. Major landforms include deep, steep-sided dry valleys (**wadis**) and flat-topped hills (**buttes** or **inselbergs**). At the base of the mountains there is often a gently sloping rock surface – the **pediment**. Some writers think that, as the mountain retreats, the pediment expands to form a pediplain (**pedimentation**). In Africa, pediments are features of semi-arid areas and not of desert basins as in the U.S.A.

The origin of these features is very problematical.* A further area of controversy is whether major desert landforms developed in the past, when rainfall was heavier.

Evidence of past humidity in deserts

1) The Valley of the Kings (Egypt) seems to be water-eroded; the tombs of the kings in the valley show no evidence of water action. Therefore rainfall had been higher before the tombs were built, 4000 years B.P.
2) Wadis in many areas are too long and well connected to have originated from precipitation at present-day levels.
3) Lake Chad has several abandoned shorelines above present-day levels.
4) Archaeological evidence shows evidence of human occupation in the now deserted Gilf Kebir highlands of Egypt.

Many examiners stress present conditions in desert questions:

Q. 28. Describe the main processes which are operating, and have operated, in tropical desert environments, illustrating your answer by referring to characteristic landforms which result from these processes.

[WEL; part]

Clearly, the distinction between *present* and *past* processes is an important one.

---

* Small, op. cit., pp. 322–7.

Present processes in arid areas

Weathering

(i) *Thermal expansion.* The alternate heating and cooling of rock was thought to cause disintegration. Grigg (1936) heated and cooled granite for the equivalent of 244 years, but no change was detected. He repeated the experiment, but now cooling the rock with water. The rock disintegrated in a period equivalent to 2½ years.

(ii) **Onion weathering**. Whether due to thermal expansion, water action or pressure release, sheets do split from bare rock surfaces (**exfoliation**), both in deserts and in the humid tropics.

(iii) *Salt action.* Steel railway sleepers in Mauritania have been eroded to a flaky mass by the saline surface sand. Some water *must* be present for this to occur.

(iv) *Granular disintegration.* Different minerals absorb heat, and hence expand, at different rates. This differential expansion causes the rock to disintegrate.

Ground-level weathering is now thought to be more important than:

Wind

'Only one important type of desert landform is today considered to be the outcome of wind "erosion"':* the **deflation hollow**. **Deflation** is the transport by wind of sand and dust. Deflation is thought to be the process responsible for the Qattara Depression (Egypt).

Small-scale features formed by wind abrasion are **yardang** ridges, orientated in the direction of the prevailing wind and separated by furrows developed along lines of weakness in the rock.

Wind is of importance in shaping sand structures, notably the crescent-shaped **barkhan** dune and the longitudinal **seif**. You should be able to draw diagrams of the differences between the two, the formation of the barkhan and its transformation into the seif.

Water

Many desert areas experience rare, but violent, flash floods. It is uncertain whether these floods could have formed the extensive wadis which do exist, but flash flooding is certainly responsible for lateral erosion by corrasion, especially where the streams come out into the lowlands. In 'hyper-arid' conditions, like those in much of the Sahara

---

* Small, op. cit.

and Arabian deserts, flash floods do not occur and the major landforms must be attributed to past periods of water erosion.

Dynamic equilibrium in arid environments

Barkhans seem to be in a state of equilibrium.

Sand dunes tend to have a limiting height since wind speeds increase with height, and sand is deposited in the 'lee'.

The slopes of pediments may be just enough to keep material moving downslope.

Further reading

Goudie, A., and J. Wilkinson, *The Warm Desert Environment*, Cambridge Educational.

10. Atmospheric processes

> Then we get on to the weather, and then we get stuck.
> (Arnold Wesker, *Roots*)

Many candidates find weather questions difficult. If you do get stuck, persevere, because the questions are very straightforward.

1. The atmosphere

The **atmosphere** is a layer of gases* and water vapour enveloping the earth. Fig. 67 shows how it is conventionally divided:

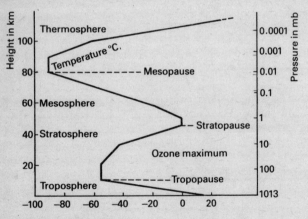

Fig. 67 *Vertical distribution of temperature and pressure (after Barry and Chorley)*

The **troposphere**:
(a) contains 75% of atmospheric gases and virtually all the water
(b) shows a temperature decrease with height (*average* 6.5°C per 1,000 m)

* Nitrogen 78%; oxygen 20.95%; argon 0.93%; carbon dioxide 0.03%.

192

(c) is the location of most weather phenomena and turbulence

(d) has a 'weather ceiling': the tropopause.

Q. 1. (a) Describe the troposphere.

(b) Show, with a diagram, the layers into which the atmosphere is divided, marking the changes in temperature and pressure with height.

Part (b) of Question 1 is straightforward enough – if you have a photographic memory. Try a rhyme, starting at 15°C, 1000 mb, ground level (spelled-out figures = distances in km above ground; numbers = temperature):

> From ground to ten, temperature falls,
> Drops 70 degrees in all.
> Stands still to twenty then it soars
> To 0 degrees: the stratopause.
> At fifty km,* pressure's one
> And now the mesosphere's begun.
> A shorter still stand, then a drop:
> It's minus 90 when it stops.
> Eighty km: mesopause,
> And stable temps ten km more.
> Thus, finally, the thermosphere:
> We think it gets much warmer here.

A sketch diagram, from the above, with accurate heights and temperatures, will suffice. For short distances, temperatures may rise with height: an **inversion**.

Atmospheric circulation

Winds (horizontal atmospheric movements) occur because **insolation** (sun's energy received at ground level) varies with

- the angle of the sun's rays (linked with latitude)
- day length
- cloud cover.

VARIABLE HEATING PRODUCES PRESSURE DIFFERENCES.

Other factors causing unequal heating are sea currents, distance from sea, relief. Be prepared to sketch summer and winter conditions (use your atlas and Fig. 68).

* Pronounce it kay-em for this 'poem' – which can be sung to the tune of 'Ninety-nine red balloons'.

The **pressure gradient** reflects the rate of pressure change: the closer the isobars, the greater the gradient and the stronger the wind. Note that in Fig. 68 winds do not blow directly from HIGHS to LOWS, but are deflected by the spinning earth (**coriolis force**); **geostrophic winds** occur when pressure gradient and coriolis force are perfectly balanced, so that they blow parallel to the isobars: *for the northern hemisphere*: WIND ON BACK, LOW PRESSURE ON LEFT.

Geostrophic winds in the middle and upper troposphere encircle the world in meandering paths known as **Rossby waves**.

Rossby waves: **high index** = no waves; mild, windy weather in the U.K.

average index = three to six encircling waves guide depression tracks

low index = pattern broken up; polar and equatorial air can move south or north.

Centripetal force and the frictional drag of the surface also affect wind direction.

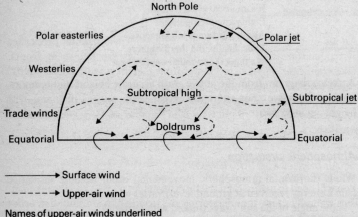

------→ Surface wind

------→ Upper-air wind

Names of upper-air winds underlined

Fig. 68 *Surface and upper-air wind belts: northern hemisphere*

Upper air-pressure patterns differ from ground-level conditions. In Fig. 69 the cold air column ends at 2 km, whereas the warm air extends to 3 km (because warm air is less densely packed). Consequently, at 2 km there is a pressure difference, and therefore a wind, also deflected by coriolis force: the **thermal wind**, blowing at right angles to the pressure gradient.

194

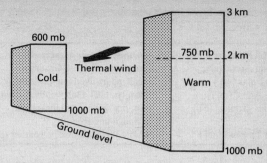

Fig. 69 *A model to explain thermal winds*

Jet streams are intense thermal winds. It seems that the core of a jet stream is often located above and behind the cold front in a depression (p. 201) and helps to 'deepen' it.

2. *Air masses*

An **air mass** is a large body of air, with similar horizontal properties of temperature and moisture. Its boundaries are known as **fronts**. Like winds, air masses are named from their region of origin: arctic, polar, tropical or equatorial. This gives us some idea of the temperature and humidity to expect. This classification is extended by noting whether the region of origin is on land – **continental** – or over the sea – **maritime**.

A. *Air masses and British weather*

You will need to understand the term **unstable** (p. 198) and the mechanisms whereby snow, thunderstorms and frontal rain are caused in order to answer Question 2 fully.

Q. 2. *Explain how air masses affect British weather:*
    (i) in winter;
    (ii) in summer.

Use Table 35 (overleaf) to help you with your answer.

195

Table 35.   Air masses and British weather

Air mass	Weather experienced
continental Polar (cP) ⎫	Indistinguishable at ground level.
continental Arctic (cA) ⎬	Extremely cold (−5°C), dry
maritime Polar (mP) ⎫	Small, short-lived low-pressure systems.
maritime Arctic (mA) ⎭	Snow (p. 199). Dull weather. Unstable
continental Tropical (cT)	Hot, dry, little cloud formation, although unstable
maritime Tropical (mT)	Warm, moist, thundery weather (p. 199)

B. Air masses and tropical climates

Q. 3. What are 'air masses' and how does information about them assist our interpretation of climate in the tropics?   [SUJB]

Until the 1930s tropical air masses (with far fewer contrasting character-istics than temperate ones) were thought to be responsible for **trade-wind weather**. The mT air masses **subside** (descend from height) over the eastern halves of the oceans and move westwards and equator-wards. There is a temperature inversion (p. 193) at about 700 m, below which is a layer of broken cumulus. Conditions are warm and dry, becoming hotter and more humid in equatorial regions.

Meteorologists now know that tropical weather systems are much more variable than this. Other important features are:

(a) **wind convergence zones**, e.g. the **intertropical convergence zone (I.T.C.Z.)**, formed where the trade winds meet, causing convection and clouds

(b) the **equatorial trough** (low-pressure system). There is a connection between the seasonal position of the trough and

(c) **hurricanes (typhoons)**. These intense, low-pressure systems de-velop thus:

1) An initial disturbance . . .

2) . . . grows into a depression, then a storm.

3) Strong pressure gradients force air inwards.

4) Air rises at the centre when pressure gradients can no longer force it inwards.

5) The rising air cools and condenses, releasing heat energy to 'fuel' the system.

6) High-level anticyclones help the risen air to flow outwards.

Should the conditions in (5) or (6) change, or the typhoon pass over cool seas or land, the system will rapidly fail.

Use Fig. 70 to describe the dimensions, cloud systems and weather associated with the tropical hurricane.

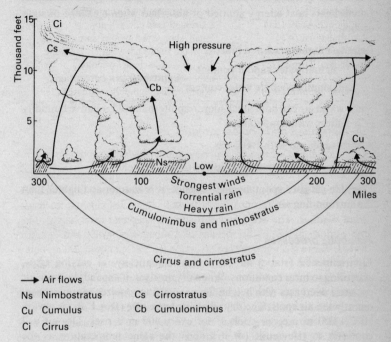

Fig. 70 *The structure of a tropical hurricane*

3. Atmospheric moisture

To understand this section, you must be sure of the vocabulary:

Adiabatic change: occurring without external heat transfer. Pressure, volume and temperature are intimately connected in a gas. If pressure and/or volume changes, so does temperature.

Adiabatic lapse rates only apply to moving air. See 'Lapse rate', below.

Condensation: **change of state** from gas to liquid.

Condensation nuclei: tiny atmospheric particles – smoke, dust, ice, salt – necessary for condensation of water vapour.

Dry air: in meteorology, not **saturated** (see below).

Lapse rate: rate at which temperature falls with height.

Latent heat: heat energy emitted or absorbed when a change of state occurs.

Relative humidity (r.h.): a ratio:

$$\frac{\text{actual water vapour content}}{\text{maximum possible water content}} \text{ expressed as a percentage.}$$

Since warm air can hold much more vapour than cold, relative humidity (r.h.) alters with temperature.

Saturated air: air with 100% r.h.

Stable air: will rise only when forced to, e.g. by relief.

Unstable air rises spontaneously because it is warmer and lighter than the surrounding air.

Adiabatic processes

Environmental (static) **air** cools non-adiabatically, at varying rates, according to local conditions. When dry air rises, it expands because air pressure decreases with height. This expansion requires energy; consequently the air cools. The **dry adiabatic lapse rate (D.A.L.R.)** is always 10°C/1,000 m, i.e. air cools 1° for every 100 m it rises. Dry air will continue to rise until: (a) it attains the same temperature as the environmental air, or (b) lower temperatures make the air saturated. In (b), it will then continue to rise, but cooling more slowly. The temperature drop due to pressure fall is partly offset by the release of latent heat as condensation occurs. The **saturated adiabatic lapse rate (S.A.L.R.)** is always less than the D.A.L.R. If sufficient condensation occurs, the air mass may become 'dry' again.

Q. 4. Why is the relative humidity of the air an important factor in determining whether the air is stable or unstable? [NI; part]

Saturated air, cooling slowly, remains unstable (i.e. warmer than its surroundings) to greater heights than dry air. The temperature at which air becomes saturated (**dew point**) will depend on how much vapour is already in the air (r.h.).

Other adiabatic processes include the **chinook** winds of Alberta and the **föhn** winds of the Alps. As they rise, they cool slowly at the

S.A.L.R., and relief rain falls. On the leeward side of the mountains, having lost most of their water, they warm up on descending at the D.A.L.R., causing dramatic temperature rises when they occur (see Fig. 75, p. 208).

4. Precipitation

You should have learned **orographic** (relief), **convectional** and **frontal** rain for O-level.* Add to this the knowledge that not all clouds form rain. BERGERON suggested that water vapour needs ice crystals as condensation nuclei for droplets to form around. Droplets coalesce and usually melt as they fall to give rain. No melting = snow.

Rain does fall without temperatures within the cloud falling sufficiently to make ice, e.g. in the tropics. Other condensation nuclei (p. 197) may be operating.

Often a crystal falls some distance and is then caught in up-currents. This may recur several times. Each time, the crystal acquires a coating of ice until it is heavy enough to fall as **hail**.

Thunderstorms

Unstable air rising very quickly (a **thermal**) can cause strong updraughts, 'fuelled' by latent heat released during condensation. The top of the cloud spreads out (**anvil shape**) and becomes positively charged. Heavy rain falls. In non-rain sections, the bottom of the cloud becomes negatively charged. **Lightning** bridges these areas of opposite electrical charge. This causes rapid expansion and hence vibration of the air: **thunder**.

Fog

'All fogs simply result from condensation of atmospheric water vapour.' This is a useful quotation. Classifications of fog acknowledge this basic fact, and are based on (a) the mechanism causing condensation; (b) the atmospheric feature concerned: stable air masses or fronts. **Stable air masses** develop when a warm (mT or cT) air mass moves poleward. The base is cooled, i.e. an inversion develops.

---

* If not, see Mayhew, op. cit., pp. 32, 33.

Stable air mass fogs

(i) ADVECTION FOG may form when mT air moves over a cooler surface to cause condensation, e.g. in summer, over the California current.

(ii) RADIATION FOG: night-time radiation – aided by cloudless skies and long nights – causes rapid cooling of the land surface. This then chills the air mass. Radiation fog is usually dispersed by the sun by mid-morning.

For types (i) and (ii), enough wind and/or turbulence must exist to keep a new supply of moist air moving on to the cool surface: wind speed around 16 km/h (force 3) seems best. Too much wind lifts the fog, and **stratus** (layer) cloud often forms.

(iii) STEAM FOG may occur when cP or cM air moves over a warm, evaporating sea. The vapour emitted is chilled by the air mass, e.g. **Arctic sea smoke**.

Frontal fog

Sometimes warm raindrops, falling from nimbostratus cloud at a warm front, evaporate and then re-condense in the cold air below. This only occurs if:

1) the rain is much warmer than the cold air
2) winds are light.

Practise selecting relevant information by considering Question 5.

Q. 5. Why are fogs common along coasts? [NI; part]

Clouds*

Layered – **stratiform** – clouds are classified by height, as in Table 36.

Clouds with vertical development are: fair-weather cumulus, cumulus, or cumulonimbus.

Cloud vocabulary

Alto-: high, used for middle clouds

Cirrus/o: wispy

Cumulus/o, cumuliform: horizontal base, rounded masses

Nimbus/o: rain cloud

Stratus/o: layer

* See Strahler, op. cit., pp. 168–9, for diagrams and photographs (*not* Strahler and Strahler).

Table 36.   Cloud classification

Group	Height in km	Type and abbreviation		Composition
High	6–12	Cirrus	Ci	
		Cirrocumulus	Cc	
		Cirrostratus	Cs	
		Halo		
		Altocumulus	Ac	Crystals and water droplets
Middle	3–6	Altostratus	As	
		Nimbostratus	Ns	Dense, precipitation falling
Low	2	Stratus	St	Dense
		Stratocumulus	Sc	

5. Low-pressure systems in temperate latitudes

Low pressure results from the removal of air, reducing the weight of the atmosphere by:
– local over-heating (**thermal depressions**)
– partial vacuums in the lee of uplands (**lee depressions**)
– warm air rising above cold at fronts (**frontal wave depressions**).

Britain is in the temperate latitudes – or mid-latitudes – which extend from 30° to 60°, north and south of the equator. The major meteorological factor in these latitudes is the meeting of polar and tropical air masses, producing frontal activity.

The frontal wave depression

A **depression** (or **cyclone**) is a roughly circular area of relatively low pressure, covering an area 1,500–2,000 km in diameter. Frontal wave depressions are associated with the meeting of two contrasting air masses. A wave develops at the junction of these masses. The presence of a trough in an upper-air Rossby wave (p. 194) and the location of the jet-stream core (p. 195) seem to strengthen this wave form.

Q. 6.   (i)   Describe the nature of Rossby waves, the polar jet stream and depressions in the northern hemisphere.
(ii)   Explain the relationships between each of these.   [OXF]

For Question 6, you should point out that you are discussing mid-latitude, frontal depressions, not thermal or lee depressions, thus

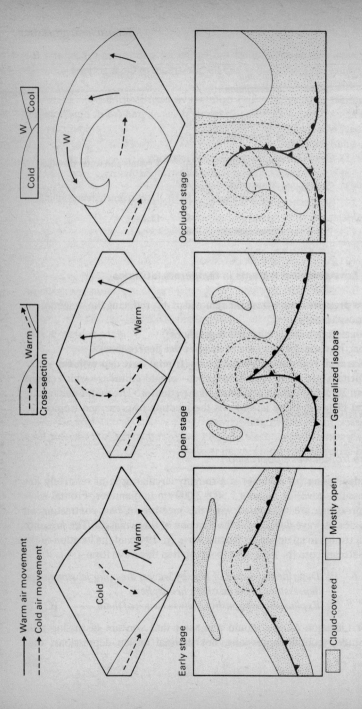

Fig. 71 (above) Stages in the development of a mid-latitude depression (from Strahler); (below) corresponding cloud systems (after Boucher and Newcomb)

showing your knowledge of the variety of depression types, and the relevance of Rossby waves and the jet stream to the first type.

Weather associated with frontal wave depressions

An active front, with *unstable* rising air, is an **ana-front**: here weather activity is in the following sequence:

(a) ana-warm front
    (1) Cirrus forms, thickening and lowering to . . .
    (2) . . . cirrus, cirrostratus and altostratus.
    (3) Sun obscured, drizzle begins.
    (4) Stratocumulus at the front gives light rain.
(b) warm sector
    (1) Wind **veers** (changes direction clockwise).
    (2) Temperature rises.
    (3) Rain: intermittent or ceases.
(c) ana-cold front
    (1) Nimbostratus cloud.
    (2) Brief, heavy downpours.

The cold front is of shorter duration than the warm.

Kata-fronts are characterized by stable air. Weather activity is subdued. Kata-cold fronts are marked by thick stratus clouds.

An **occlusion** occurs when the cold front catches up with the warm front.

Occlusion weather

In a **warm occlusion**, the leading air is colder than the following air. In a **cold occlusion**, the following air is colder.

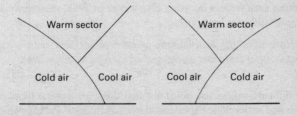

Fig. 72 *Warm and cold occlusions (after Pergley)*

Occlusion weather brings continuous rain and gloom, but eventually the moisture content in the uplifted warm sector is exhausted so that precipitation ceases altogether.

Do read meteorology questions carefully. Question 7 asks only how **precipitation** (rain, drizzle, sleet, snow and hail) occurs in *all* low-pressure systems: frontal wave (frontal rain), thermal (convectional), lee and, of course, monsoons (pp. 217–23). It does not ask how the systems form.

Q. 7. Describe the development of precipitation in low-pressure systems.

6. Anticyclones

Here high pressure (over 1012 mb in the U.K.) is caused by subsiding air, warmed adiabatically as it descends, and marked by an inversion. The air mass is stable and, in warming, can absorb any water vapour.

Cold anticyclones occur:

(a) when air above a cold surface (as in continental interiors, e.g. Siberia) cools and contracts, causing an upper-level inflow; these are the great **seasonal anticyclones**

(b) when mP intrudes between depressions, i.e. **transitory** (short-lived) **anticyclones**.

Warm anticyclones are difficult to explain. Permanent warm anticyclones occur over the subtropics, e.g. the Azores high. Temporary ridges sometimes extend from the Azores to Britain.

Anticyclones and British weather: NO RAIN.

Summer anticyclones: bring fine weather.

Transitory winter anticyclones: can bring **anticyclonic gloom** with moist air, trapped beneath the inversion, forming stratocumulus sheets. These disperse at night, and radiation fog (p. 200) may develop.

Blocking anticyclones occasionally (winter of 1961, summer of 1976) stabilize weather for long periods.

Q. 8. How does the mid-latitude weather associated with a typical depression differ from that associated with a typical anticyclone?

[NI; half]

This is difficult, unless you point out that there are several types of depression and anticyclone experienced in mid-latitudes. Perhaps ana-type frontal depressions are typical. From a fifty-year study, it seems that summer anticyclones are *marginally* the most frequent type in Britain.

7. Reading weather maps

Weather-map questions are very common:

Q. 9. (a) Compare Figs. 73a and b (p. 206) with regard to pressure, winds, air masses and precipitation.

(b) Describe and account for the weather shown on each of the figures.

For Question 9, part (a):

(i) Check 'compare' on p. 123. Work systematically through the comparisons in the order given in the question.

(ii) Learn to recognize high-pressure systems, low-pressure and fronts.

(iii) Describe winds in terms of: (a) direction (westerlies come *from* the west): wind tail shows direction into circle; (b) speed: tail 'feather' indicates strength.*

(iv) Deduce air masses from:

    (a) precipitation – present: probably maritime
                       – absent: possibly continental (except for summer mT: see p. 196)

    (b) temperature – warm 20°C+ summer ⎫ probably tropical
                    15°C winter ⎭
                 – cold 10°C and below, summer ⎫ probably
                       40°C and below, winter ⎭ polar.

If you can recognize on the weather map the systems outlined on pp. 201–4, you can then explain them. Watch the 'weather man' on TV every time you can (*not* the 'idiots' guides' – catch the one with isobaric maps on BBC-1, 9.25 p.m.). Listen to his explanations. Take a daily paper which has a weather map. Note the situation it shows for your region and see how it compares with what you see outside your window.

You may be given a satellite photo. Make sure you have seen plenty of them (again on TV) *and their related synoptic charts. Do not neglect* to invoke the terms 'instability' and 'unstable' whenever precipitation occurs on the synoptic chart. Re-read sections 3–6 in this chapter (pp. 197–204) and make a table with the headings 'stable' and 'unstable'. Note each weather phenomenon under the appropriate heading.

---

* Mayhew, op. cit., p. 38.

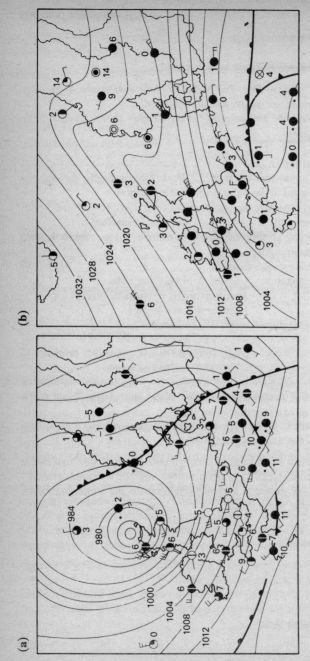

Fig. 73 *See Question 9*

8. Local weather

Land and sea breezes

These are best explained using isobaric cross-sections:

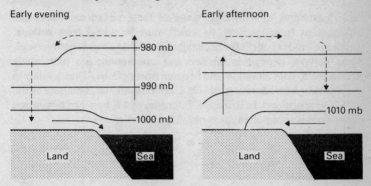

Fig. 74 *Isobaric cross-sections, showing land and sea breezes (from Barry and Chorley)*

In the evenings the sea retains its warmth while the land cools rapidly. The air over the sea expands, causing air from the land to flow as an **offshore (land) breeze**. This is compensated for at higher level. Land breezes also occur as winds flow downslope to the sea.

During early afternoons air expands over the more rapidly heating land. There is a 'pressure slope' from sea to land, down which winds blow.

Note that these winds depend on the differing heating and cooling rates of land (rapid) and water (slow).

SEA BREEZES can affect local weather greatly. On the Gulf Coast of the U.S.A., the cool air can form a minor front, marked by cumulus clouds. In Britain things are (naturally) on a smaller scale, but temperatures can be lowered up to 50 km inland.

Other local winds

Anabatic (upslope) winds occur when valley sides are heated more than the floor. The flow is up the valley sides.

Katabatic (downslope) winds occur at night when heavier, cold air from the hilltops (or from an ice cap) flows downhill. These are also called **mountain winds**.

Valley winds, like anabatic winds, develop during warm afternoons, but here the flow is up the valley axis.

Q. 10. Describe and account for the local variations in climate created within mountain ranges.   [O and C]

Fig. 75 attempts to summarize some of these variations. Check the explanations from the text, to which must be added **frost hollows**. Katabatic winds result in the accumulation of cold air over cold ground. Some valleys, depending on size and orientation, are particularly vulnerable to cold air inflow and become frost hollows. Thus a valley in the Austrian Alps has recorded −28°C on the floor and, simultaneously, −2°C 150 m upslope. In Britain, a difference of 4°C between hilltop and valley floor is common in areas of fairly low relief.

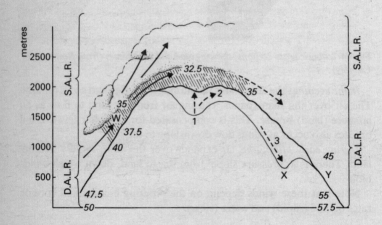

1 Valley wind	W = Orographic rain
2 Anabatic wind	X = Frost hollow
3 Katabatic wind	Y = Rain-shadow area
4 Föhn wind	Italic numbers = temperatures

Fig. 75 *Some weather variations associated with mountains*

You should revise this topic in a regional setting, especially AEB candidates.

9. Urban climates

1) Pollution from burning coal (sulphur dioxide) is declining; pollution from oil and petrol is rising. **Smog**, **pollution domes** (a hemisphere of polluted atmosphere over the city), and **pollution plumes** (domes extended by the wind) result.
2) Temperatures are higher in cities (**urban heat island**), due to:
   (a) changes in atmospheric composition (see above)
   (b) production of heat by human activities: heating, lighting, cooking, etc.
   (c) reduction of heat loss as airflow patterns are broken up by buildings.
3) Humidity is lower because run-off is rapid through drains and sewers and because of lack of vegetation – lower transpiration.
4) Rain may increase because of the orographic effect of large buildings and the increased density of condensation nuclei.

Local winds and urban effects may alter weather substantially from that forecast.

10. Microclimates

There is some controversy over the field of this study. Barry and Chorley* limit microclimatology to the study of climates beneath a vegetation cover; Miller and Parry† also include variations around buildings or across streets and gardens. Define your terms before you begin.

Forests reflect and trap heat. The temperature range at the canopy is much greater than at ground level. Wind speeds are reduced, increasing the prospect of frost in high-latitude forests. Drifting fog is filtered out by forests.

The three layers of the tropical rain forest (p. 234) cause greater temperature stratification than occurs in temperate woodlands.

Standing crops can shelter ground surfaces from sun and wind, making them cooler and more humid.

Buildings heat up rapidly on their sunny side, thus reducing humidity. Whereas wind speeds over a whole city may be lower than average, narrow 'canyon' streets can cause strong gusting.

* Barry, R. G., and R. J. Chorley, *Atmosphere, Weather and Climate*, Methuen, 1982.
† Miller, A. A., and M. Parry, *Everyday Meteorology*, Hutchinson, 1975.

Q. 11. How may microclimates be affected by man? [NI]

For Question 11, re-read this section and work out the likely effects of: forest removal; tree planting; crop planting and harvesting; building and demolition.

11. Weather forecasting

You may be asked to predict future weather from a given synoptic chart and summary. You must assume that the winds will continue to move as they have moved. To help with this, you can use a geostrophic wind scale:

Fig. 76 *Geostrophic wind scale at 1:30,000,000*

Lay the appropriate scale (for the representative fraction of the chart) at right angles to the isobars, so that one isobar cuts the base-line, and read off where the next isobar cuts the scale, to obtain wind speed. This can also be used across the isobars at fronts: fronts move at two-thirds of the wind scale.

You must also be familiar with the weather associated with cold fronts, warm fronts and anticyclones.

11. World climates

> Let us blame the climate for it.
> (John Masefield, *So Long to Learn*)

Climatology is the study of climates. **Climate** is the summary of average weather conditions and weather variations from studies lasting at least thirty years.

Factors affecting climates include:

A. Latitude

The amount of insolation received at the earth's surface is dependent on the angle of the sun's rays. Rays at right angles to the surface (**overhead sun**) are much more powerful than oblique rays.

The earth is tilted on its axis in relation to its orbit. Consequently, those portions receiving overhead sun vary throughout the year. From the earth's surface, it seems that the position of the overhead sun varies thus:

21 March (equinox) – at the equator
April and May – moving northwards until . . .
June – overhead at Tropic of CaNcer (mnemonic: N = Northern tropic)
July and August – moving southwards until . . .
22 September (equinox) – overhead at the equator
October and November – continues southwards until . . .
December – overhead at Tropic of Capricorn.

Maximum temperatures occur at the tropics because the apparent motion of the sun is rapid at the equator and slows as it reaches the tropics:

Latitude	Days experiencing overhead sun
6°N–6°S	30 at each equinox
17°N–23.5°N } 17°S–23.5°S	86 consecutive days

Furthermore,

(a) the summer tropical days are long, whereas length of day is always around 12 hours at the equator

(b) amounts of cloud are lower in the tropics: less insolation is intercepted.

B. Land and sea

Albedo (the percentage of solar radiation reflected back) varies with the nature of the surface. The sea reflects little, absorbing much radiation, and this is stored as heat. Land surfaces have reflection coefficients (albedo) between 8% and 40%. Add to this the difference between the specific heats of land and sea (p. 207) and we can understand **continentality**: the climatic characteristics of continental interiors, which include:

1) rapid heating: maximum temperatures occur one month after sun is highest
2) rapid cooling; hence:
3) large temperature ranges
4) little modification of temperatures by the sea
5) lower precipitation levels.

   Maritime climates are dominated by oceanic influences and are:

(a) **equable** (small **diurnal** (daily) and seasonal ranges) because of the slower heating and cooling rates

(b) (*not invariably*) cloudy and rainy from oceanic moisture in the air.

C. Ocean currents

Warm ocean currents: Gulf Stream
                        North Atlantic Drift
                        Brazil
                        Kuro Siwo

tend to bring higher temperatures to subtropical east coasts, and to western Europe, and increase evaporation.

   Cold currents: the California
                      Peruvian
                      Benguela
                      West Australia

bring lower temperatures to west-coast deserts. The connection between cold currents and deserts is discussed on p. 187.

D. Pressure and winds

Throughout the year, there are seasonal changes in the distribution of high and low pressure and the location of the wind belts:

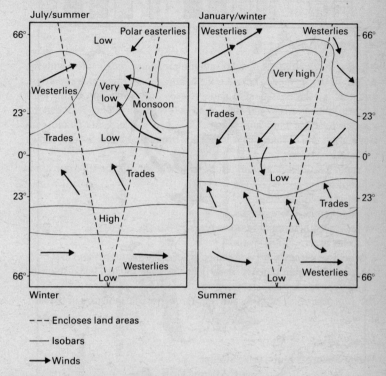

Fig. 77 *Pressure and winds: a model of seasonal changes*

Classification of climates

Climatic types based on temperature and rainfall characteristics have been suggested, notably by Köppen and Miller, who backed up their systems with the evidence of the resulting vegetation type.

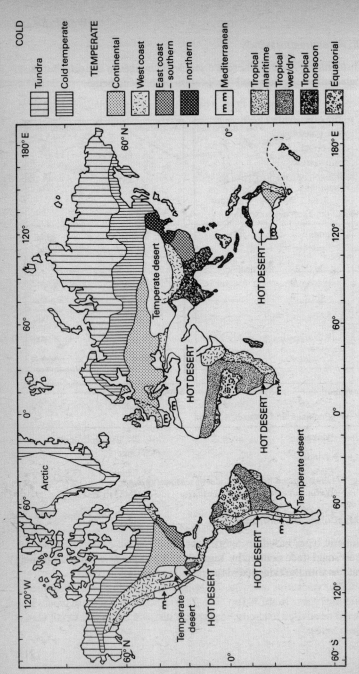

Fig. 78 *World climates*

COLD
- Tundra
- Cold temperate

TEMPERATE
- Continental
- West coast
- East coast – southern
- – northern
- Mediterranean

- Tropical maritime
- Tropical wet/dry
- Tropical monsoon
- Equatorial

Climate questions

Q. 1. Identify and explain the characteristics which distinguish maritime from continental climates. [LON]

Use a detailed example here. Thus, the temperate type (see Fig. 79, p. 216) may be divided into:

1) west-coast ⎫
2) east-coast ⎭ maritime
3) continental

The figures below illustrate this:

Table 37. Temperate climates

		Summer temp.	Winter temp.	Rain total (in mm)
MARITIME	West coast	warm 20°C	cold 0°C	650
	East coast	very warm 25°C	cold 1°C	1,000
	Warm east coast	hot 27°C	cool 6°C	1,200
	Continental	very warm 24°C	very cold −5°C	500

		Rain distribution	Locations
	West coast	even	U.K., British Columbia, S. Chile
	East coast	summer max.	N. China, N.E. U.S.A.
	Warm east coast	summer max.	S. China, S.E. U.S.A.
	Continental	summer max.	Great Plains, steppes, veld

Re-read 'factors affecting climates' (pp. 211–13) in order to explain the variations in this subdivision.

Other questions ask you to explain the distribution and nature of climatic types. Table 38 (pp. 218–19) is a summary of these types. You would be advised to choose four specialities (i.e. find more detail than is given here):

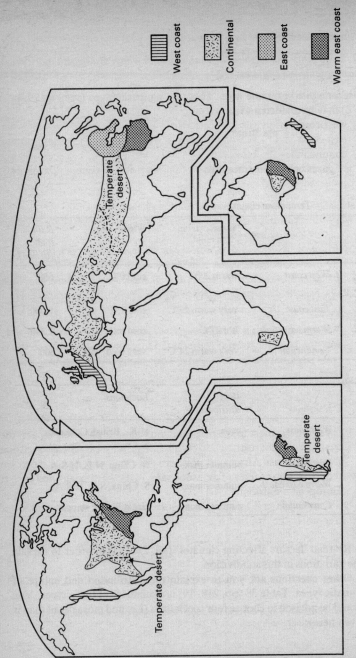

Fig. 79 *Subdivisions of the temperate zone*

West coast

Continental

East coast

Warm east coast

– one high latitude (cold climate)
– one low latitude (tropical)
– one humid
– one arid
for which you know
1) temperatures – reasons for
2) precipitation: total
                 reasons for any seasonal changes in amount and intensity.

Be prepared for questions on climates to include queries on associated vegetation, e.g.:

Q. 2. For either equatorial or Mediterranean areas:
(a) describe and briefly explain the characteristics of the chosen climatic regime, quoting specific figures;
(b) show, with the aid of sketches or diagrams, how the natural vegetation has adapted to the climatic regime you have described in (a);
(c) discuss the extent to which the climatic type you have chosen has influenced agricultural practices in the region(s) where it occurs.

                                                   [SCO.T]

If you are taking a regional paper, you would be well advised to note the climatic zone(s) represented in your regions and use the relevant regional detail to improve your climatology answers, and vice versa.

Monsoons

These are the most frequently examined *climatic* phenomena, and their occurrence is not restricted to South-East Asia. West Africa (the **Guinea monsoon**), East Africa and northern Australia experience monsoons, and some writers refer to monsoon rains in the Caribbean* and even the 'European monsoon'.†

A **monsoon** is a large-scale seasonal reversal of winds, rainfall and pressure in the tropics.

Q. 3. On a world map, indicate the areas of monsoon climate. Explain why the Indian monsoon is the best developed of these.   [OXF]

Note that Question 3 does not ask you to describe the development of

---

  * Horrocks, N. K., *Physical Geography and Climatology*, Longman, 1981.
  † Barry and Chorley, op. cit., p. 237.

Table 38. Climatic types: a summary

Climatic region	Temperature			Rainfall	
	summer	winter	range	total	annual distribution
Cold climates					
I Tundra	mild	extremely cold	extreme	light	even
II Cold temperate (boreal)	warm	very cold	extreme	moderate	summer max.
Temperate climates					
III Continental	very warm	very cold	extreme	moderate	summer max.
IV Temperate west coast	warm	cold	moderate	moderate	even
Va Temperate east coast	very warm	cold	moderate	moderate	summer max.
Vb Warm temperate east coast (as above, but warmer, wetter)	hot	cold	moderate	heavy	summer max.
VI Mediterranean	hot	mild	moderate	moderate	winter max.
Tropical climates					
VII Tropical maritime	hot	warm	small	moderate	even
VIII Tropical wet-dry	very hot	very warm	small	moderate	summer rains, winter dry
IX Tropical monsoon	very warm	very warm	small	heavy	monsoon rains
X Equatorial	hot	hot	small	heavy	even

Main influences on climate	Example					Other locations
	name	*summer*	*winter*	*range*	*rainfall total*	
high latitude	Dawson City (Canada)	14°C	−30°C	44 deg.	315 mm	N. U.S.S.R., Greenland coast
high latitude	Winnipeg (Canada)	18°C	−15°C	33 deg.	530 mm	north central U.S.S.R.
middle latitude; distance from sea	Denver (U.S.A.)	24°C	− 5°C	29 deg.	510 mm	Russian steppes, S. African veld
middle latitude; warm sea currents	Oxford (U.K.)	18°C	0°C	18 deg.	630 mm	British Columbia, S. Chile, New Zealand
middle latitude	Washington (U.S.A.)	25°C	1°C	24 deg.	1,064 mm	N.E. U.S.A., N. China
subtropical latitudes	Hankow (China)	25°C	6°C	19 deg.	1,300 mm	S.E. U.S.A., S. China
subtropical latitudes, depressions in winter	Marseilles (France)	26°C	10°C	16 deg.	580 mm	S. California, central Chile, southern tips Africa and Australia
low latitudes, moderating effect of sea	Rio de Janeiro (Brazil)	28°C	24°C	4 deg.	110 mm	east coast Africa
low latitudes, overhead sun brings rains	Zungeru (Nigeria)	34°C	26°C	8 deg.	1,100 mm	central Brazil
low latitudes, intense heating leads to low-pressure systems	Calcutta (India)	25°C	21°C	4 deg.	1,600 mm	N. Indonesia, N. Australia
equator – equal lengths of day and night, no seasons	Entebbe (Uganda)	24°C	23°C	1 deg.	1,500 mm	Amazon, New Guinea

the monsoon. India is the classic area of monsoon climate because the underlying cause of the monsoon is the effect of continentality (p. 212) on temperatures and pressures, and the continental area of Inner Asia is larger and further from the sea than any other area affected by monsoons. Use Fig 80 to help you answer the question.

January

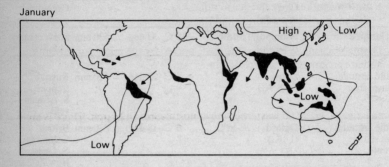

July

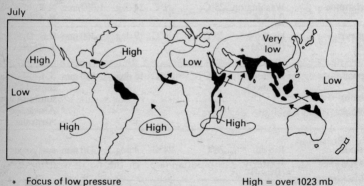

✳ Focus of low pressure	High = over 1023 mb
⬛ Monsoon lands	Low = under 1011 mb
➝ Selected winds	Very low = under 1005 mb

Fig. 80 *Monsoonal areas and associated pressure systems*

The Asian monsoon

Upper-air movements seem to be vital in the timing of the monsoonal burst:

(i) Winter

(a) UPPER AIR: Above 3,000 m, pressure over Central Asia is low. Westerly air currents result.

(b) GROUND LEVEL: Pressure is high over Central Asia. Air subsides beneath the upper westerlies to give
– northwesterlies over northern India
– northeasterlies over Burma and Bangladesh
– easterlies over peninsular India.
Depressions move from west to east, guided by the upper-air currents, and are an important source of winter rain.

(ii) Spring

(a) UPPER AIR: The westerlies move northwards in March. There is an upper-air low at about 85–90°E in May.

(b) GROUND LEVEL: A thermal low develops over the northern Indian subcontinent. Early summer rains in Bengal, Bangladesh, Assam and Burma are related to the upper-air trough.

(iii) Early summer

(a) UPPER AIR: The circulation switches to a summer pattern: a high-level easterly jet stream about 15°N. When this recurs, at . . .

(b) GROUND LEVEL: The monsoon 'bursts'. No one is sure which is the 'chicken' and which the 'egg' here.

(iv) Summer

(a) UPPER AIR: Easterly jets predominate. In the north-west air is subsiding.

(b) GROUND LEVEL: Pressure remains low. Rainfall is at a maximum, closely linked with the easterly jet, which also steers 'monsoon depressions'. Relief also influences rainfall distribution. The subsiding upper air prevents rainfall in the arid north-west (Thal and Thar deserts).

(v) Autumn

(a) UPPER AIR: The westerly jet re-establishes itself in October.

221

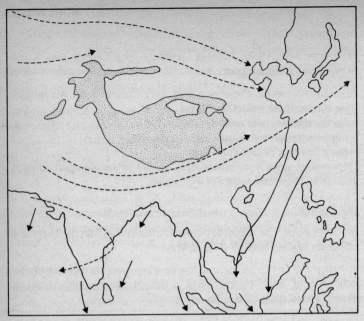

----➤ Air at 3 km (10,000 ft)

——➤ Surface winds

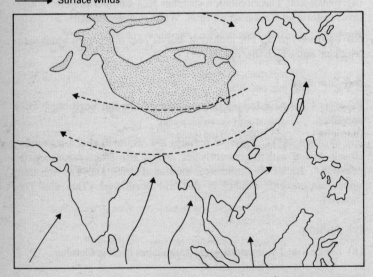

Fig. 81 *Ground- and upper-air motion over Asia: winter (above), summer (below)*

(b) GROUND LEVEL: Trade winds dominate. Cyclones in the Bay of Bengal bring rain to Bangladesh and south-east India.

Q. 4. To what extent can the monsoons of India and Asia be considered simply as large-scale versions of land and sea breezes? [NI]

First you must describe both systems. Next, bring out the similarities – pressure differences generated over land and sea – then the differences, i.e. the vital role of the upper air in the monsoon system.

Climatic hazards

This is a topic directly examined only by AEB, at the time of writing.* A **climatic hazard** is a *largely unpredictable*, sudden climatic change which adversely affects the environment. Thus, drought is scarcely a hazard in a desert, nor is torrential rain in the tropical wet/dry zone. Climatic hazards include:

Table 39. Some climatic hazards

Type	Definition	Examples
Drought	Over 20 days with <30% normal precipitation	U.K., 1975: June, July 1976: June–August[1] Sahel, 1968, 1970–4[2] Ethiopia, 1984
Flood	Submergence of land not usually covered with water, *or* an increase of water depth in a partially submerged area, e.g. padi field.	Australia, 1983[3] North Devon, 1952[4] Bangladesh, 1974[5]
Tropical cyclone (hurricane)	Deep low-pressure system originating over tropical seas (pp. 196–7). Wind speed >120 mph	Florida, 1935[6]
Tornado	U.S.A.: violently rotating, small, low-pressure system. Winds up to 300 mph. African tornado: less severe. Forms squalls	Great Plains, U.S.A.[7] West African coast
Frost	Atmospheric moisture freezing to ground, especially in valley-floor inversions	California[8]

* 1984.

For each hazard, you should know the causes and the consequences. You can find information on the numbered hazards in Table 39 in the following works:

1) King, C. A. M., *Physical Geography*, Basil Blackwell, 1980, p. 112.
2) Grove, A. T., *Africa*, Oxford University Press, 1978, p. 148.
3) Rees, H., *Australasia*, Macdonald & Evans, 1968, p. 28.
4) Miller, A. A., and M. Parry, *Everyday Meteorology*, Hutchinson, 1975, p. 266.
5) Reed, A., *The Developing World*, Bell & Hyman, 1979, pp. 13–15. Miller and Parry, op. cit., p. 225.
6) Dury, G. H., and R. Mathieson, *The United States and Canada*, Heinemann Educational, 1976, p. 218. Miller and Parry, op. cit., p. 225.
7) Miller and Parry, op. cit., p. 225.
8) Dury and Mathieson, op. cit., pp. 218, 233.

Candidates are frequently 'caught out' by imprecise reading of the question:

Q. 5. Illustrate the influence of natural hazards* upon the process of economic development in DEVELOPING COUNTRIES.   [AEB]

The words I have put into capitals constitute a precise geographical term. Look it up and select your information accordingly.

Climate and soils

DOKUCHAIEV was the first to develop the idea that soil is an independent body whose character is determined by climate and vegetation. Since vegetation develops in response to climate (among other things), the link between climate and soils becomes stronger.

Why are climate and soils linked?

Basic vocabulary is needed for this section:

Colloid: in soil; a minute particle of clay or humus, a vital reservoir of minerals and water. Without colloids, soils are dry and inactive.

Leaching: the downward movement of material in solution or in colloidal suspension.

---

* Not solely climatic; see Haggett, *Geography: A Modern Synthesis*, Chapter 6.

Q. 6. What factors determine the speed and efficiency of leaching?
[O and C]

Consider water input; losses through evaporation; solubility of soil components; factors encouraging throughflow – in detail, with examples.

Soil horizon: a layer of soil, parallel with the ground surface.

A horizon: contains a large proportion of humus; most soluble minerals removed by leaching.

B horizon: (**subsoil**) receives material, leached from A horizon, which sometimes concentrates into a hard pan.

C horizon: mainly parent material, partly weathered.

Regolith: A to C horizons inclusive.

MANY SOIL-FORMING PROCESSES ARE A FUNCTION OF CLIMATE:

(i) **Weathering rates** increase as precipitation and temperatures rise (p. 155).

(ii) **Bacterial action** is closely linked with temperature.

(iii) **Vegetation** varies with rainfall. In temperate latitudes, trees grow in areas of over 750 mm, and thrive on and promote acid soils. Grasses, associated with precipitation below 750 mm, thrive on and promote basic soils.

(iv) **Podzolization.** A **podzol** has:

A HORIZON: ashen colour and sandy; iron compounds, clays, bases leached out.

B HORIZON: receives leached products from A; thick, dark iron pan forms.

CLIMATE: wet enough (over 700 mm) for leaching, and larger green plants; cool enough (below 15°C) to inhibit evaporation and bacteria – little humus.

CLIMATIC TYPES: cold temperate (**boreal**), temperate west coast at height.

(v) Laterization (**laterite**: deep tropical soil, with silicates and alkalis removed, leaving an iron–aluminium-based thick red clay.) Laterites have:

HORIZONS: none.

HUMUS: little or none.

CLIMATE: warm enough (25°C) for bacteria to consume humus; wet enough (1,500 mm) for **desilication** (leaching of silica).

CLIMATIC TYPES: all tropical and equatorial.

(vi) Calcification: forms **pedocals**, e.g. chernozem (p. 236), chestnut soil (p. 387); slightly alkaline (basic). Pedocals have:

A HORIZON: humus-rich. Bases abundant and brought to soil surface by grasses.

B HORIZON: nodules and slabs of calcium, brought up from parent rock by capillary action and evaporated out.

CLIMATE: dry enough (<600 mm) to inhibit leaching. Dry season necessary. Warm enough in summer (20°C) for evaporation to act.

CLIMATIC TYPES: temperate continental; tropical wet-dry.

(vii) Gleying: bacteria in saturated clays, lacking oxygen from soil air, remove oxygen from clays, which become blue/grey. **Gley soils** have:

A HORIZON: thick accumulations of undecomposed peat.

B HORIZON: gleyed.

CLIMATE: cool enough (10°C summer) to inhibit humus development and inhibit evaporation; wet enough, with low evaporation rates, to keep soil saturated.

CLIMATIC TYPES: tundra; bog areas of cold and temperate continental.

(viii) Salinization: the accumulation of soluble salts in the soil (sulphates and chlorides of sodium and calcium).

CLIMATE: hot desert (25°C, 250 mm rain).

Soils which are strongly related to climate are called **zonal soils** (see Fig. 82).

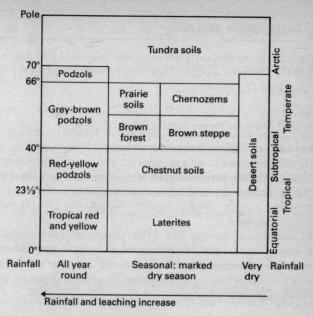

Fig. 82 *Zonal soils and climates (after Horrocks)*

Q. 7. Discuss the extent to which the distribution of climatic types provides a sound basis for distinguishing major soil types. [LON]

Intrazonal soils do not correlate with climate because other factors:
– relief
– drainage – e.g. peat formation, gleys
– parent material, e.g. limestones form
              terra rossa (southern Europe)
              black waxy soils (Alabama),
override the influences of climate and vegetation.

Young **azonal** soils (without horizons) have not yet had time for the climatic/vegetational processes to operate.

12. Ecosystems and soils

Every breath you take, every move you make, every bond you break . . .
(Lyric by The Police, © 1983, Virgin Music (quoted by permission))

Every breath, movement and bond made or broken by any organism affects another. **Ecology** is the study of how (1) living organisms relate to: (2) the **lithosphere** (crust and upper mantle), notably the parent rock and soil; (3) the **biosphere** (the parts of the earth and atmosphere where life exists, notably the land surface and shallower seas); and (4) the **atmosphere**, notably climatic aspects. Collectively, (1)–(4) may be called the **ecosphere**.

We have already seen (pp. 224–7) that climate and soil are frequently inter-related. Any study of an area which stresses the interactions between the organisms and the environment is said to use a **systems** approach and to be looking at **ecosystems**. Ecosystems vary in scale from the Sahara Desert to a hedgerow.

Features of ecosystems

A. There are four basic components:

1) **abiotic** (non-living), e.g. water, soil
2) producers (**autotrophs**), i.e. green plants which can **photosynthesize** – use the sun's energy to make food from atmospheric CO_2
3) consumers (**heterotrophs**), i.e. animals which eat plants or other animals
4) **decomposers** – agents of decay like bacteria and fungi.

B. Energy from the sun flows through the ecosystem via food chains and more complex food webs.

Oak leaf → Hairstreak caterpillar → Thrush   →   Hawk
(producer)   (herbivore)   (carnivore) (carnivore)

Fig. 83a *Food chain*

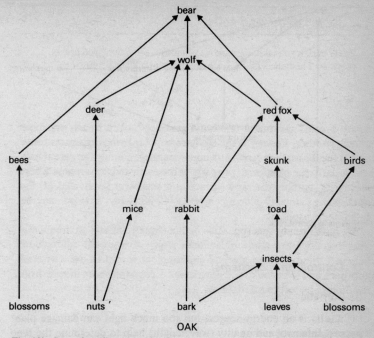

Fig. 83b *Part of an Illinois food web*

Each step from the plants in a food chain is a **trophic level**. Usually, the weight of living material (**biomass**) in any ecosystem decreases at each trophic level: the **trophic pyramid**. This is a result of the energy losses *between* each level, as mass is converted, and *within* each level, via heat loss.

C. Nutrients 'flow' through ecosystems in cycles.

Nitrogen, oxygen, water, phosphorus, calcium, magnesium and carbon dioxide are conserved in an ecosystem. Input and loss are small compared with the volume which circulates within the system. Here is a model of nutrient flow in a forest:

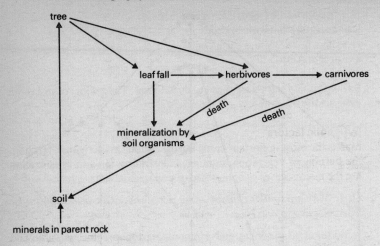

D. Controls on ecosystems:

(i) Climatic

(a) LIGHT is an energy source, but too much light can damage plant tissues. Intensity and quality (wavelength) help to determine the type of plants which grow, e.g. **heliophytes** (light-lovers) or **sciophytes** (shade-lovers). Light intensity can vary greatly within an ecosystem – see 'Tropical rain forest', pp. 234–5.

(b) TEMPERATURE: Tropical plants cannot stand temperatures below 15°C; temperate plants usually fail below −2°C. Warm-blooded animals can be more independent of temperatures (using insulating fur, shivering and sweating, for example) than can cold-blooded species.

(c) WATER is vital to life. In plants:

Xerophytes are adapted to arid conditions.

Halophytes tolerate saline conditions.

Hydrophytes live entirely underwater.

We have already seen how trees require more rainfall than grasses (point (iii), p. 225).

(ii) Topographic (relief) influences include:
– temperature fall with altitude
– relative humidity and altitude
– aspect and insolation.

(iii) Edaphic factors are those to do with soil. The major control is the **pH** – acidity or alkalinity – of the soil.

(iv) Biotic factors
Man is the most important biotic factor. Among his activities, farming, the burning of vegetation, hunting, industrialization and urbanization are the major causes of obliterated or polluted habitats.

Q. 1. Why are similar climatic zones not always associated with similar assemblages of plants? [OXF]

In addition to outlining and exemplifying topographic, edaphic and biotic factors, you could also mention the local variations within climatic zones (pp. 207–9) and the separate evolutions of Australia, Europe and the Americas. Use your regional sources to compare the vegetation developed under, for example, 'Mediterranean' climates in the continents named above.

Large ecosystems

Questions on climate/soil/vegetation zones, i.e. ecosystems, are normally very straightforward. The multiple question which follows is based on a number of examination papers.

Q. 2. For a given climatic/vegetation zone:
  (i) Describe the physical conditions under which vegetation has developed.
 (ii) Describe the composition and structure of the vegetation with regional variations.
(iii) Discuss the adaptation of vegetation to the environment.
 (iv) Suggest how its characteristics have enabled the vegetation type to be maintained as the climatic climax vegetation.
  (v) Explain why a sub-climax vegetation is to be found in some locations.
 (vi) Write an explanatory account of the ecosystem.
(vii) Discuss the factors which have led to the development of the dominant soil type in this zone.

(viii) Outline the effects of man on the ecosystem.
(ix) Compare and contrast one ecosystem with one other.

You could be asked any two or three of these.

Climax vegetation is the final stage of the natural process of succession in a plant community. It is in equilibrium with its environment and maintains a balance between production and consumption in its ecology.

Sub-climax vegetation occurs when a plant community has been prevented from reaching true climax by natural or man-made factors.

Unless you are specializing in world ecosystems, you should find that a knowledge of the following ecosystems is sufficient:

(a) coniferous forest
(b) tropical rain forest
(c) temperate grasslands
(d) tropical savanna
(e) semi-deserts.

Summaries of these ecosystems are given below, following the structure of the multiple question above.

A. Coniferous (boreal) forest

(i) Winter, $-15°C$; short summer, $18°C$; precipitation mainly snow, 600 mm.

(ii) Few species dominate:
 – Europe: pine and spruce varieties
 – Asia: fir and spruce varieties, more subsidiary species
 – America: fir, spruce, pine, tamarack.

 Pure stands (vegetational areas of single species) are common. Little undergrowth.

(iii) Trees are evergreen. Leaves are needle-shaped, restricting surface area and preventing moisture loss by transpiration. Soils lack nutrients because of leaching, and are acid: only the conifers can stand these conditions.

(iv) Conifers alone can tolerate acid podzols (see above). Seeds can withstand forest fires. Evergreen cover restricts light and therefore undergrowth.

(v) (a) Lumbering. Overcutting prevalent in U.S.S.R. 10 million hectares (ha) of the cutting between 1950 and 1960 has not regrown.
 (b) Fire (U.S.S.R.: 1 million ha/year).
 (c) Reservoirs (U.S.S.R.: 18 million ha of **taiga** now flooded).

(vi)

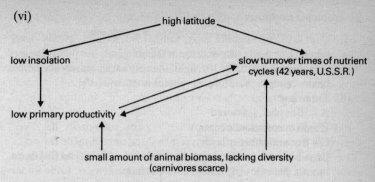

(vii) Soil types vary. Podzol dominant (p. 225).

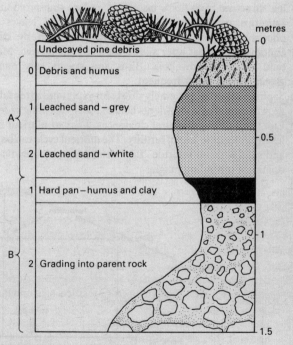

Fig. 84 *Podzol profile beneath pine forest (after Eyre)*

(viii) See (v), above.

B. Tropical rain forest

(i) Over 25°C throughout year, rainfall >1,500 mm, evenly distributed, r.h. high. Seasonal contrasts minimal, *but* microclimates very diverse (pp. 209–10), light intensity varies greatly above and below canopy, therefore sciophytes at ground level.

(ii) Three layers:
A – 50 m plus, scattered
B – 30 m continuous canopy
C – 8 m understorey layer.
Broad-leaved, evergreen trees, thin barked. **Epiphytes** (living on, but not parasites of, trees), parasitic **lianas** (vines). Little undergrowth. Profusion of flora and fauna. African forests poorer than Indo-Malayan and Latin American.

(iii) 'A' layer gains light from extra height. Leathery leaves protect leaf structure from fierce insolation, reduce transpiration losses. Drip-tips enable speedier leaf drying – wet leaves cannot photosynthesize. Lianas gain height and light by climbing. Epiphytes trap leaf litter and re-use nutrients therein. Mammals tend to be tree-dwellers. Birds and insects very numerous, ground-dwellers less frequent.

(iv) Saplings can grow extremely slowly for years until a tree falls, then growth is meteoric. Nutrients held in roots – leaching proof.

(v) Lumbering or agricultural clearances. Lack of nutrient input of leaf litter leads to loss of fertility. The nutrient cycle can be broken and soils become infertile. Less demanding, xerophytic species dominate secondary jungle.

(vi)

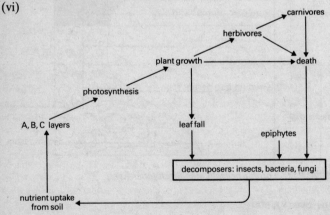

(vii) Laterization (p. 226), but only on non-acid parent rock. Desilication (p. 226) widespread.

(viii) Shifting cultivation (pp. 394–5). Lumbering – all Indonesian rain forest now cleared and sold. Agricultural clearance. Brazilian rain-forest clearances for pastoralism. Result of clearances: lack of cover → soil erosion → silting up of rivers, irrigation canals → flooding → destruction of short-stemmed, high-yield crops of the 'Green Revolution'.

C. Temperate grasslands

(i) Precipitation varies: 250–1,000 mm, summer maximum; winter −5°, summer 25°C.

(ii) The grass type and height vary with rainfall, e.g. U.S. prairies, wetter areas: bluestem grass 1 m high; drier areas: buffalo grass, bunch grass 20 cm high. Rare trees – willows, poplars – occur along watercourses. Small mammals (gophers, shrews) have few predators. Birds abundant.

(iii) Grasses can remain dormant in cold winter, resist fire (below), need less rain.

(iv) Temperate grasslands probably do not represent a climatic climax since they have everywhere been altered by man.

(v) Fires have encouraged the growth of fire-resistant species (grass, with the majority of roots below ground, can withstand fire well). Grazing has modified rather than replaced vegetation.

(vi)

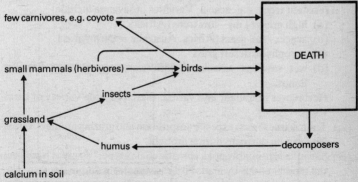

(vii) The intensive root-networks decay into humus implanted into the soil by the vegetation. Soils are deeply fertile, with a fine crumb structure between the roots, and are pervious – thus well-draining. The two soil types associated with temperate grasslands are **chernozems** and **prairie soils**: they are not the same.

Table 40. Contrasts between chernozem and prairie soils

	Chernozem	*Prairie soil*
Dominant process	calcification	leaching of calcium (wetter climate)
Humus content	very high	very high
Colour	dark brown-black	brown
pH	basic	slightly acid
Other	calcium nodules	no calcium deposits

(viii) Perhaps 40% of temperate grasslands are not natural, but occur by clearances and/or fire. The boundaries of this ecosystem do not correlate with climate, suggesting another causal factor: man. Major changes have been destruction of bison; over-cropping leading to soil erosion, gullying, dust bowls.

D. *Tropical savanna*

 (i) Temperatures usually above 25°C, but there is no climatic type linked closely with savannas.

 (ii) Grasses (elephant grass), sedges (marsh grass), thorny or drought-resistant trees, e.g. acacia. Varieties of savanna include:
   (a) high grass (4 m) – low trees (Africa)
   (b) acacia – tall grass (Africa, Australia = eucalyptus)
   (c) xerophytic desert grass
   (d) wet savanna associated with waterlogging, e.g. Brazilian llanos.
   Herbivores abundant and varied, therefore wide variety of carnivores.

(iii) Thorny trees resist excess transpiration and grazing animals. Grassland can be dormant during drought.

(iv) Savanna is probably not a climatic climax type,* so great have been the modifications by man. Fire-resistant trees dominate.

 (v) Burning and grazing.

* See Eyre, S. R., *Vegetation and Soils*, Edward Arnold, 1968, pp. 239–49.

(vi) Low biomass.

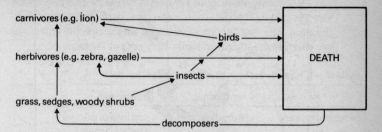

(vii) No dominant soil type associated with savanna.

(viii) Savanna thought to be man-made; see Eyre.*

E. Semi-deserts

(i) Rainfall 360 mm. Temperatures vary; we will consider hot (25°C plus) areas.

(ii) **Succulents**, e.g. cacti; low scrub, ephemeral (short-lived) grasses.

(iii) Succulents store water, spring leaves cut down transpiration losses. **Ephemerals** have short life-cycles which will be initiated by rare precipitation. **Gourds** have extensive dry root systems. Creosote bush can withstand extreme aridity and high temperatures. Insects, reptiles (rattlesnake), mammals (pigmy rabbit), birds (roadrunner) are all adapted to drought.

(iv) The types above are the only vegetation which can stand the heat and aridity, i.e. xerophytic vegetation.

(v) Irrigation: provides food sources without predators – locust plagues are one result.

(vi) This is an extremely fragile ecosystem, and links are not so close between plants because they are so scattered.

(vii) Desert soils (**sierozems**). Upward capillary action brings lime and gypsum to the surface (salination). Humus content is low because vegetation is sparse.

(viii) Irrigation: see (vi). Radioactive testing in American deserts 1945–60.

You would be advised to supplement these summaries with examples from your regional studies, so that you can be much more specific on species and locations.

* op. cit.

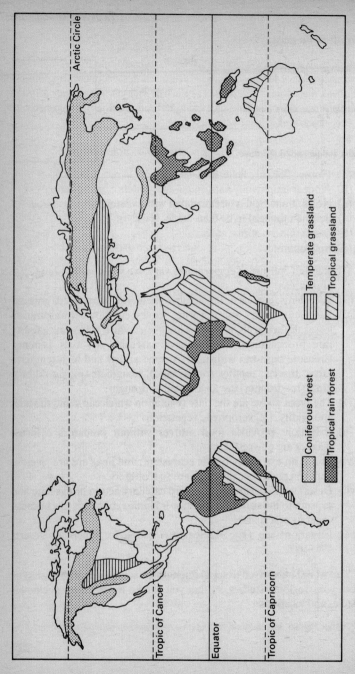

Fig. 85 *Some major world ecosystems*

Arctic Circle

Tropic of Cancer

Equator

Tropic of Capricorn

Temperate grassland

Tropical grassland

Coniferous forest

Tropical rain forest

Small-scale ecosystems

The idea of a climax vegetation (p. 232) indicated that there would be a **succession**, or orderly sequence, of communities, from earliest colonization to the climax. There is: (a) **floristic** (plant) succession; and (b) **faunistic** succession (a sequence of animal communities), but the second is very much controlled by the first.

The succession on a bare rock surface in middle latitudes

1) (a) **Pioneer** flora are lichens.
   (b) Pioneer fauna: only ants, mites and spiders can live here.
2) (a) Acids from lichen break down rock. Small accumulations of dust → moss patches.
   (b) Small spiders, spring-tails.
3) (a) Soil accumulates in moss mats. Isolated grasses spread.
   (b) Worms, grubs (larval insects).
4) (a) Small tree seedlings appear.
   (b) Small mammals, birds, reptiles.
5) (a) Trees emerge.
   (b) Food web now complex and complete.

This succession may be represented at one time by a series of zones:

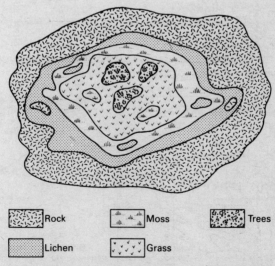

Fig. 86 *Vegetational zoning on a rock outcrop (after Knight)*

A woodland ecosystem

Q. 3. With reference to any temperate woodland, explain:
(a) the morphology and structure of the vegetation;
(b) how energy flows and is utilized in the ecosystem. [NI]

A typical British oak forest would comprise:
– a discontinuous canopy of oak trees
– scattered shrubs, e.g. hazel and hawthorn
– shade-loving herbs: bluebell, dog's mercury, wood sorrel, flowering
  before tree foliage cuts out the light.
Part (b) of Question 3 is most easily answered by a flow diagram.

Nutrient cycles similar to those in Fig. 87 occur for iron, copper, sodium, phosphorus and zinc. As you can see, the calcium is stored at some points in the cycle (Ⓢ = storage).

Most oakwood soils are in the brown forest zone: dark, humus-rich. The A layer is freely draining but not strongly leached. The B horizon is not distinct. Soils are neutral or slightly acid. *Soil variations* – more acid

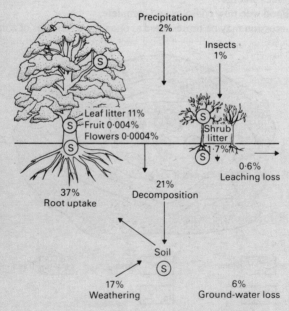

Fig. 87 *The calcium cycle in an oak forest (after Simmons)*

on sandstones, with some podzolization on gritstones, sands and gravels.

Q. 4. Explain, with suitable examples, what happens when the soil/ plant/water/man relationships are thrown out of balance in an ecosystem.
[O and C]

Use examples from this chapter and from Chapter 15, 'Agriculture'. This is an excellent area for your own fieldwork – any patch of wasteland can be investigated.

Heathland and dune colonization and ecology are also sometimes examined.

A major clash of interests occurred in the Cooloola Dune area of the Queensland coast. This area is the home of many rare species, in a complex ecosystem, and there are majestic cliffs of coloured sand. These sands contain rutile, zinc, ilmenite and monazite, which mining companies wished to extract. It took eleven years of action by conservationist groups to ensure the safety of Cooloola Dunes by having the area zoned as wilderness, with legal constraints upon mining and forestry.

Soils

Soils can be classified by:
1) colour: black/brown: indicates high humus content
   red: iron oxide, well drained or limestone
   yellow: hydrated iron oxide
   grey: low humus or from gleying (p. 226)
2) acidity:

Table 41.   pH and some major soil types

4	4.5	5	5.5	6	6.5		7	8	9
very acid		strongly acid		slightly acid		NEUTRAL	weakly alkaline	alkaline	strongly alkaline
rare; podzol		grey and brown; tundra		brown forest; chernozem; tropical; black			chestnut; prairie		black alkali

241

3) texture (diameter in mm):
   – sand   0.1–1
   – silt   0.002–0.1
   – clay   below 0.002.

Through sieving and the use of pipettes, the proportions of the three constituents are calculated, and the results plotted on a ternary diagram, to determine the soil type:

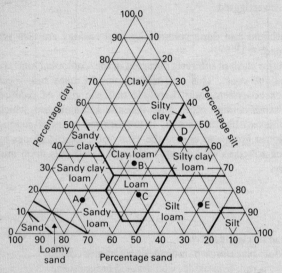

Fig. 88 *Soil texture classes*

Data-response exercises often require you to read the percentage composition at sample points, e.g. A–E above. Check that you are using the relevant scales and axes.

Q. 5. (a) *In a small area of your choice (not exceeding 4 km²) how would you set about making a soil map?*
   (b) *What factors would cause the soils you had mapped to vary over the area?*   [OXF]

You might use any *one* of the three classifications outlined in this chapter.

Factors affecting soil

(a) PARENT MATERIAL: vital in young soils, especially if limestone occurs (terra rossa, black waxy soils).

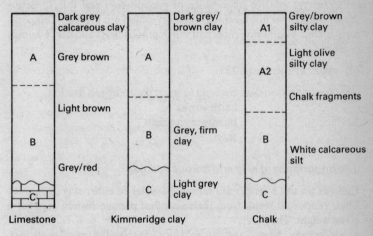

Fig. 89 *Parent material*

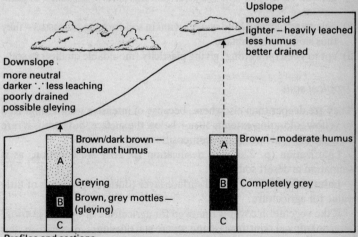

Fig. 90 *Soils and slope*

(b) RELIEF: flat areas: leaching
             gentle slopes: better drained
             steep slopes: faster run-off; less percolation.

(c) CLIMATE: relative importance of precipitation and P.E.T. determines whether or not leaching, capillary action are present. Temperatures affect: weathering rates and soil depth; bacteria and hence humus content.

(d) VEGETATION: see p. 225.

(e) LIVING ORGANISMS: bacteria (above) plus nitrogen fixation
                       earthworms
                       burrowing animals
                       MAN.

The importance of clay and humus colloids

Colloids (in soil science) are minute particles of either clay or humus. Their properties result from their very vast particle surface area for a given weight. They are:
1) electrically charged and can hold ions (dissolved chemical particles). Ions of calcium, magnesium and potassium are bases, vital for grass growth. Hydrogen ions are acid. Colloids control exchange of plant nutrients
2) able to attract and hold water – vital in soil-forming processes – they thus slow down drainage
3) apt to swell on wetting, giving **plasticity** (mouldable quality) to soil.

Tropical soils

They are deeper than elsewhere, because of intensive weathering. Red or yellow coloration extends 10 m+ below the surface, but humus is rare because of rapid bacterial decomposition.

    Laterization (p. 226) and desilication (p. 226) are common, as is salination in desert soils.

    Laterites often have a hard surface layer (duricrust) which is of little value for agriculture.

    If the vegetation cover is removed for agriculture or by over-grazing, intense tropical rainstorms cause severe soil erosion.

    Over-cropping causes fertility to fall rapidly.

    Not all tropical soils are poor, e.g. Indo-Gangetic plain, Western Ghats of India, alluvial deltas of South-East Asia.

Check from Fig. 135 (p. 387) which are the main tropical soils. You will need more information to draw horizons – Strahler* has photographs of yellow podzol (Puerto Rico), **latosol** – lateritic soil (Puerto Rico), grey desert soil and red desert soil among others. Learn from your regional geography how man has degraded tropical soils.

Tundra soils

Plant life on the tundra is restricted by:
(a) the **physiological drought** (where water is available, but frozen, so cannot be used by plants) of the long winter
(b) the short growing season
(c) cold, strong winds.
Trees are few, shrubs are low-growing.

For the same reasons, decomposition of plant material is very slow. Hence tundra areas are characterized by:
(a) **peat** formation: partially decomposed, waterlogged plant material
(b) lack of horizons due to frost heaving (p. 184)
(c) gleying.

Soil erosion

This has been mentioned before (pp. 235, 236). Chase up and expand relevant regional references, to answer:

Q. 6. 'The removal of vegetation is a major cause of soil erosion.' Discuss. [O and C]

* op. cit., p. 308.

13. Population

> Poor Malthus. Everyone regrets him.
> (Sydney Smith, *Letters*)

A. Distribution

Race

Racial classifications are based solely on biological features:

Table 42.   Racial classifications

Type	Height	Face	Skin	Hair	Indigenous areas
Caucasoid	medium	narrow/ medium	'white'	straight/ wavy	Europe, Middle East, West Asia
Mongoloid	short/ medium	broad	yellow/ red-brown	straight	North and East Asia, Red Indian, Eskimo
Negroid	medium	medium	yellow brown/black	curly	Africa

Australoid and Capoid races also exist; numerically they are very small. This is not the only classification.

For an explanation of racial distribution, see Beaujeu-Garnier.*

Geography of population

Other ways in which people are classified are by: (a) language; (b) religion.

B. Population density

Crude population density is the number of people per square kilometre, and any world maps you may see of this are of necessity very generalized. Densities vary widely; generalized groupings are:
(a) **high (densely populated)**: over 200 per km^2

---

* Beaujeu-Garnier, J., *Geography of Population*, Longman, 1978.

(b) **moderate**: 50–200 per km^2

(c) **low**: 5–50 per km^2

(d) **sparse**: less than 5 per km^2.

Overpopulation is an excess of population in an area in relation to resources. This is often reflected in living standards, which are indicated by several indices or measurements (see p. 384). Fig. 91 (overleaf) is based on **gross domestic product*** (**G.D.P.**), i.e. the market value of goods produced within a nation in one year, on a per capita (per head) basis, i.e. G.D.P. divided by population. In the figure:

'Rich' = G.D.P. per capita over \$2,000†

'Moderate' = G.D.P. per capita \$1,000–2,000

'Poor' = G.D.P. per capita under \$1,000

'Dense' population = over 50/km^2

'Sparse' population = under 50/km^2

Fig. 91 is a choropleth (see p. 77). The *national* statistics used hide *regional* variations. Thus, for example, the densely populated East Coast of the U.S.A. does not show up on this map. You will need to consult a map of world population density to help with part (ii) of Question 1.

Q. 1. (i) *Distinguish between the concepts of dense population and overpopulation.*

(ii) *Describe and explain the distribution of the major areas of dense population in the world and assess the degree to which each may be overpopulated.* [OXF]

Those regions classed in Fig. 91 as 'poor, densely populated', are overpopulated. The countries with the lowest levels of G.D.P. per capita and the highest population densities can be roughly ranked by dividing G.D.P. per capita by density per km^2. The poorest, most densely populated nations emerge, from this ratio, as:

1) Bangladesh

2) India

3) Haiti

4) Pakistan

5) South Korea

6) Philippines

7) Indonesia.

* **Gross national product** includes income earned abroad and excludes income of foreign nationals.

† 1979 figures from *Universal Atlas*, George Philip. This atlas is an excellent source of material for A-level.

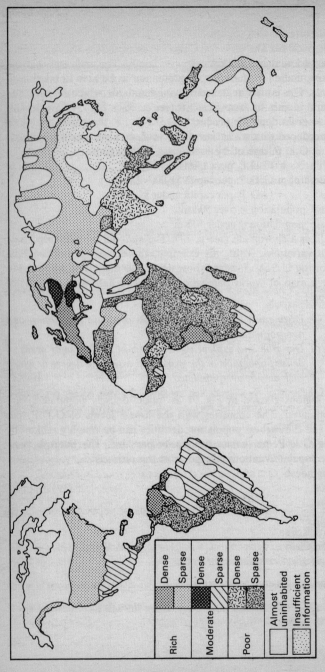

		Dense		Sparse
Rich				
Moderate				
Poor				

Almost uninhabited

Insufficient information

Fig. 91 *Population and living standards*

Points to stress:
  (i) No data are available for China. Present (1984) Chinese policy aims to limit childbirth to one per family. This indicates that the government feel that overpopulation is a problem in China.
 (ii) Nations need not be densely populated to be overpopulated. The country with the lowest G.D.P. per capita is Mali, with a density of 5 per km^2.
(iii) Overpopulation is not restricted to the Third World countries. Pollution, pillage of the countryside and exhaustion of resources in parts of Britain, West Germany, U.S.A., etc., are indications of overpopulation in the developed world.

Methods of relieving the pressure of population on resources

(a) **Limiting population growth**
India has a policy of free family-planning methods, backed by intense propaganda; China uses a system of fines and job demotion for over-productive parents.

(b) **Development**
  (i) Natural resources: see pp. 400–402.
 (ii) Agriculture: see pp. 283–4.
(iii) Industry: see p. 403.

Use Question 2 as a basis for research on this topic, preferably selecting examples from the regions you are studying: developed and underdeveloped.

Q. 2. With reference to named overpopulated areas selected from contrasted countries, analyse the causes of overpopulation and suggest ways in which the pressure of population on resources could be reduced.

[WEL; part]

Some Boards like to consider the question of population density in more detail:

Q. 3. Critically examine the view that rural population density is related to the level of agricultural production. [LON]

(Note the word 'rural' in this question.)

Q. 4. Examine the extent to which the population distribution of a rural area is influenced by the physical environment. [LON; adapted]

These are essentially regional geography questions and point up the crucial fact that a 'human' geography paper demands good 'regional' knowledge.

C. Population growth*

Precision of vocabulary is important here:

Birth rate: *usually* number of births per thousand people, per year.

Crude rate: any of the 'rates' in this list which have not been adjusted for the age and sex structure of the population.

Death rate: *usually* number of deaths per thousand people, per year.

Fertility rate: *usually* number of births per thousand females, per year.

Infant mortality: death of infants under one year old.

Natural change: change in a population due to birth and death *only*.

Q. 5. With reference to one named country with a high rate and one named country with a low (or negative) rate, analyse the main factors responsible for differences in rates of natural increase of population.

[WEL; part]

Negative rates of natural increase result from an excess of deaths over births. East Germany has a negative rate of natural increase (−0.2%).

Low birth rates are generally correlated with high living standards, and factors are inter-linked:

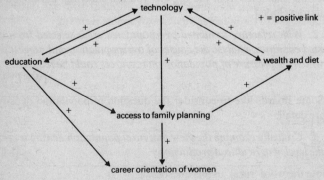

Fig. 92 *Some factors reducing birth rates*

* All rates in this section refer to 1970–77.

Candidates probably 'waffle' on these topics more than on most: a diagram like Fig. 92 saves time; but do not follow it with a repetitious explanation: it is self-explanatory. To this diagram can be added: (a) religious beliefs which may determine whether contraception is allowed; (b) social customs, e.g. age at marriage.

High birth rates show the other side of the coin. Low living standards are linked with birth rates of 25, and over, per thousand. The poorest and most undernourished peoples tend to high rates, but no one has identified the cause clearly. Two suggestions are:
 (i) diet and sexual appetite are linked
(ii) where infant mortality levels are high, people might be having more children in the hope that some will survive to adulthood.
Even with a high birth rate, natural increase may be low, if death rates are high.

Positive rates of natural increase result from an excess of births over deaths. In countries with high birth rates, but where modern medicine and international relief agencies have lowered the death rate, rates of annual increase can be very high. Kenya's death rate of 14/1,000 is the same as that of East Germany, but the birth rates are 51/1,000 and 14/1,000 respectively. Kenya's natural increase is 3.6% – the highest in the world.

Low death rates are linked with higher incomes, because wealth generally brings: better housing and sanitation; better diet; and better medical services. Death rates are also affected by place of residence. In the developed world, death rates are lower in country areas, perhaps because pollution, overcrowding and traffic are less.

It is important to remember that very different birth and death rates can combine to result in various rates of annual increase:

Table 43.   Births, deaths and annual population increase, 1970–77

Nation	Birth rate per 1,000	Death rate per 1,000	% annual increase
Gabon	32	23	0.9
Colombia	34	9	2.9
Chad	44	23	2.1
Taiwan	26	5	2.1

Models of population growth

Thomas MALTHUS (1766–1834) claimed that:
– population increases **geometrically**, i.e. by increasing amounts (as in 1, 2, 4, 8, 16 . . .)
– agricultural output increases **arithmetically**, i.e. by a constant amount (as in 1, 2, 3, 4, 5 . . .).

Consequently he believed that the population of each country would inevitably outstrip its **carrying capacity** (the largest number of a population that the environment can support). At this point, Malthus predicted that the following curbs on population (**Malthusian checks**) would occur:

1) 'misery' (famine, disease and war)
2) 'vice' (abortion, sexual perversion and infanticide)
3) 'moral restraint' (sexual abstinence and late marriage).

N.B.: Too many candidates know only the first type of Malthusian check.

Q. 6. Explain why the predictions for the world's population made by Malthus have not been fully realized. [AEB]

Note that the wording of this question indicates that you should outline some of the incidents which have fulfilled Malthus's predictions:

 (i) famine: Ireland, 1845: 750,000 deaths
 (ii) malnutrition: calorie intake in the Third World is two-thirds British
(iii) disease: malnourished populations have higher infection rates, and are more likely to die when infected
(iv) war: Japan's wars of 1904 and 1941–5 are thought by many historians to have been triggered by a need for more land for her population. (Find out what Hitler meant by the German term *Lebensraum*.)

 The failure of Malthus's predictions to apply everywhere may be explained by the following:

(a) *new land areas* have been brought into production
(b) *industrialization* has created revenue and technology for agricultural improvement so that . . .
(c) *agricultural output* between 1800 and 1970 grew much faster than Malthus predicted. Yet, beyond a certain point, increased agricultural inputs (fertilizers, pesticides, mechanization, improved strains) add progressively smaller increases in output: the 'law' of diminishing returns

(d) *population control techniques* have cut birth rates. (Malthus would see high abortion rates – Soviet women on average have three abortions each – as 'vice'. He might see contraception as 'moral restraint'.)

The 'Club of Rome' – an international group of economists and social scientists – commissioned several reports on population in the 1970s. 'The Limits to Growth' is the most famous; it predicted that all Malthus's prophecies, plus environmental disasters, would occur. This report has been heavily criticized by those who agree in part with Question 7:

Q. 7. The problem with world population is not too many people, but maldistribution of world resources. Discuss.   [OXF]

(**Maldistribution** is unequal distribution.) They feel that the benefits of *production* are unequally distributed. The classic example is Brazil, where G.D.P. per capita has soared but the benefits have been enjoyed by the elite few, and where thousands are landless or shanty-town dwellers. Others argue that the famines of the 1970s – Bangladesh, Bihar (India), Kampuchea, Ethiopia and the Sahel – prove the Club of Rome to be right.*

A third view is that resources are sufficient, but that they are improperly managed: Oxfam believe the Ethiopian–Sudanese famines (1984–5) to be due to bad land use, not drought.

The demographic transition model

A study of Swedish population† shows that birth and death rates have gone through four distinct phases as industrialization and urbanization have increased (Table 44):

---

* See Jones, H. R., *A Population Geography*, Harper & Row, 1982, pp. 170–79, for an excellent summary of thinking on population and resources.

† Figures from Royal Ministry for Foreign Affairs, Stockholm, 1974; quoted in Haggett, *Geography: A Modern Synthesis*.

Table 44.   Population in transition

Stage	Births/ thousand	Deaths/ thousand	% children	% over-65s	% employed in agriculture
1) High, stationary (pre-1810)	high (36)	high (27)	33	6	not known
2) Early expanding (1810–70)	high (33)	falling (26→18)	32	5	72% (1870)
3) Late expanding (1870–1930)	falling (30→14)	low (12)	25	9	39% (1930)
4) Low, stationary (1930→)	low (13)	low (11)	20	15	19% (1975)

Some population researchers (**demographers**) believe that this pattern, often shown in graph form (Fig. 93), is a model, and that every country must go through all the stages before world population stops growing.

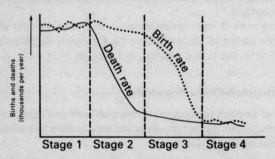

Fig. 93 *The demographic transition model*

Although no major country is still in the high, stationary phase, certain regions in the equatorial forests of Brazil and Central Africa still have high birth and death rates. Examples for the other stages are:
– stage 2 (B.R.>35; D.R.>15):   Algeria, Bolivia
– stage 3 (B.R.>20; D.R. 15 and below):   Egypt, Korea, Brazil
– stage 4 (B.R.<20; D.R.<15):   Japan, Australia, U.K., U.S.A.
Must the model be followed everywhere? You will need to read a specialized book,* but don't expect a clear 'yes' or 'no'.

* Jones, op. cit., p. 168.

You must know that the stages relate to: (a) economic development levels (p. 363); (b) the age structure of the population. Look at the fall in the percentage of under-14s and the rising numbers of over-65s in Sweden between 1810 and 1975. This takes us directly to the next topic.

D. Population structure

Strictly speaking, **population structure** is a breakdown of all the characteristics of a population which can be measured.

Geographical studies of population structure tend to be restricted to three aspects: age, sex (gender), and occupational structure.

Age–sex population pyramids

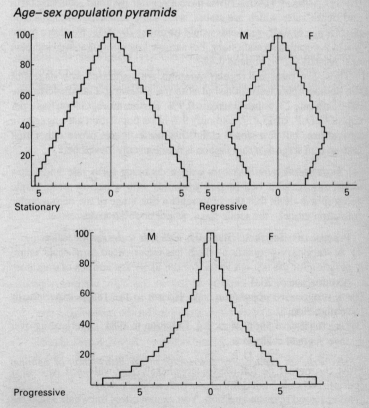

Fig. 94 *Stationary, regressive and progressive population pyramids*

255

You should be familiar with the horizontal bar graphs which show the percentage of males and females in five-year age groups (Fig. 94).

(a) PROGRESSIVE POPULATIONS have high birth rates – reflected in the width of the first three to four layers – and low death rates. In the main, these are low because so many of the people are under 20. Progressive pyramids represent stage 2 (early expanding) and stage 3 (late expanding) in the demographic transition. If you are given a wide-based pyramid to comment on, total the numbers (male *plus* female) for the 0–15 age groups, using the scale.

Stage 2 should show above 35% under 15.
Stage 3 should show 30–35% under 15.

(b) STATIONARY POPULATIONS have a regular pyramid reflecting birth and death rates which are stable, with some minor fluctuations. The percentage of 0–15-year-olds would be about 28–29%. Nowhere in the world is population stationary, but sample low rates of annual increase are: Austria 0.2%; Finland 0.4%.

These low rates and regular pyramids are associated with stage 4 of the demographic transition, but note the following: Gabon: birth rate 32; death rate 23; annual increase 0.9%. Furthermore, Gabon has a per capita G.D.P. of $5.677, and only 9% of its population are engaged in agriculture, but few would claim that these figures prove either that Gabon is in stage 4 or that Gabon is economically 'developed'.

(c) REGRESSIVE POPULATIONS with a declining birth rate and a low death rate exhibit bell-shaped pyramids with a narrow base. Some geographers think that this represents a fifth stage of the demographic transition model – the senile stage, where population decreases.

Practise drawing sketch pyramids *with side scales* for the following:
1) A stationary population which has experienced large-scale immigration for the last ten years (for the likely age and sex of migratory groups, see p. 263).
2) A progressive population, e.g. Britain in the 1850s, experiencing emigration.
3) A progressive population, e.g. Lebanon in 1984, experiencing over five years of civil war.

Q. 8. Write an explanatory description of the distribution of national population pyramids of various shapes, worldwide.

This is a good revision question. You cannot cover the whole world but check on growth rates for major countries.

– Progressive, early expanding: over 3% increase, e.g. Kenya.
– Progressive, late expanding: 1–3%, e.g. India.
– Low, stationary: 0–1%, e.g. U.K.

Implications of population-pyramid features

(a) VERY WIDE BASE: even if family size reduces, population will continue to increase as the under-20s group grow up and reproduce.

(b) NARROW BASE: with under 25% under 15, and over 6% over 65. This indicates that the nation concerned is likely to have problems with **age dependency**, i.e. the increasing proportion of pensioners dependent upon the workforce. If a population is increasing at less than the **replacement rate**, i.e. less than the rate required to keep population figures stable, there will be increasing problems of financing and caring for the elderly.

Of course any predictions based on age–sex ratios are unlikely to be totally accurate because there is a further component of population change: migration. You will need to re-read pp. 250–53 and pp. 261–3 to answer the next question:

Q. 9. Discuss the extent to which information on the age structure of a population assists in the prediction of population growth.　　　[LON]

The common pitfall in answering Question 10:

Q. 10. What is 'population structure' and how is it important in a study of the geography of population?　　　[OXF]

is to neglect the third element of population:

Occupational structure

The breakdown of population in any nation into major occupational groups, agriculture, industry and service is said to reflect its stage in the demographic transition. Thus, for 1977:

Table 45.　Population by occupation

Stage	Country	% in agriculture	% in manufacturing
2	Bolivia	52	3
3	Brazil	40	11
4	Belgium	5	32

You can see that employment in agriculture falls and employment in manufacturing rises through the transition.*

Other components of population structure

(a) RELIGION. This can be the basis of disputes:
– Ulster (1960 →   )
– Punjab (Sikh versus Hindu, 1983–4)
– Nigeria (Muslim extremists 1983–4)
which frequently lead to deaths.

(b) SOCIAL CLASS. In the U.K., the Registrar-General defines social class by occupation of the male (wives take their social class from their husbands, whatever their occupation, in this classification).

Table 46.   Registrar-General's classification

I	professional (e.g. doctors, lawyers)
II	managerial and lower professions (e.g. managers, teachers)
III N.	non-manual skilled (e.g. shop assistants, clerks)
III M.	manual skilled (e.g. bricklayers, carpenters)
IV	semi-skilled (e.g. postmen)
V	unskilled (e.g. porters, labourers)

Class structure is important because, as you go from I to V, the death rate rises, quite terrifyingly. This is thought to be due most largely to variations in lifestyle. Occupational danger and poor access to doctors also play their part.

The relationship between class and family size is less clear-cut. Jones† claims that the highest and lowest classes have the larger families, with lower fertility in groups III and IV.

* N.B. Countries do not all fit neatly into the demographic transition model. Birth rates, death rates, age structure, employment structure, per capita G.D.P. and level of development do not go neatly hand-in-hand, but the broad trends do exist.
  † op. cit.

14. Migration

And yet we must consider how we advance . . .
And yet we must consider towards what we advance . . .
(George Seferns, *An Old Man on the River Bank*)

Add to the above the consideration of 'from what we advance', and you have the whole study of migration in a nutshell.

Apart from compulsory migration, every migratory movement is seen as a response to: (a) *push* factors, unsettling the migrant; (b) *pull* factors, attracting the migrant. In Question 1, therefore, you would be advised to divide your answer into two parts: pushes and pulls.

Q. 1. Give an explanatory account of the factors tending to promote a shift of population from rural areas to urban areas. Illustrate your account with reference to specific answers. [LON]

(For rural depopulation, see pp. 264–6.) As part of your revision you might apply all the migration questions in this chapter to a country or countries within your particular regional studies: try not to confine your answers to the U.K.

Classification

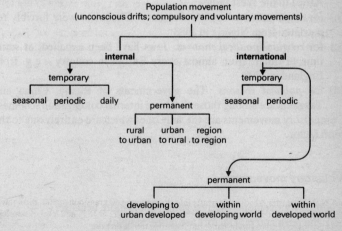

Fig. 95 *Population movements – a classification (after Whynne-Hammond)*

Some of the movements in Fig. 95 have specific names:

(a) permanent international movement: **emigration** (from country); **immigration** (into country)

(b) seasonal internal movement (can be international in Africa): **transhumance** (agriculture only)

(c) daily internal movement: **commuting**

(d) permanent rural to urban: **rural depopulation**.

You could construct a diagram selecting from the relevant parts of Fig. 95 to answer Question 2.

Q. 2. Suggest a simple classification of those parts of the world now experiencing rural depopulation.   [OXF; part]

Use the 'permanent' groups within the national and international sections.

Unconscious drifts include the type of movement that caused Mongoloid peoples from Asia to cross the Bering Straits and occupy North America, where they were termed 'Red Indians'. These movements have now been halted due to action by national governments.

Compulsory movements

Compulsory movements occur:

(a) for *economic reasons*. Examples include the slave trade from West Africa to the West Indies

(b) for *mixed economic/political reasons*. Ghanaians were forcibly repatriated from Nigeria in 1983

(c) for *religious/political motives*. Jews have been expelled, at some time or other, from almost every European country – e.g. from England in 1290

(d) for *political reasons*. The governments of Russia, China and Tanzania are among those that have internal colonization schemes.

Compulsory movements are the only ones which are entirely due to the *push* factor.

Voluntary movements

Voluntary movements interest geographers more because:

(i) the push and pull factors are more complex

(ii) changing factors may alter migration patterns over time

(iii) voluntary movements greatly exceed compulsory ones

(iv) geographers have found certain patterns and 'rules' from studying voluntary movements.

International migration (emigration / immigration)

The movements of Europeans to the 'New World' exhibit the two types of factor noted at the beginning of this chapter:

Push factors (not in ranked order):

1) mechanization of agriculture: led to surplus agriculture populations

2) changes in land tenure: e.g. the clearances of the Scottish Highlands

3) mechanization during the first phase of the Industrial Revolution caused unemployment among hand-workers

4) political persecution caused mass exoduses of Russian and East European Jews to the U.S.A.

5) famine. Between 1845 and 1900 the population of Ireland fell from 8.5 to 6.5 million. Of these 1 million were emigrants; mostly young, mostly male.

Pull factors:

1) new agricultural lands: Great Plains, prairies, pampas, veld, south-east Australia

2) governmental inducements: e.g. assisted passages (notably Australia), very cheap land (Homestead Acts, Canada 1872; U.S.A. 1862)

3) freedom from persecution/trial: these range from the high ideals of the Pilgrim Fathers to the movements of Nazis to Latin America in 1945

4) material inducements: in early 1984, 300 East Germans per week moved to West Germany. The majority came from the Dresden area – that region of East Germany which cannot receive West German TV.

Other factors

In 1883 Emma Lazarus wrote a sonnet on the Statue of Liberty, 'The New Colossus'. It contains these lines:

> . . . Give me your tired, your poor,
> Your huddled masses . . .

But it was not the poorest, congested countries that dominated emigration to the United States. This indicates that: (a) knowledge about emigration; (b) private means to pay for transport; and (c) existing transport facilities are as important as the inequalities expressed in the *push/pull* factors.

Present international migration tends to be:

1) FROM: the less developed countries of southern Europe, Asia, Africa and Latin America
2) TO: U.S.A., Canada, Australia and New Zealand – the major receiving countries (in that order)
3) SELECTIVE:
   (a) by the **quota system**, whereby the U.S.A. would receive immigrants in proportion to the numbers of that national descent already in America
   (b) by *skills*. Some claim that Third World countries are experiencing a 'brain drain'; doctors and engineers are accepted where others may not be. Canada has a 'points' system based on education, training, age, occupational skill and occupational demand in Canada. Potential immigrants have to score over 50 points out of 100 before they are allowed to enter. However, within Europe, we see unskilled migrant workers, notably Turks, being allowed into West Germany to do the unpleasant manual work which their hosts are not attracted to. During times of recession there are calls for the repatriation of migrant workers
   (c) *by family ties*. This is the major basis of immigration into the U.K., and the necessary entry condition for East Germans who wish to move to the West
   (d) *by religion*. Falasha Jews, Ethiopia to Israel; revealed in January 1985.

Q. 3. 'The movement of people from place to place can be viewed as a spontaneous human effort to achieve a balance between population and resources.'* Discuss. [LON]

This question should be answered in two parts. Your first section should deal with international migration (see above), and you should note that 'from the end of 1973 one host country after another has imposed severe restrictions and, in some cases, total bans on the recruitment of foreign labour, although not of seasonal workers'.† This may be attributed to: (i) public hostility to immigrants; or (ii) world recession.

The second part of your essay for Question 3 should deal with internal (domestic) migration. Before moving to that, we will consider:

The effects of migration

Q. 4. What factors have led to the migration of workers from less to more developed countries and what have been the effects on population distribution and structure in the countries of origin and in the host nations?

[SUJB]

Forced migrations obviously decrease the numbers of the group concerned, e.g. Ugandan Asians (in the 1970s), in the country of origin, and increase those numbers in the host country.

In general, however, it is the young, male element of the population which is most likely to move. They usually leave areas of population pressure, like Bangladesh (population density 588/km^2). It is in the nature of most immigrants to gather in distinct areas. Fig. 96 (overleaf) shows how this was reflected in the 'zoning' of New York.

Similarly, Ugandan Asians have settled in a limited number of areas in Britain, creating small **ghettos** (areas of a city in which members of a particular cultural/ethnic group are concentrated). The existence of a ghetto area in a city convinces the indigenous population that there are more immigrants than in fact there are. Government policies to disperse immigrants within Britain have had little success.

A further result of immigration can be hostility between groups: the Protestants in Ulster were originally immigrants (encouraged to migrate from 1690 onwards).

---

* Whynne-Hammond, op. cit.
† Jones, op. cit.

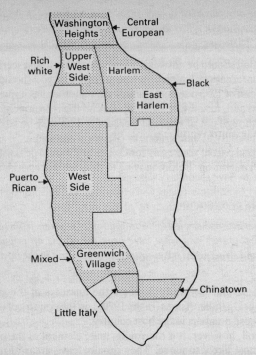

Fig. 96 *Ethnic zoning in New York (after Wreford Watson/Taussik)*

Internal migration

Rural–urban movement: rural depopulation

The major reason for rural–urban migration is the inequality between city and countryside.

Push factors have been:
1) agricultural unemployment, due to better farming technology in the developed world, and landlessness in the Third World
2) decline of country occupations. Technology is making blacksmiths, wheelwrights, thatchers and potters redundant
3) poor social conditions. The inequalities between services in city and country are greatest in the Third World, where electricity and piped water are usually unavailable and doctors and schools are few.

Within the developed world, there is evidence that health care is worse in rural areas
4) famine. Harvest failures are common in the Third World and are a stimulus for people to move to the cities.

Pull factors include:
1) employment. The greater chance of getting a job in the city often turns out to be an empty dream for many migrants (see 'Urbanization in the Third World', pp. 335–6)
2) education. Children in remote rural areas – from the Scottish Hebrides to the plains of Sudan – may be forced to move to cities if they are to have secondary schooling
3) services. In addition to gas and electricity and hospitals, cities have the more frivolous attractions of cinemas, football stadiums, etc. People think they will be less bored in cities.

Problems created by rural depopulation

Some geographers* believe that there is a **vitality threshold** – a level of population below which complete decline becomes irreversible. Emigration from St Kilda (western Scotland) was so severe that in 1930 the demoralized and aged remnants of the island's population were evacuated.

Vital community services like shops, churches, schools, doctors and transport will be withdrawn if the population falls too much. (When my next-door neighbours moved to a village in Wales, their two children increased the village school numbers by 20% – much to the relief of the teacher.)

Rural depopulation results in the numerical decline of the 'economically active' population and an increase in the proportion of the 'inactive': those who are too young or too old to travel to look for employment. This is exemplified by the population structure of the South African Bantu 'homelands'.

Q. 5. 'Out-migration represents the haemorrhaging of the regional body.' To what extent do you agree? [NI]

Look up 'haemorrhage', and don't forget that 'To what extent' means give both sides of the argument (see p. 123).

---

* Beaujeu-Garnier, op. cit.

Remedies for rural depopulation

1) Forcible returning of migrants: Tanzanians without the necessary papers are returned to their villages.
2) Improvement of rural services: British examples are the provision of minibuses, postal buses.
3) Provision of rural employment, notably light engineering, encouraged by grants, etc., from local councils.

None of these remedies has been particularly effective. In Nairobi, Kenyan policemen bulldoze the shanty towns (dodomas) built by migrants from the country, but these are quickly rebuilt.

Urban–rural movements

These are largely confined to the developed world and include:
(a) prosperous workers (usually classes I and II) who can afford to commute long distances, are not dependent on public transport, and enjoy the country environment
(b) retired people
(c) **suburbanization**. A suburb is a residential district, dependent on the city for occupational, shopping and recreational requirements.

Q. 6. Explain the rapid growth of suburbanization since 1930.

Answers to Question 6 should include:
 (i) *natural increase in urban populations* which will lead to a demand for more housing
 (ii) *the movement of some industry to the suburbs.* **Footloose industries** are not tied to a location (by raw materials, power, etc.). These industries are usually in the **service** or **quaternary sector** and include administration, finance and management (office work); education and research. Such industries can locate in the less congested suburbs
(iii) *improvements in transport.* **Commuting**, i.e. travelling daily to work over a considerable distance, depends on fast transport. The most common form of commuting is between a city workplace and a suburban home
(iv) *amenity.* For many, the suburb presents a way of life which satisfies family and leisure requirements
 (v) *cost.* According to **bid-rent theory**, urban land-use is the result of competition between different types of user:

(a) Shops require central locations and can outbid other land-users.
(b) Industry would benefit from, but cannot afford, central locations but can pay for locations outside the C.B.D.
(c) Housing cannot compete with shops and industries, so suburbs develop where bid-rents are lower: at the edge of the city. Suburbs grow because agriculture is outbid by residences; therefore agricultural land is sold for housing.

Urban–urban movements

This is most characteristic of the developed world, and is usually related to unemployment or job promotion. Its relative rarity in the Third World results from the small number of urban areas other than the primate city (p. 331) in Third World countries.

Rural–rural movements

These occur in areas of agricultural development. New cocoa-farming developments in south-eastern (Volta region) and south-western (Brong Ahafo region) Ghana have contributed to population increases of over 100% in the past 20 years.

Theories of migration

RAVENSTEIN propounded the earliest theories (*Laws of Migration*, 1885). His major ideas were:

Table 47. Ravenstein's migration theories

Theory	Comment
(a) Most migrants move short distances	(a) Over half the 'moves' made annually in England and Wales are within the same local-authority area
(b) Long-distance migrants go to urban areas	(b) The largest urban centres in the U.K. receive a higher proportion of migrants
(c) Migration occurs in small steps: 'the inhabitants of the country immediately surrounding a [city]	(c) See Friedmann's model, p. 359

Table 47 continued

Theory	Comment
flock into it, the gaps thus left . . . are filled up by migrants from more remote districts, until the attractive force of [the city] makes its influence felt, step by step, to the most remote corner'*	
(d) Each migration has a compensatory (but not necessarily equal) movement in the opposite direction	(d) One example in south-eastern England can be expressed as in Fig. 97, below
(e) Women are more migratory than men over short distances	(e) Perhaps because women, on marriage, move to husband's workplace

* Ravenstein, *Laws of Migration.*

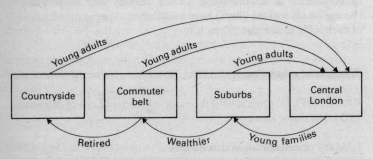

Fig. 97 *A migration cycle*

It is the first idea (a) in Table 47 which has attracted most research, particularly with the evolution of the concept of **distance decay**: that reactions decrease with distance, because: (i) greater distance incurs greater cost; and (ii) available information on long-distance opportunities decreases over distance.

Gravity models are derived from Isaac Newton's law of gravitation: 'Any two bodies attract each other with a force that is: (i) proportional to the sum of their masses multiplied together; and (ii) inversely proportional to the square of the distance between them.' (See 'Sphere of influence', p. 61.) The idea of distance decay is incorporated in part (ii) of the gravity model and is used in the **inverse distance law**: 'The volume of migration is inversely proportional to the distance travelled by migrants.'

Zipf derived this law and stated it mathematically:

$$Nij \propto \frac{1}{Dij}$$

where Nij = the number of migrants between town i and town j
$\propto$ means 'is proportional to'
Dij = the distance between the towns.

He later altered this model to take into account the 'gravitational' pull of the population of the two towns, thus:

$$Nij \propto \frac{Pi \times Pj*}{Dij}$$

where Pi = population town i
Pj = population town j.

You will see both equations in examinations. The first is less satisfactory because it ignores the gravity model effects.

N.B.: There is an enormous difference between the symbols = (which means 'equals') and $\propto$ (which means 'is proportional to').

No calculations are possible for you until mathematicians can express the equations using an equals sign. This is done by inserting a constant (k). So:

$$Nij = k \frac{Pi \cdot Pi}{Dij}.$$

Many researchers considered Zipf's idea to be oversimplified. Other geographers have built in factors like unemployment rate (U), labour force (L), wages per head (W), to derive equations like:

$$Nij = k \left(\frac{Ui}{Uj} \quad \frac{Wi}{Wj} \quad \frac{Li \cdot Lj}{Dij} \right).$$

You need not learn this equation, but remember that when it is tested, this model shows that population or labour force and distance are the predominant factors.

---

* Mathematicians 'drop' the multiplication sign ($\times$) and may insert a mid-spaced dot so that the equation is usually shown as $Nij \propto \dfrac{Pi \cdot Pj}{Dij}$.

Questions on these models usually give you:

(a) an equation to describe and explain

(b) a map of migration flows to interpret, i.e. for you to identify the theory involved. Fig. 98 is one such map:

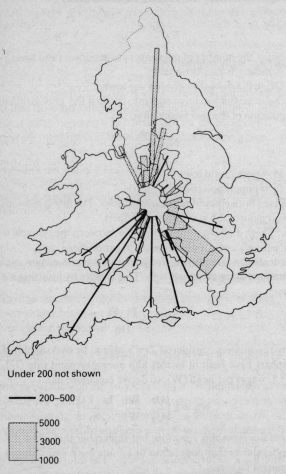

Under 200 not shown

—— 200–500

5000
3000
1000

Fig. 98 *Migration to Birmingham, 1965–6 (after Johnson, Salt and Wood)*

In Fig. 98 it looks as if population is more important than distance: use the distance and the number scales to illustrate this for Question 7.

Q. 7. Fig. 98 shows numbers of migrants into Birmingham.

(i) Describe the relationship between migration and distance shown on the map.

(ii) How might such a map be used as a starting point for further analysis of the relationship between migration and distance?

(iii) What factors other than distance might help explain the pattern depicted? [OXF; adapted]

Commuting: daily migration

Maps of commuting patterns may be given in data-response questions. If so, you would outline the theory that commuter numbers will fall with distance from place of employment (i.e. distance decay), and give examples, using percentages and distances derived from the map given in the exam.

Next you should look for **anomalies** (data which do not fit into the pattern): **positive anomalies** are found where numbers are greater than expected, **negative anomalies** are found where numbers are lower than expected. Should you be asked for explanations, note the factors of ease of travel and unemployment rates.

A third factor in explaining the anomalies might be:

Intervening opportunity

STOUFFER believed that opportunities for economic activity which occur between the point of origin and the intended destination of the migrant (intervening opportunities) may disrupt the simple models of gravity and distance decay.

The hypothesis of intervening opportunity is that 'the number of persons going a given distance is inversely proportional to the number of **intervening opportunities**'. Applications of this model have shown that it predicts migration numbers very well, e.g. within French-speaking Belgium. When movement for the whole of Belgium is studied, the model does not fit, because there are cultural differences in operation – Belgium is divided between French and Flemish speakers.

Question 8 is a useful revision question. The information on pp. 260–61 covers your needs, but you will have to be very concise.

Q. 8. Identify and assess the relative significance of the various factors which affect the migration of population at different geographical scales.

[O and C]

Migrant labour

Question 9 is an excellent basis for revision on this topic:

Q. 9. Study Table 48. The areas or countries in group B supply migrant labour to those in group A.

(i) Discuss the social and economic conditions in group-B areas or countries which lead to large-scale out-migration and the factors in group-A countries which attract migrant workers. (Your answers should refer to specific examples.)

(ii) Describe the type of employment undertaken by migrant workers in their host countries.

(iii) Discuss the socio-economic problems which may and do arise in host countries as a result of large-scale in-migration.   [SCO. A]

Table 48.   Destination and origin of
            migrant workers in Europe

Group A	Group B
France	Portugal
West Germany	Yugoslavia
Netherlands	Turkey
North Italy	Spain
Denmark	Greece
	South Italy
	Algeria

15. Agriculture

This is a wide topic, and there are marked variations in the themes chosen by different Boards. To prepare the topic properly:
1) check – by using the appropriate syllabus or by asking your teacher – what you should know. Few candidates will need all of this topic
2) familiarize yourself with the vocabulary:

Table 49.   Agriculture: a glossary

Agribusiness: industries dealing with farm produce and farm services

Agriculture: practice of cultivating the soil and rearing animals

Agricultural practice: farming methods

Arable: crops

Bush fallowing: clearance and farming of land for limited time. Fallow period of 10–15 years before re-cultivation

Capital: wealth, especially as invested in future production

Cereals: grains, e.g. wheat, maize, barley, oats, rye, rice, millets and sorghums

Commercial agriculture: wholly for financial returns

Consumer: industry or individual using agricultural product (not confined to edible goods)

Co-operative: farm, etc., for production and distribution of goods, costs and profits being shared by members

Dairying: care of cattle for milk production

Economic rent: in agriculture, profit made by farmer; see 'Agricultural theories', p. 285

Efficiency: ratio of agricultural output to inputs (see below) indicated by yields per unit area, or per worker

Environment: the ecosystem (p. 228). Agriculture *always* produces environmental consequences, i.e. affects the ecosystem

Extensive agriculture: characterized by low inputs of labour, low yields and large farm units, e.g. Australian cattle ranching

Farm unit: individual farm

Highest use: land-use yielding highest economic rent. This concept is central to VON THÜNEN's ideas (pp. 279, 285)

Hill farming: farming practice in developed world adapted to more difficult conditions (cooler, wetter climate, thinner soils, poor communications) of uplands. Usually pastoral

Holding: land held by farmer either as owner or tenant

Inputs: agricultural inputs can be:
(a) *technological*: fertilizers, insecticides and/or pesticides, mechanization
(b) *physical*: irrigation, drainage, terracing, reclamation
(c) *human*: labour

Intensity of land-use: amount of input per unit area

Intensive agriculture: characterized by high inputs and (usually) high yields. Many agricultural products may be produced either under extensive or intensive conditions, except for market gardening and dairying which always demand intensive practice

Land reform: change in land tenure aiming to benefit poorer individuals

Land tenure: the system of land ownership in agriculture, e.g.
(a) **owner-occupation**. Farmer owns and farms his land. Examples range from modern family farms to peasant systems where a whole group may own the land
(b) **tenant farming**. The user pays the landlord (i) in cash, (ii) in crops – **sharecropping**, (iii) in labour, or combinations from these three
(c) **plantation agriculture**. Owned by an institution, e.g. a private company, worked by hired labour
(d) **collectivist**. Land owned by group, for example by village: *ujamaa* (Tanzania); *kibbutz* (Israel)

Market gardening: intensive cultivation of vegetables, soft fruit and flowers (U.S.A. = **truck farming**)

Margin: point at which cost of inputs = value of output (i.e. economic rent is zero)

Mechanization: in agriculture, use of machinery for cultivation of soil (ploughs, harrows, seed drills, sprayers, etc.) and collection of produce (harvesters, milking machines, etc.)

Mixed farming: animals and crops produced. Crops are often for **fodder** (animal foods)

Movement minimization: reduction of transport (and therefore transport costs) to lowest possible level. Transport costs are an important component in determining economic rent

Pastoral farming: rearing of livestock

Peasant agriculture: usually subsistent (see below)

Reclamation: bringing into agricultural production:
(a) wetland – marsh or coastal shallows – by drainage, etc.
(b) arid land – by irrigation
(c) infertile land – by improved technology
(d) abandoned land

Shifting cultivation: clearance and cultivation of land for limited period. New land then farmed; original land abandoned, e.g. bush fallowing

Subsistence agriculture: pure subsistence farming has a total absence of cash, all the produce being consumed by the producers or bartered. Most modern subsistence involves some sale of crops or stock for cash

Viticulture: cultivation of grape-vines, usually for wine

Agricultural systems

Examiners' reports show that many candidates write poor essays on farming systems because they have no detailed examples – case studies – to draw on. If you pick case studies from your regional geography you will cut down the amount of material to be learnt (although it may be that plantation agriculture is not practised in the regions you are studying).

For each system you *must know*:
(a) *the physical setting*, notably relief, drainage, climate (with figures) and soils
(b) *relevant human factors*: (i) *economic*: labour, markets, technology; (ii) *social/cultural*: division of land, labour, traditional methods and crops
(c) crops and livestock produced
(d) scale (approximate area) and methods of farming
(e) problems.

You should aim to know case studies of the following systems:
1) subsistence farming: intensive or extensive (less important)
2) commercial farming: extensive; pastoral or arable
3) commercial farming: plantation, notably for Cambridge candidates
4) commercial farming: intensive pastoral or intensive arable, e.g. market gardening
5) commercial farming: intensive mixed farming

Questions 1 and 2 typify those set on case studies.

Q. 1. (a) *Explain what is meant by intensive subsistence farming.*
    (b) *With reference to one named area of intensive subsistence farming assess the relative contributions of physical, economic and cultural factors in the development of that form of agricultural production.*   [WEL]

Q. 2. (a) *Define what is meant by 'extensive agriculture'.*
    (b) *Examine the factors which affect the distribution of any one extensive agricultural system.*   [LON]

Questions on plantation agriculture are concerned with:
 (i) its essential features
 (ii) location of major plantation areas
(iii) economic advantages
(iv) problems.

Factors affecting agriculture

The use of an area for a particular type of farming is conditioned by a variety of factors, which are themselves inter-related. The examples given below will make little sense to you unless you follow them up, particularly the ones set in your 'special' regions.

Physical factors

Relief

SLOPES may inhibit arable farming since:
 (i) machinery cannot operate on slopes greater than 11°; all cultivation is environmentally impossible on 18°+ slopes
 (ii) tilling of soil on slopes can lead to soil erosion.
This factor can be overcome by **terracing**: cutting a series of 'shelves' into the slope. These are stabilized by retaining walls. Terracing is used in *Europe*: for viticulture, e.g. Rhine valley, Yugoslavia; in *Asia*: for rice culture, e.g. China, Java.

ALTITUDE
 (i) generally lowers temperatures by about 6°C per 1,000 m. This cooling is advantageous in the tropics, notably in the erstwhile 'White Highlands' of East Africa (7°C cooler than at sea level). However, European hill farmers are faced with shorter growing seasons

(ii) often increases precipitation: annual precipitation in Strathclyde (Scotland): Oban (sea level): 1,250 mm; Ben More (1,130 m): 2,500 mm.

Drainage

TEMPERATE WETLANDS have to be drained before they can be cultivated, for instance the German *watten* and the Somerset levels.

TROPICAL WETLANDS are an asset, since rice may be cultivated without irrigation, as in the flood plains of the South-East Asian rivers (Hong (Red) River, Mekong delta; both in Vietnam).

Soils

Soils are influenced initially by rock type, and subsequently by climate, vegetation and soil organisms.

Outstandingly fertile soils include:

(a) **alluvium** – silt deposited by rivers. Examples are:
 – *Europe*: Fenland (East Anglia)
 – *Africa*: Nile valley
 – *Asia*: Vietnam (see above), Yangtse delta (China)
 – *North America*: Great Valley (Sacramento River, California)
 – *South America*: Paraná River (Argentina)

(b) **basalt-derived soils**:
 – *Asia*: Deccan plateau (India)
 – *North America*: Snake Plateau, U.S.A.

(c) **loess soils** – fine yellow/grey soils deposited as wind-borne dust in periglacial conditions:
 – *Europe*: from Normandy to Kiev, forming major agricultural areas
 – *Asia*: eastern China
 – *North America*: Mississippi plains.

Climate

TEMPERATURE: Little will grow below 6°C. Some approximate minimum growing-season temperatures are: barley 12°C; wheat 15°C; maize 20°C; cotton 25°C.

PRECIPITATION: Water is essential for all plant growth, but some crops demand more, e.g. cotton 550–1,150 mm; rice 1,500 mm; rubber 1,700 mm. It is easier and cheaper to increase water by irrigation than to raise temperatures (greenhouses are expensive – the more so when heated).

LENGTH OF GROWING SEASON is a major control on possible crop varieties.

Climatic hazards
OCCASIONAL FROSTS threaten crops from oranges (California) to coffee (Uganda).

'HAIL can kill a county full of wheat in half-an-hour' (John Gunther, *Inside U.S.A.*).

WINDS: The cold **mistral** (South of France) and the hot dry **sirocco** winds can cause crop losses. Hurricanes destroyed the Dominican banana crop in 1980.

Vegetation
Usually a product of climate, natural vegetation may be exploited for food by 'hunters and gatherers'. In Ghana, selective forest clearances have left oil palms *in situ*, such that an oil-palm belt now exists.

Animal life (including diseases)
Everywhere the farmer wages war against pests. Examples of pests are:
- *Europe*: Colorado beetle (potato)
- *Africa*: locust; capsid bug (cocoa)
- *North America*: boll weevil (cotton)
- *Central America*: Panama disease (bananas).

Economic factors

Demand (market)
A commercial farmer will only produce those commodities which are sufficiently profitable. Price changes are reflected in agricultural land-use:
- in *Europe*: Common Market (E.E.C.) subsidies have stimulated grain farming: barley is replacing sheep over the chalklands of southern England
- in *Africa*: northern Nigeria's production of groundnuts has almost ceased as farmers turn to vegetables, for which high prices are paid by oil-rich workers

– in *Asia*: rising oil prices have made synthetic rubber dearer; this has led to an increase in the rubber acreage of Malaysia
– in *North America*: Americans are eating less bread and potatoes, more meat. Great Plains farmers are increasingly raising cattle on irrigated pastures
– in *South America*: in 1962, Brazil launched a programme to uproot 2,000 million coffee bushes and replace them with maize, rice, beans and cotton because of overproduction of coffee.

Increasingly, **marketing boards** try to stabilize prices and control stocks, to protect farmers against fluctuations in demand.

With the information in this section, you should find Question 3 simple.

Q. 3. Explain how changes in agricultural land-use patterns may result from changes in consumer demand. [O and C]

Labour
The success of certain Third World export crops is based on cheap labour: notably Malaysian rubber and Sri Lankan tea.

Transport
Von Thünen's model (p. 285) was based on the assumption that transport time and costs were the major factors in determining the nature of agriculture. High-value commodities, like early fruit and vegetables (**primeur** crops), or exotic crops, like avocado pears, can withstand high transport costs, however.

Social factors

The factors listed in Question 4 are social because they reflect the way a society is organized – land tenure and co-operatives – and how land is inherited: holdings often grow smaller if they are divided up between the farmer's heirs (**fragmentation**).

Q. 4. Explain with examples how any two of the following can affect farming:
(a) modes of land tenure;
(b) co-operatives;
(c) size of land holdings.

Different modes (or types) of land tenure are explained on p. 274.
From Malaysia, there is evidence that yields of rubber are higher on

279

plantations than on peasant plots, perhaps because of the ability of the plantation owners to pay for better inputs (pp. 274, 398–9), and because of the **division of labour** possible on the plantation, where groups of workers, specializing in one particular task, increase efficiency.

Some economists would argue that the small farmer produces more because of his personal stake in farming. This seems to be the case in Belgium, where average farm size is 1.8 ha (1 ha = 10,000 m^2 or 0.01 km^2), cultivation is intensive (often by hand), and crop yields are among the highest in Europe.

Co-operative farming

This has played a vital part in Denmark's agricultural growth. Danish farms are middle-sized, around 36 ha, but farmers can economize by joint purchases of machinery and fertilizers, and transport, process and sell their products more effectively through the co-operatives.

Whether the establishment of co-operatives will help the Third World is a moot point. China has had limited success with state co-operatives and is now allowing more private enterprise; *ujamaa* villages in Tanzania (see p. 274) have failed, but Oxfam has had success with co-operative ventures in the Sahel zone of West Africa.

Farm size

Question 5 is entirely devoted to this topic, whereas this book gives only enough information to answer half the question, as in Question 4; therefore you may need to consult a specialist book.*

Q. 5. What relationship is there between size of farm unit and efficiency of production?   [O and C]

Small farms are unlikely to be economically viable (practicable) in areas of poor physical conditions. In more favoured areas, production can be very high on small farms (see Belgium, above), but in general a larger farm, with larger fields, makes for more economic use of machinery. In consequence, many fields have been 'merged' in East Anglia,† and miles of hedgerow have been removed.

The largest farms – in Australia and the Great Plains – are not highly productive. Stock (animal) numbers per hectare and crop yields per hectare are so low that only a very large farm unit is viable. Australian

---

* Try Morgan, W. B., and R. J. C. Munton, *Agricultural Geography*, Methuen, 1971.

† Some East Anglian farmers claim that they have been forced to mechanize because skilled labour (e.g. hedgers and ditchers) is unavailable. Larger field sites then become vital.

cattle stations can exceed 10,000 km^2 (1 million ha). Prairie and Great Plains farms are smaller – around 200 ha, but increasing in size.

Clearly there is no simple relationship between efficiency of output and farm size if the whole range of environments is considered.

Be prepared to discuss the influence of the following factors:
(a) temperature
(b) precipitation
(c) transport and marketing
(d) population density
(e) government policies
on *specific* farming areas.

Question 6 stresses the need for you to note the inter-relationships between 'agricultural factors':

Q. 6. The use of an area for a particular type of farming is conditioned by the interplay of a variety of factors, some of which are indicated on the figure below.

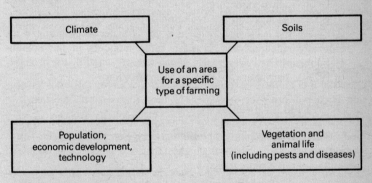

Fig. 99 *See Question 6*

Discuss one distinctive farming type which you have studied in an area of the developed world, and one type in the developing world. In both cases relate your answer to the figure above and emphasize the inter-relationships between the factors listed there.   [SCO. A]

Agricultural problems

Production

Q. 7. In what ways can the world increase its output of food to feed a rapidly increasing population? [SUJB]

Question 7 poses the major agricultural problem: to feed the world.
Agricultural output may be increased by:

(i) Bringing more land under cultivation:

It is estimated that only 4,000 million of the 11,000 million ha of cultivable land are actually farmed. There are two major difficulties:
1) *cost.* In addition to the normal agricultural inputs, an **infrastructure** is needed: the underlying services, such as transport, communications, power supplies, water, etc., needed for any development
2) *environmental consequences.* Ecologists are worried that the clearance of tropical rain forest, especially in Brazil, will affect the world's hydrology and the evolution of new species. In other tropical areas the ecological balance is very fragile. A programme to eliminate smallpox and increase cattle numbers in the Somali Republic initiated overgrazing which was worsened by the drought of 1973–5. Now there are fears of desertification.

(ii) Increasing the irrigated acreage:

Increases in food production in Pakistan have been aided by the irrigation of 10 million ha in the Indus valley. Fig. 100 shows the Third World countries which have the highest irrigated areas – clearly there is potential for much more irrigation.
However, there are problems:
1) *financial cost*: the Gezira-Managil scheme in Sudan, said to be 'the largest and most successful scheme in Africa',* cost £43 million, spread over 40 years. This is very cheap. At today's prices it would cost ten times as much, and foreign bankers do not like lending on irrigation projects – the returns are too low
2) *social cost*: 80,000 people had to be resettled as a consequence of the Volta River Project (Ghana)
3) **bilharzia**: a tropical disease, transmitted by worms parasitic on snails. 2,000 million people suffer from this debilitating disease.

* D. N. McMaster, in Clarke, J. I., *et al.*, *An Advanced Geography of Africa*, Hulton Educational, 1975.

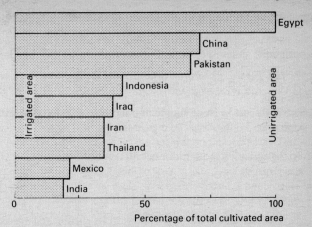

Fig. 100 *Irrigation: top nine Third World countries ranked by % of cultivation under irrigation*

Any increase in tropical water area increases the risk of bilharzia. There is a chemical which will kill the snail without endangering any other species, but it is expensive – yet another cost of tropical irrigation schemes

4) **salination**: occurs when surface evaporation induces the movement of ground water to the surface, causing a crust of salts to form. It is a frequent consequence of irrigation in the tropics, from Ghana to the Indus plain. Reclamation – by deep ploughing and regular flushing, or chemical treatment – is again expensive

5) *water rights*: some rivers cross national boundaries, notably the Indus (India and Pakistan) and the Mekong (Vietnam, Laos, Cambodia, Thailand). Complex treaties have to be negotiated.

(iii) Increasing yields per acre:

The **Green Revolution** is the increase in cereal productivity begun in the late 1960s by using:

– **hybridization**: breeding new crop strains which grow faster and yield more, notably 'miracle rice'
– hormones. Minute amounts of hormones can increase yields dramatically
– pesticides, insecticides, herbicides, fungicides
– fertilizers.

These techniques have boosted output: Mexico and the Philippines now have a grain surplus where once there was a deficit.

Has the Green Revolution worked?*

1) Costs of conversion to new wheat and rice strains are high, because substantial amounts of fertilizer and water are needed. Landless and poverty-stricken peasants cannot afford the inputs.
2) Increased production can lead to price falls; costs may not be covered.
3) Fertilizers are in short supply and increase in price with every oil price rise.
4) Miracle rice doesn't taste nice!

Increasing agricultural output alone will not feed everyone (see 'Hunger and food', p. 391).

Problems of intensive agriculture

Intensive agriculture in the developed world is encouraged by:
  (i) pressure on land: since land is in short supply, high economic rents are necessary to 'outbid' other land-users
 (ii) high demand, so that affluent societies are prepared to pay high prices
(iii) large markets, which encourage market gardening, even if physical conditions are not ideal. Profits are such that costs of greenhouses, fertilizers, etc., can be absorbed.

Consequently, many areas which are not naturally fertile are over-farmed.

   Some problems which arise include:
(a) **gluts** (overproduction): in 1978, plums were offered in the Vale of Evesham at 3p per lb. The weight of plums was breaking tree branches. Gluts cause financial problems
(b) *costs*: since oil prices began to rise in the early 1970s, greenhouse owners have been faced with ever-increasing heating bills
(c) *soil exhaustion*: this is a problem, for example, in the intensively cultivated *huerta* (market gardens) of Mediterranean Spain
(d) **monoculture** (single crop cultivation) is particularly prone to the rapid spread of crop disease.

Q. 8. Outline three problems of dependence upon intensive agriculture in a developed country.

With a question like this, do have the sense to choose three *different* potential problems.

* Further reading: Morgan, W. B., *Agriculture in the Third World*, Bell & Hyman, 1978, pp. 110–13.

Agricultural theories

J. H. von Thünen published *The Isolated State* in 1826. He attempted to explain land-use patterns in terms of economic rent (p. 273), and held that the main factors affecting profits were:

1) *land values*: rural land values decline with distance from the city. Consequently high-value agriculture would occupy the more expensive land, and low returns would be acceptable on the distant, cheap land

2) *transport costs*: bulky products (i.e. with a large tonnage per unit of production area) will rapidly become expensive to transport with increasing distance. Lighter or more transportable produce remains profitable over much greater distances. Look at Fig. 101:

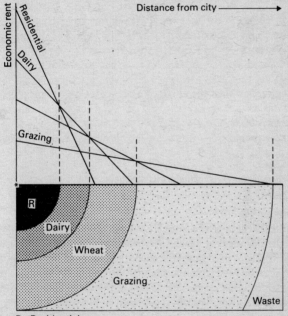

Fig. 101 *Bid-price curves and land-use rings*

The **bid-price** (or bid-rent – they are the same thing) can be explained as a trade-off between the convenience of being near the city – reducing transport costs – and the high cost of land there. In Fig. 101, *dairying*, an intensive form of land-use, stands to gain from location near the city, but the high transport costs quickly make it uneconomic as you move further from the city. In other words, dairying has a steep bid-rent curve. *Wheat* is less lucrative, but transport costs are lower, so it occupies the cheaper land further from the city. Notice that the broken lines mark the points at which one type of land-use 'outbids' another and therefore becomes the more profitable land-use.

Questions on graphs resembling Fig. 102 are common.

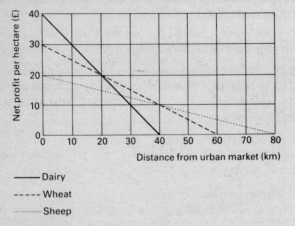

Fig. 102 *Interpreting bid-price graphs*

Interpreting Fig. 102:
(i) Land-use will appear as a series of rings around the urban market. Use the distances at which (1) wheat 'outbids' dairy and (2) sheep 'outbid' wheat to indicate the changes in the land-use.
(ii) Costs can be read from the slope of the graph. Reading the wheat line, we see that profits are £20/ha at the market and £10/ha at a distance of 40 km. Transport costs (given the von Thünen assumptions) are therefore: £20 − £10 = £10 for 40 km. Therefore £10/40 for 1 km, i.e. 25p.
(iii) To deduce the results of lowered cost, draw a new line for the crop, parallel to the old line but starting, say, £10 higher (since lowered costs = higher profit). The opposite could be done for higher transport costs.
(iv) If market prices increase, net profits increase.

Von Thünen's model and reality

This model only applies if several assumptions are made:
1) No trading with other areas occurs; the state is isolated.
2) No variations in soil fertility, relief or climate exist in the area – it is a featureless, uniform plain, or **isotropic surface**.
3) The farmer is an entirely rational **economic man** – one who has perfect knowledge in order to maximize profits.
4) Transport costs are directly proportional to distance from the city.

These assumptions were made to simplify the real world in order to understand some of it.

Q. 9. Using specific examples illustrate the factors which will distort the pattern of agricultural land-use developed by J. H. von Thünen. [AEB]

To answer Question 9, you must first outline the pattern predicted by von Thünen, and the assumptions he made. You can then deal with the assumptions, showing how real-world situations differ and what effects these differences have, e.g.:

1) Britain is part of the E.E.C.
Present low prices of European U.H.T. milk may seriously reduce the pattern of dairying in the U.K. We are not an 'isolated state'.

2) (i) Variations in *soil fertility*

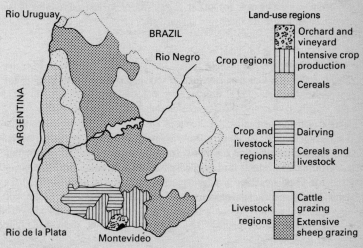

Fig. 103a *Uruguay: land-use (after Tidswell)*

287

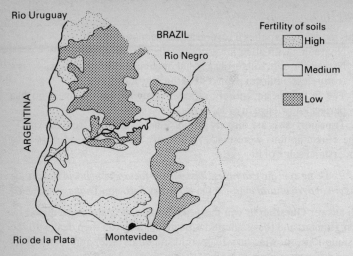

Fig. 103b *Uruguay: soil fertility in land under 200 m (after Tidswell)*

Trace Fig. 103b and fit it over Fig. 103a. Note that:
 (i) intensive crop production occurs around Montevideo, even on soils of low fertility. Look for other proofs of von Thünen's theory
 (ii) dairying does not occur on the less fertile land to the east of Montevideo. Look for other areas where fertility encourages or discourages more intensive agriculture.

2) (ii) Variations in *relief*
Fig. 103 omitted areas of high relief. Use a tracing overlay on Fig. 104 to see if the areas of low apple production can be explained by relief features.

3) Economic man
If a farmer organizes his farm to maximize profit and minimize transport costs, it follows that his own farm will also be zoned. Chisholm has shown that, in Finland, output decreases with distance from the farmhouse. A model farmer would organize his dairy farm as in Fig. 105a (overleaf). An actual dairy farm is shown in Fig. 105b.

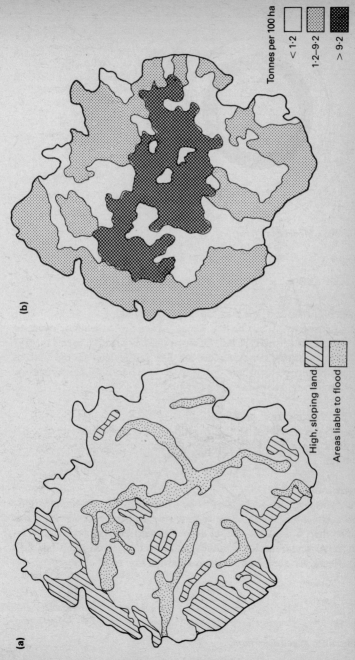

Fig. 104 Herefordshire: (a) adverse terrain, (b) zones of decreasing intensity of cider apple production (Tidswell)

High, sloping land

Areas liable to flood

Tonnes per 100 ha

< 1·2

1·2–9·2

> 9·2

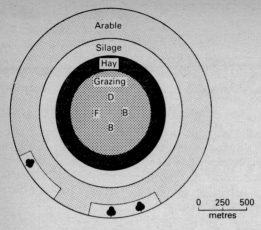

Fig. 105a *Model dairy farm*

B – Barns

F – Farmhouse

D – Dairy unit

0   250   500
metres

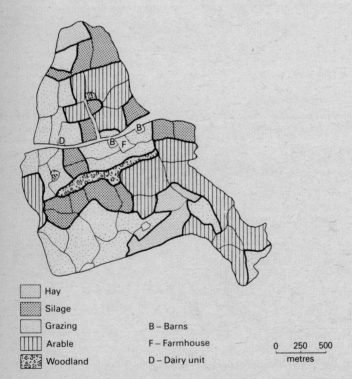

Hay

Silage

Grazing

Arable

Woodland

B – Barns

F – Farmhouse

D – Dairy unit

0   250   500
metres

Fig. 105b *Actual dairy farm*

You need this detail to answer Question 10.

Q. 10. Explain the principles underlying the model of dairy farming shown in Fig. 105a and suggest reasons for the differences between the farm in Fig. 105b and the model. [WEL; adapted]

4) Transport costs

A good transport route may alter transport costs. Von Thünen recognized this and built a navigable river into his model. Today, it will be motorways and trains which allow intensive cultivation at great distances from major urban centres. Note the concentration of dairying in Devon and Cornwall in Fig. 106; measure the average distance of these areas from London and the Midlands.

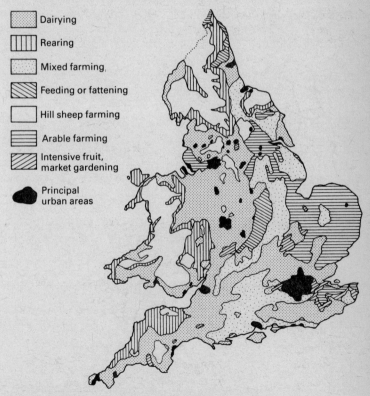

Dairying

Rearing

Mixed farming

Feeding or fattening

Hill sheep farming

Arable farming

Intensive fruit, market gardening

Principal urban areas

Fig. 106 *The main types of farming in England and Wales*

Question 11 combines the ideas of von Thünen with the agriculture factors discussed on pp. 276–81.

Q. 11. Study Fig. 106 which shows types of farming in England and Wales and then, making reference to theoretical studies, discuss the factors which may have led to the pattern shown. [SUJB]

Other agriculture questions, like Question 12 below, are best answered with reference to one country whose agricultural geography you have studied; but Fig. 106 and an atlas should give you enough for an answer.

Q. 12. How important are physical factors in the creation of agricultural land-use patterns? [O and C]

16. Industry

Mr Weber tried hard to explain
Plant location with isodapanes.
He said, 'Every boss
Will reduce transport costs
To markets on featureless plains.'

Industry is defined as economic activity concerned with the extraction of raw materials, the production of goods and the provision of services. **Manufacturing industry** refers solely to the production of goods. Note these terms as they are used in Questions 1 and 2:

Q. 1. Assess the usefulness of elementary industrial location theory in explaining real-world patterns of industrial location. [O and C]

You can consider any type of industry from lumbering to the 'pop music industry'. See pp. 304–5 for a discussion of this question.

Q. 2. Examine the main arguments for and against the spatial decentralization of manufacturing industry, at different geographical scales.

[O and C]

Here, you must restrict yourself to the production of goods. See 'Secondary industry', p. 296.

Table 50. Industry: a glossary

Accessibility: *in industry*, not as precisely defined as in networks. Refers to distance and ease of transport

Agglomeration: concentration of industries close to one another

Agglomeration economies: savings made by producers in agglomerations because they use infrastructure collectively

Behaviourism: *in industry*, the idea that businessmen are not perfect 'economic men', but beings with varied knowledge and abilities when decisions are made

Concentration theory: suggests that there is a hierarchy of agglomerations, from individual plants to industrial belts, within a developed nation, with a ratio of 2:1 upwards between each level (THOMPSON)

Criterion (plural: **criteria**): factors and/or standards considered in decision-making. As in:

Q. 3. What would be your general criteria for locating:
(a) a steel works using imported raw materials;
(b) a butter and milk-powder factory;
(c) an office and warehouse for a mail-order business? [SUJB; part]

Cumulative causation: the theory that economic development leads to an increase in differences between regions, due to agglomeration economies (MYRDAL). See also p. 357

Decentralization (deglomeration): the movement, e.g. of industry, from urban centres. This may result from (i) overcrowding, congestion, high land prices, pollution; (ii) government inducement to move to areas of high unemployment

External economies: cost advantages (savings) from sources outside the industrial organization, e.g. skilled labour-force, research and training institutions, the existence of ancillary industries providing materials. External economies are especially important to small firms

Footloose industry: see p. 266

Functional linkage: links between industries. Can be *strong* (e.g. between Lucas components and British Leyland) or *weak* (e.g. between Lucas components and stationery suppliers)

Inertia: tendency of industry to remain in a location after reasons for being there have gone

Inputs: *in industry* these are: Finance, Administration, Components, Technology (machinery, machine parts), Raw materials, Electricity (the initial letters appear in the word FACToRiEs), and represent some of the functional linkages of an industry

Isodapanes: lines joining up total transport costs (i.e. for moving materials and finished product). They are constructed by: (i) plotting isotims (transport-cost contours) around raw-material source; (ii) plotting isotims around market; (iii) joining intersecting points where the total costs are the same. Practise this by drawing in the isodapane for 9 and 10 units of transport cost on Fig. 107

Isotim: see 'Isodapanes'

Labour: the workforce may vary in: skills, cost, mobility, stability (likelihood of strikes, absenteeism), supply

Least-cost location: location judged to be **optimal** (economically best) because costs are lowest

Locational factors: *in industry*:
  1) **amenity**: congenial living conditions. Very important in footloose industries
  2) *raw materials*: industries which lose much bulk and/or weight during manufacturing locate near raw materials. Water is a major raw material

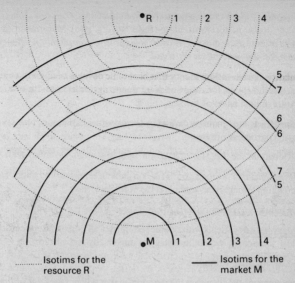

Fig. 107 *Isotims for isodapane construction*

3) *power*: electricity is very mobile. Only large power-users, e.g. aluminium processors, locate near cheap, usually hydro-electric, power
4) **capital expenditure**: the costs incurred in setting up and running an industry. In some areas these costs are low because: (i) pre-existing buildings can be cheaply converted; (ii) local authorities reduce rates, provide facilities. Such areas will particularly attract small industries. Also, *money attracts industry*: the City of London and New York have become industrial centres
5) *labour* (see p. 294)
6) *management skills*: very difficult to quantify (put into numbers), but obviously important
7) *transport* is measured in **economic distance**, i.e. cost and time are more important than mileage. Motorways are magnets for industry
8) *markets*: the customer, who can be: (a) another firm; (b) the public
9) *human factors*: *in industry*, this means chance or whim. Dayton, Ohio, the home of the Wright brothers, is now a centre for aerospace research
10) *politics*: governments influence industrial location: (i) to relieve unemployment; (ii) for defence purposes

Location quotient: see pp. 117–18

Market-orientated: those industries depending heavily on access to markets, e.g. consumer goods

Material index: weight of raw materials ÷ weight of finished goods. Material index >1.0 → raw-material-orientated industry, e.g. steel. Material index <1.0 → market-orientated industry. *Always introduce this consideration whenever the importance of raw materials is discussed*

Maximum-revenue location: location judged to be optimal because income is greatest. The least-cost location and maximum-revenue location for one industry are almost never at the same place

Multiplier effect: the reactions caused by the opening, expansion, reduction or closure of a particular firm

Optimal location: see 'Least-cost location' and 'Maximum-revenue location'

Outputs: *in industry*: finished goods (to consumer); semi-finished goods (to another factory); machinery and parts (to other factories)

Primary industry: extraction *only* of natural resources, e.g. mining

Quaternary industry: deals with people; comprises all personal services, e.g. education, finance. A *class* of industry not universally recognized

Real-world situation: examples

Satisficer concept: the idea that the decision-maker will not look for optimal economic answers because he has other criteria, e.g. social benefits, low risks

Secondary industry: manufacturing goods

Spatial: see p. 127

Sub-optimality: choosing less than the optimal location; see 'Satisficer concept'

Substitution principle: the idea that firms try to minimize costs by looking for cheaper substitutes for a location

Tertiary industry: distribution, i.e. transport, wholesaling and retailing

Value added by manufacturing: a measurement of the economic importance of an industry, this is calculated as value of finished goods minus value of raw materials

---

Why do candidates perform badly on industry questions?

One reason is that it is difficult to tell from the question which technical terms the examiner is looking for. Some examples may help here.

Q. 4. 'Locational decisions in manufacturing industry are taken in order to minimize costs.' Discuss. [LON]

This is a 'discuss' question; therefore you must:
1) note when and why the statement is borne out (p. 374). Include the substitution principle
2) explain when and why the statement is not borne out (see p. 298).

In part (2), you should include, and explain, the following: maximum-revenue locations; satisficer solutions and sub-optimality; behaviourism in decision-making.

Q. 5. (a) *With reference to specific examples, show how large industrial regions develop.*

(b) *Why might industrial firms move from large industrial areas to a fresh location?*

In (a), you should note and explain: cumulative causation and agglomeration economies; multiplier effects of an industrial development; functional linkages and external economies. Part (b) refers to deglomeration.

Even when the terms are given, candidates do not always show a good understanding of them.

Q. 6. *How far do the following factors explain the present-day location of industry:*
(a) *accessibility to a port;*
(b) *nearness to raw materials;*
(c) *closeness to markets;*
(d) *agglomeration economies and external economies?*

Questions 1–6 of this chapter need the supporting evidence of 'real-world' examples. Some of these you will find under 'Theme 7: Industry' (Chapter 22, p. 374). At this point, I am directing you to the 'Themes in regional geography' sections in order to hammer home the importance of linking human and regional geography.

Themes in industrial geography

Q. 7. *(i)* *Discuss the changing significance of raw materials as a control on the location of manufacturing industry.*

(ii) *How has this influenced the changing world distribution of ONE major manufacturing industry?* [NI]

Re-read 'Material index' (Table 50, p. 296) to establish that the significance of raw materials varies according to the material index of the product. In addition, you should note that the importance of raw materials as a locational factor is declining. This is due to:

1) improved technology. Many materials are partly processed near the source (Liberian iron ore undergoes **beneficiation**, i.e. partial refining, before export)
2) improved transport
   (a) in the areas of primary extraction (e.g. Kedia d'Idjil to Nouadhibou railway, Mauritania. Each diesel-electric train carries 10,000 tonnes of ore)
   (b) to the industrial agglomerations. Examples include supertankers, and the St Lawrence–Great Lakes waterway, completed in 1957
3) the increased importance of other locational factors. This can be seen if the oil industry is chosen for part (ii) of Question 7. Notice how different factors come into play over time.

Changing locations in world oil refining

1) 1859–1940. The earliest refineries were oilfield (*raw material*) based because of the high proportion of waste (50% in Pennsylvanian oil); the 'heavier' fractions (portions) of the oil, e.g. diesel oil, were unwanted until around 1910 when diesel began to be used to fuel furnaces, ships, trains and lorries. Production was predominantly on U.S. oilfields (70% of world total in 1938).
2) 1940–60. *New technology* – supertankers – made transport cheap from Third World fields (Middle East, North Africa, Caribbean). Technological advances (in plastics, paints, fertilizers and in air transport) mean that 95% of crude oil is saleable. This decrease in the amount of waste has led to the development of *market-orientated refineries* and thus to the growth of oil refining in non-producing countries, especially in western Europe.
3) 1960–70. Oil refineries were increasingly located in the consumer countries of North America and western Europe with precise *physical requirements*:
   (a) large, flat land area on firm geological foundations
   (b) deep-water site for supertankers
   (c) availability of large quantities of low-cost water.
4) 1970–84. Two trends should be noted:
   (a) The tidewater locations described above (Fawley, U.K.; Hamburg, West Germany; Philadelphia, U.S.A.) are proving to be

located too far from some *markets*. Pipelines have been constructed to take crude oil to the source of demand. The Central European Pipeline runs from Genoa to Ingolstadt in the south of West Germany; the Interprovincial Pipeline takes oil from the Canadian prairies to Toronto.

(b) Third World refineries are developing in producer nations (raw-material-based). Nations concerned include:
   – Africa: Nigeria, Gabon
   – Middle East: Kuwait, Saudi Arabia, Iran, Iraq
   – Far East: Indonesia
   – Central America: Mexico
   – Latin America: Venezuela.

But the high construction costs deter many Third World countries from building their own refineries. Furthermore, eight companies (three European, five American) control most of the world's crude oil production, and they prefer to keep refineries on land they can be *politically* sure of, i.e. Europe and the U.S.A. Iran and Nigeria are among the states which have appropriated European-financed refineries. Finally, Europe and the U.S.A. have the largest number of skilled oil engineers and technicians (*labour supply*).

(c) *Further technological advance* has made submarine oil production possible – in the North Sea and the Gulf of Mexico.

Changing locations in the steel industry

Some Boards stipulate a specific industry. Steel is the favourite:

Q. 8. With reference to named examples drawn from contrasting areas of either steel or textile manufacturing, assess the extent to which the present-day distribution of the industry can be explained in terms of past choices of least-cost locations. [WEL]

The contrasting areas should include at least one from the developed and one from the developing world.

The U.S. steel industry

The traditional raw materials of the industry are coking coal, iron ore, limestone, water and scrap. Limestone is relatively abundant and cheap and plays little part in the choice of locations.

Coking coal must have few impurities, be able to withstand pressure in the furnace, and leave little ash. Few coalfields can fulfil these requirements, and coking coalfields had a great 'pull'. Steelworks were located on coalfields, often using local ores, e.g. the Pittsburgh–Youngstown area. Cost of coking coal was at a minimum here and coal retained its pull when more distant ores were used. In the nineteenth century, iron ore moved to coal because so much coal was needed. Throughout the nineteenth century a decline in the amounts of coal needed was experienced. The required amounts of coal and iron ore – and hence their transport costs – were more equal. New steel-mills grew along the route between the Lake Superior ores (at Mesabi) and the Appalachian coal. The best sites were along the Lake Erie shore where the transport systems change from boat to rail and vice versa: at Cleveland and Toledo. Other lakeshore developments were at Chicago and Hamilton, not on the direct route.

Pittsburgh maintained its importance, however, partly by manipulating the freight rates and thus continuing to be a low-cost location. This was the 'Pittsburgh plus system'* whereby all steel sold was priced at each sale point as if it had been produced in Pittsburgh and shipped to the point of sale – even if it had been made in the city where it was purchased. Such was the power of the U.S. Steel Corporation. With the introduction of the electric-steel process and the need to import ore – from Labrador (Canada) and Venezuela – a tidewater site became the least-cost location. Steel mills were built at Fairless Hills (New Jersey) and at Sparrows Point, on the Atlantic coast.

Transport costs are not the only factor in least-cost locations. Poor-quality ore and high mining costs make pig-iron produced with local coal and iron ore at Birmingham, Alabama, dearer than the Pittsburgh product.

Scrap is an increasingly important element, easily available on the Atlantic coast and in the Chicago area, but less readily available in Pittsburgh, thus adding to the costs of the latter and hastening its decline.

Higher-cost locations have been developed on the Gulf and Pacific coasts – Houston, Los Angeles, San Francisco–Seattle, and in Utah, near Salt Lake City. These are designed to serve the West Coast consumers, where the market can stand the costs.

* Made illegal in 1924.

Steel in the developing world

'Past choices' (see Question 8) are scarcely of importance here, since most Third World steel plants are very new. Fig. 108 indicates why Ajaokuta was chosen as the site for Nigeria's steelworks.

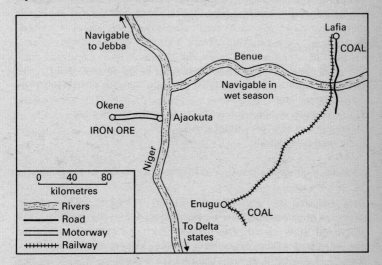

Fig. 108 *Advantages of Ajaokuta for steelmaking*

You may be lucky enough to have a question limited to one country:

Q. 9. With reference to any one country, comment on the impact of raw materials and transport on the location of one industry.

You would be wise to select an area within your chosen regions where the locations of the raw materials and the industry are few. Construct a revision map, showing transport lines and industrial centres. Such a map goes a long way to answering the question. You should discuss the Weberian principles involved (below) and note the actual distances and transport methods concerned.

Government and industrial location

Q. 10. 'Government policy is now the principal factor in industrial location.' Discuss this view with reference to two countries that you have studied. [OXF]

301

Again, this is really a regional geography question (see p. 354). Use this as a revision guide, and remember that any 'discussion' must include opposing evidence.

Theories of industrial location

Weber's model

WEBER made a number of assumptions, the critical ones being:

1) inputs necessary for industry (p. 294) are unevenly distributed on an isotropic plain
2) the markets can be located as precise points on the plain
3) labour is fixed at several locations.

He then considered:

(i) How to find the point of minimum transport costs (least-cost location)

Assuming that transport costs are directly related to distance, isodapanes can be drawn to establish least-cost locations (see Fig. 107, p. 295). These will be influenced by the material index of the product (p. 296). In Fig. 107 there is only one material source. If there are two sources, a **triangle of weights** is drawn, such that the three sides are directly proportional to the weight of material per tonne product. From this, the angles a, b and c can be found.

The following calculation is made:

$$\alpha = 180° - a$$
$$\beta = 180° - b$$
$$\theta = 180° - c$$

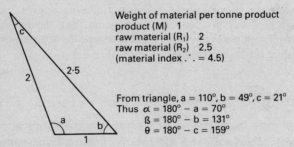

Weight of material per tonne product
product (M)   1
raw material (R_1)   2
raw material (R_2)   2.5
(material index $\therefore$ = 4.5)

From triangle, a = 110°, b = 49°, c = 21°
Thus α = 180° − a = 70°
   ß = 180° − b = 131°
   θ = 180° − c = 159°

Fig. 109a *Triangle of weights*

The angles α, β and θ fix the least-cost location within the **locational triangle** (Fig. 109b).

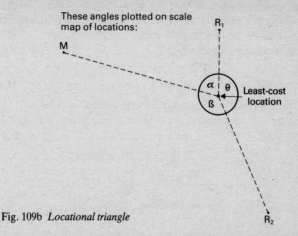

These angles plotted on scale map of locations:

Fig. 109b *Locational triangle*

(ii) How the least-cost location is deflected by other costs

(a) CHEAPER LABOUR. Isodapanes are constructed, and the isodapane with the same value as that of the cheaper labour source is noted. This is the **critical isodapane**. Fig. 110 illustrates a situation where labour is £3 cheaper on a single product at L_1 and L_2. The critical isodapane has been marked accordingly. The rule of thumb is that if the cheaper labour source is inside the critical isodapane, it is profitable to move. So in Fig. 110, L_1 is a good site for relocation and L_2 is not.

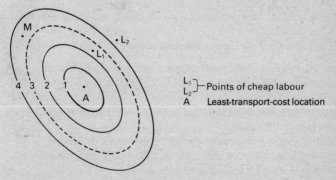

L_1 ⎤
L_2 ⎦ Points of cheap labour

A — Least-transport-cost location

Fig. 110 *Labour costs: the critical isodapane*

(b) AGGLOMERATION ECONOMIES. To find out whether, say, three firms should agglomerate, a critical isodapane is drawn around each firm. The critical isodapane is now the one with the same value as the estimated saving per product. If the isodapanes intersect, it will be profitable to locate in the overlapping area.

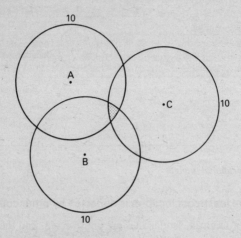

A, B and C are three firms.
The critical isodapane has
been drawn for each

▨ Overlapping area

Fig. 111 *Agglomeration economies*

Q. 11. (i) *Explain the working of A. Weber's model of industrial location.*

(ii) *What are the limitations of this model?* [OXF]

Many geographers have tried to apply Weber's model to real industries. Smith decided that the material index was 'rather a blunt tool of analysis', and that raw-material locations 'are less relevant, the more elaborately manufactured a material becomes'. Furthermore, the model does not take into account:

(i) fluctuations in freight rates (see Pittsburgh plus, p. 300)
(ii) the distorting effect of the actual transport network upon costs
(iii) the way demand is spread over large areas
(iv) the intervention of governments.

Lösch's theory

This is based on demand and assumes (a) an isotropic plain, and (b) demand spread evenly over the plain. LÖSCH determined that each factory owner would look for an area which would command the largest possible market, without overlapping on to the territory of a competitor. The result would be a region of evenly spaced factories, each with a hexagonal market area.

You should be capable of finding the weaknesses in Lösch's theory yourself – just look at the assumptions. You can use Lösch and Weber to answer Question 1 of this chapter.

17. Transport and trade

> Geography, made up of seas of treacle and seas of butter.
> (Macaulay, *Minute*, 2 February 1835)

Had he been writing today, Macaulay might have mentioned wine lakes and butter mountains. The problem of trade surpluses (p. 373) is still with us.

Transport: choice of route

In an ideal world routes can be chosen either:
(a) to minimize the length of the route, and hence the costs of construction and maintenance
(b) to maximize traffic, i.e. collect more road-users. This will raise costs, but improve access
(c) to minimize user-costs – but this may involve high construction costs.

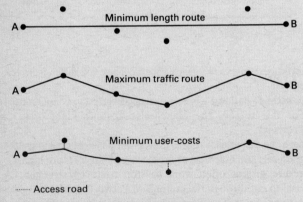

Fig. 112 *Three alternative routes between A and B*

Keep these ideas in mind when answering Question 1.

Q. 1. (a) Two road networks separated by a narrow lake are shown in Fig. 113. Alternative routes, A and B, are proposed for a new road link between *X* and *Y*. Briefly argue a case for the adoption of one of these routes.

(b) (i) If the towns *X*, *Y* and *Z* are to be linked by a road system which minimizes user-costs, draw on the map the required additions to the network.

(ii) Give reasons for suggesting that some compromise to this ideal situation might be sought. [LON]

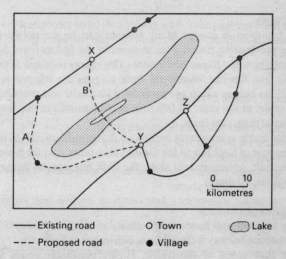

—— Existing road   ○ Town   ▨ Lake
--- Proposed road   ● Village

Fig. 113 *See Question 1*

Compromise routes are usually chosen. They will differ from least-cost routes by:

(i) **positive deviations**: where a route is diverted to collect more traffic. For this reason, the Manchester–Toronto flight often calls at Prestwick

(ii) **negative deviations**: routes may avoid physical obstacles like steep gradients and marshes, or areas where land costs are high.

Pressure groups often work to stop route construction. A road proposal to cut through the grounds of Petworth Park was opposed by the National Trust. The 'houses for people' lobby greatly influenced the decision to drop the London motorway box scheme.

307

Modes (types) of transport

A. Inland waterways and coastal shipping

Q. 2. Discuss the advantages and disadvantages of inland waterways and coastal shipping for the movement of minerals and manufactured goods.
[SUJB]

Advantages

Water transport is cheap. Many systems can be developed by improving pre-existing rivers, as in the case of the St Lawrence Seaway, the Mississippi, the Rhine and Rhône. The energy required to propel a barge is low. On the Mississippi, bulk cargoes are shipped in dumb (engineless) barges which are assembled into rafts and propelled by a motor vessel at the rear; 20,000 tons may be carried in this way. This economy of scale cuts costs.

Coastal traffic is important in the U.S.A. for bulk cargoes of iron ore from the port of Sept Iles to the Great Lakes ports, and for movements of Texan salt, potash and oil along the Gulf Intracoastal Waterway to Birmingham, Alabama.

Disadvantages include:

(a) the freezing and hence inoperability of some waterways. The St Lawrence Seaway is closed from November to February
(b) the slow speed of the traffic. Highly perishable goods are not suitable for barge transport
(c) sedimentation: the U.S. government must dredge the Mississippi continuously
(d) as barge-rafts get larger, waterways have to be straightened
(e) drought conditions can make water levels dangerously low
(f) industrial pollution, notably on the Seaway.

B. Ocean transport

Q. 3. Since the end of the Second World War there have been significant changes in the ability to carry raw materials by sea in bulk.
Outline (i) the nature of these changes;
*   (ii) their geographical consequences.*   [OXF]

(i) Ships have become: (a) faster, with improved design; (b) cleaner, with the substitution of oil for coal; (c) less labour-intensive, as oil replaced coal; (d) specialized, notably for refrigerated cargoes and oil; (e) bigger (supertankers carry 500,000 tonnes deadweight); (f) more efficient and (g) easier to load because of containerization of cargoes.

(ii) Go through the changes in the same order, noting the geographical consequences:

    (a) shipping cargo by sea remains much cheaper than by air

    (b) demand for coal has fallen: redundancies in the coalfields

    (c) number of employed seamen has fallen, e.g. stokers now unnecessary

    (d) (i) it is economic to ship oil from the producing areas to European and North American refineries

        (ii) specialized quays develop in the ports

    (e) oil ports have had to grow larger and larger. Thus new ports – with 16-m draughts – have been developed: Milford Haven, Bantry Bay

    (f) dock-side employment has fallen dramatically, and caused much hardship, notably in the East End of London and on Merseyside.

Some of this information can be used to answer Question 4.

Q. 4. Discuss the effects the increased size of merchant ships has had on the pattern of shipping lanes and on port development throughout the world.   [O and C]

Shipping lanes

Larger ships are possible on the high seas: it is the canal systems along the shipping lanes that may prove to be bottlenecks: major canal links in shipping lanes include: the St Lawrence Seaway, the Panama Canal and the Suez Canal. Try to find out how deep these canals are: can they accommodate ships with a draught of 15 m?

Port development

(i) New ports will be constructed: note the oil ports at Sullom Voe (Shetland), and above.

(ii) Existing ports may build **outports**: a port that can be reached by larger vessels than the main port that it serves. Examples include Rotterdam (outport Europoort), Hamburg (Cuxhaven), Bristol (Avonmouth).

(iii) Changes within the port. BIRD developed a model of 'Anyport' which reflects the elaboration of the docks as larger, specialized cargoes emerge (Fig. 114).

309

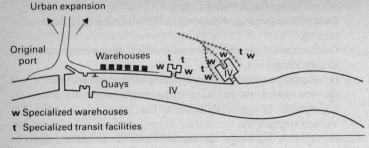

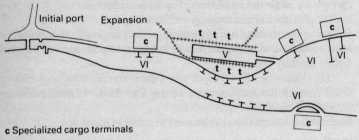

Fig. 114 *Later stages of 'Anyport' (after Bird)*

C. Railways

From 1830 until about 1940, railways were the dominant system of land transport. Purpose-built lines stimulated development in isolated regions: Russia was crossed by the Trans-Siberian Railway, North America by Canadian Pacific. Some economic historians claim that the construction of the Trans-Siberian Railway was a major factor in Russia's economic development, because of the jobs created in railway construction, railway operation, building of rolling stock; and because of the agricultural produce of the new lands (the multiplier effect).

Now, however, rail transport is declining in importance. The 'crunch' came for Britain in the early 1960s when Beeching decided that lines built to small centres to gain their custom (positive route deviations) were uneconomic.

Q. 5. Discuss the effects on railway transport of competition from road and air traffic. [OXF]

Examiners would like additional examples outside Great Britain.

Railway developments in the U.S.A.

 (i) *Passenger traffic* was at its peak in 1920. During the next decade, passenger traffic fell by 50%, mainly due to competition from the roads. Private cars now account for 90% of inter-city transport, airlines 5%, railways 2.5%.

(ii) *Freight traffic* reached its zenith during the Second World War, but declined due to competition from trucks, especially for traffic dispatched in lots of less than one carload.

Although competition has caused a rapid decline in American passenger traffic, it has forced the railways to be more efficient freight-carriers by using: (i) containers; (ii) piggy-back transport, where the bodies of trucks are carried on rail flatcars, to be hitched to motor trailers at the destination; (iii) diesel or electric power. U.S. railways have recovered to some extent, and now hold a steady 40% of the freight market.

(*Other factors* not asked for in Question 5 include pipelines, improved inland waterways, and a decline in the use of coal. All three have cut the volume of railway freight.)

D. Road transport

We saw above how severely U.S. railways suffered through competition from roads. Road traffic has a number of advantages:
1) great flexibility of service: numerous routes and destinations possible
2) door-to-door service
3) fast and cheap over short distances
4) it can handle outsize systems
5) construction and running costs borne by the state.

Q. 6. What effects has mass motorcar ownership had on:
(a) village shops and postal services;
(b) delivery services in the countryside;
(c) country bus services;
and how are rising petrol prices likely to affect rural life for the young and old in the years ahead? [O and C]

This is a temptingly easy question, but must be 'stiffened up' with real examples.
(a) Go to a small village and count the number of shops, looking for any evidence of shop closures and/or limited opening hours. Check the number of deliveries from the post office. Compare with the main city post office.

(b) Survey the shops in your nearest C.B.D. Ask them if they deliver and, if so, how far they deliver.

(c) Look at your local bus services, together with a map. Are there any villages that are off routes entirely; and any others that are served by only weekly or twice-weekly buses?

E. Relationships between different modes of transport

In the section on railways above, the effects of competition between road and rail were noted. Although competition between transport modes is an important theme, you should also think of each mode as fulfilling a particular need:

Q. 7. Describe and explain the different economic roles played by road, rail and air transport within present-day countries. [NI]

The varying importance of transport modes depends, to some extent, on the degree of development within a country. (External communications are not required here: note the stress on 'within'.)

Transport in West Africa

ROADS: A distinction must be made between unsurfaced dry-weather roads and tarmac roads. **Mammy-wagons** (privately owned lorries, driven and maintained by owners and relatives, able to change from freight to carriage to passenger by the addition of a few planks) are vital to development, providing low-cost, efficient service.

Specialized road vehicles range from heavy goods vehicles to passenger minibuses. Throughout West Africa, private cars are less numerous than other vehicles. The importance of bicycles must not be underrated. Bikes with strengthened carriers are used to carry freight and passengers, notably in eastern Nigeria.

RAIL: Over long distances, where the volume of traffic is high, railways offer cheapest transport. In Europe, railways pre-date all-weather roads; in West Africa the railways followed road development. Only Nigeria and Ghana have rail 'systems'. Traffic is largely freight (e.g. groundnuts in Ghana), and railway development has been hampered by road transport. The Ghanaian government has tried to cut back competition by preventing the haulage of cocoa and timber on roads paralleling railways, partly to prevent road damage from heavy lorries.

INTERNAL AIR TRAFFIC is costly. Initially the air services were 'flying mammy-wagons', but after an accident in Nigeria in 1954 better air-craft were used and costs rose, so that today the principal users are government officers and businessmen on expense accounts.

Transport in Britain

Table 51 shows the percentage use of road, rail and air transport for passengers and freight:

Table 51. Passenger and freight transport in Great Britain: 1975 (percentages in italics)

| | Road | | Rail | Air |
	lorries, buses coaches	private		
Passengers (thousand million passenger/km)	54 *12*	357 *79*	35 *7*	2.2 *0.4*
Freight (thousand million tonne/km)	91.8 *79*	–	23.5 *21*	–

In Britain, the railway had traditionally been a carrier over medium to long distances, but Table 51 shows the situation by 1975. Now the railway's role is in providing **inter-urban** (between cities) transport, and for commuting into large cities.

Motorways are of vital importance in passenger and freight transport, but the idea that **urban motorways** could solve urban traffic problems has been dropped because of their cost and environmental drawbacks.

Internal air transport faces competition from British Rail's 125 trains and, when it finally arrives, the A.P.T. (Advanced Passenger Train). Generally, only the rich use internal air transport: e.g. lobsters and grouse are flown from Prestwick (Scotland) to London. U.K. aircraft have failed to attract businessmen partly because it takes so long to get to and from the terminals.

F. Change

Transport networks are constantly changing:

Q. 8. Show how changes over time and space in the network of one transport mode may affect human spatial activity. [O and C]

Inland waterways make a good choice of mode for this question, since they have passed through a number of changes.

Canals in England

1) Pre 1840: a dense network of canals was constructed in England. Most of the network lay south of a Lancaster–Newcastle line and north of a Tonbridge–Ilfracombe line. Their main cargo was coal, together with industrial raw materials. Canal-side factories grew up in South Lancashire, Merseyside, the West Riding, the West Midlands and London.

2) 1840–1940: saw the decline of the canals as, first, rail and then road transport grew in importance. Few factories looked for canal-sites since the waterways were restricted to narrow (sometimes as little as 6 feet) barges, and locks made canal transport slow.

3) 1940–45: saw a resurgence in canal use because fuel was scarce during the war and canal barges are cheap to run. No new canal-side sites developed, however.

4) 1945–65: plans were made to develop further about 350 miles of our most-used canals, but little industrial development occurred as a result.

5) 1965 → : new uses are planned, all centred around recreation.

Recreational uses include boating, angling, walking, natural history and industrial archaeology; in Huddersfield, for example, an old canal wharf has been turned into a pleasant marina. It will cost £1 million annually to keep canals in good repair for recreation but Buchanan* concludes that 'Britain will need every mile of this pattern of waterways to assist in the provision of worthwhile recreational outlets'.

G. The dominant mode

The dominant mode of freight and passenger transport (road, rail, air, sea and inland waterway) varies in importance according to:
(a) the level of economic development
(b) the physical characteristics of the land
(c) the size and location of the state.

Passenger-use is measured in kilometres, and freight in tonne/kilometres.

(a) In less developed countries, road-users predominate. Take your examples from Table 52. Do not be misled by the small numbers of cars in Algeria and Upper Volta into thinking roads unimportant: re-read 'Transport in West Africa' (pp. 312–13). What is of interest

---

* Quoted in Kirby, D. A., and H. Robinson, *Geography of Britain: Perspectives and Problems*, University Tutorial Press, 1981.

Table 52.   Transport in four countries

	Cars in use (thousands)	Railways		Airlines	
		passenger/ km	tonne/ km	passenger/ km	tonne/ km
Algeria	400	1,452	2,016	1,723	9.2
Australia	2,139	7,308	9,624	10,944	14
U.S.A.	120,485	16,452	1,252,800	404,556	10,387
Upper Volta	11	none	none	140	13

here is the relative importance of air transport in Upper Volta, which has no railway system.

(b) In the U.S.A. the dominant mode of freight transport is inland waterways, partly because of large natural systems: the Great Lakes, Mississippi–Ohio, etc.; and the relative absence of relief obstacles along them. Furthermore, their very length makes them more cost-effective. Britain's small size and absence of large flat areas make modern waterway developments expensive.

(c) This has been touched on in (b), above, and is further illustrated by Fig. 115, which shows how different transport modes become profitable over greater distances.

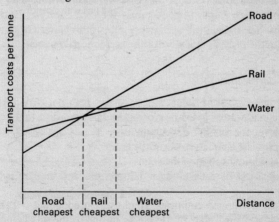

Fig. 115 *Transport costs graph*

Factors (a), (b) and (c) can be used as a basis for answering:

Q. 9. Discuss the factors which cause the density and connectivity of road networks to vary from place to place.   [LON]

315

Revise the definition of 'connectivity' (p. 109) and take examples from your specialized regions.

Question 10 asks for more explanation:

Q. 10. Explain how economic factors influence the development of communication networks and the provision of transport services.

[O and C]

This is best answered by using a model. The most famous was derived by TAAFFE (and others):

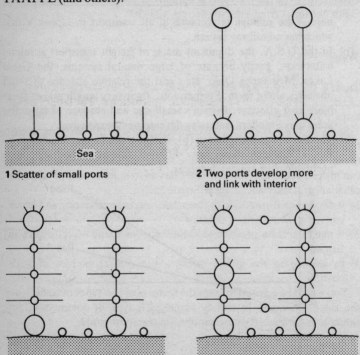

1 Scatter of small ports

2 Two ports develop more and link with interior

3 Feeder routes develop

4 Interconnections begin

Fig. 116 *The development of a transport network (after Taaffe, Morrill and Gould)*

Stage 1 shows a scatter of sea ports. In stage 2, two of these ports grow more rapidly and develop links with the interior to exploit natural resources, or for political or administrative reasons. In stage 3, the two large ports enlarge their hinterlands as feeder routes develop. Small nodes grow up at the junction of these feeder routes. In stage 4, some of the nodes grow larger, perhaps because of economic development, and make connections of their own. If the interior develops fully, high-speed connections will be made from interior to port.

Q. 11. The transport network of a nation is more closely related to the distribution of population than to relief and drainage. Discuss.

[LON; adapted]

Use this to revise the transport geography of your chosen regions.
For network (graph) theory, see pp. 109–10.

Trade

Trade is the buying and selling of goods and services between areas. It can be within the country (**domestic**) or international. The latter is most usually questioned.

Some economists explain the benefits of trade by the **law of comparative advantage**: only a small relative advantage in terms of costs is necessary to make trade of benefit to all participants, because the seller can make a profit and the consumer has an item more cheaply than he can make it. Other advantages of trade are:
1) it allows some countries to specialize, increase efficiency and lower costs, e.g. Danish dairy produce
2) it makes certain produce available all year round – e.g. apples in Britain
3) by expanding the global market, it makes economies of scale possible.

You would be advised to learn the features of two types of trade. Use the same structures in writing about each type of commodity; for example (a) origins, (b) destinations, (c) transport mode.

Trade in fuels

Coal
There is little trade in coal since the major producers (U.S.A.: 25%; U.S.S.R.: 21%; Poland: 7.5%; U.K.: 5%) are among the main consumers. Poland and East Germany export coal to other **Comecon** (Communist Common Market: not China) countries. East European coal is moved by rail or barge.

317

Oil

The major exporters are Saudi Arabia, Iran, Iraq, Libya, Kuwait, Venezuela and Nigeria: Third World producers who do not have the capacity fully to utilize the resource within their economy, and who are heavily dependent on oil revenues. Other producers – like the U.S.A., U.S.S.R. and U.K. – use all their own oil, and still import more. The major importers are the industrialized nations of the West, and Japan.

Oil is moved by pipeline or supertanker.

Natural gas

This shows similar patterns to oil.

Algeria is the major Third World exporter. Among the European producers (U.K., Norway, West Germany and the Netherlands), only the last named has an exportable surplus. Russia is to export natural gas to western Europe.

Trade in manufactured goods

The pattern is almost the reverse of the oil trade: almost every Third World country imports manufactured goods and hardly any export them. The exceptions are the **N.I.C.s** (the **newly industrializing countries**), e.g. Hong Kong, Taiwan and the Philippines.

Developed countries almost all engage in both the export and import of manufactured goods.

Thus the degree of development is one of the factors influencing the international trading pattern of a nation:

Q. 12. Discuss TWO of the important factors that influence the international trading patterns of nations. [NI]

Question 12 does not ask for examples, but you should give them, from the oil trade and manufactured goods trade (above). The second factor is:

Trade controls

These include:
1) total bans. It is illegal to trade in cocaine in the U.K., for example
2) customs duties or tariffs
3) **exchange controls** which limit the amount of money which can be spent abroad

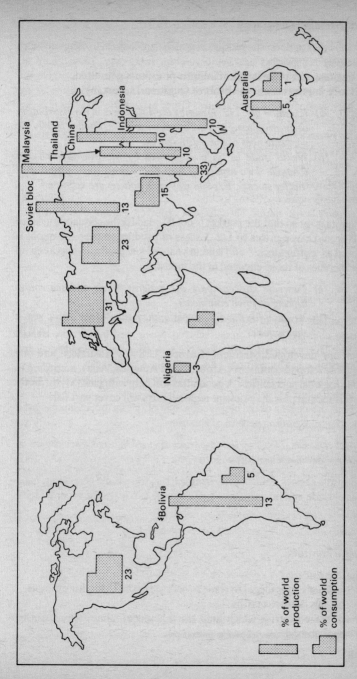

Fig. 117 *World tin: production and consumption*

4) subsidies to domestic producers which enable them to compete more easily

5) **quotas**: maximum levels of imports or exports permitted.

Trade controls are at the heart of Question 13, part (b).

Q. 13. (a) Examine Fig. 117. Describe the differences in the distribution of tin-producing and tin-consuming areas. Outline briefly the consequences of these differences.

(b) World trade in tin is controlled by the International Tin Council. Two aspects of their policy are 'export quotas' and 'buffer stocks'. Explain why such policies are necessary.

[SCO. A]

A quota is set so that the market is not flooded by the commodity, since this would cause prices to fall. Excess of production over the quota is stored as 'buffer stock'* and sold in years of low production to keep up the incomes of those engaged in the industry.

Q. 14. (a) Describe and compare the patterns of air and sea routes linking any two continents.

(b) Account for the differences in the nature of the traffic which they handle. [AEB]

Pick one developed continent (Europe, U.S.A., Australia), and one underdeveloped continent (Africa, Latin America, Asia), according to your regional specialities. A good atlas will help with part (a); the notes in this section plus the relevant regional texts will cover part (b).

* Wine lakes and butter mountains are examples.

18. Rural settlement

> God made the country, and man made the town.
> (William Cowper, *The Task*, 1771)

Today country and town are less distinct and, in Europe at least, both are now definitely man-made landscapes.

Settlement classification

Settlement classification is usually by size, function and form. Table 53 shows the criteria for separating urban from rural settlement.

Table 53. Distinctions between rural and urban settlements

	Rural	*Urban*
Size (in km^2)	Under 2,000	Over 2,000
Industry	Mainly primary	Mainly secondary, tertiary and quaternary
Services*	Limited provision of banks, schools, etc.	Chain-store, hospital, amusements, education
Administration	Parish council	From rural district to metropolitan borough
Size of administrative unit	About 8 km^2 (larger in sparsely settled districts)	Can be a whole county, or larger

There are many exceptions, however:

Size: Woodstock (Oxon) has the administrative status of a town, but its population is below 2,000. Kidlington, nearby, has a population of 10,000, but no chain-store or hospital.

Industry: Settlements of over 2,000 do exist which depend on primary industry, like the towns of the Leicester coalfield, e.g. Measham.

* See indicator functions, p. 63.

Services: Some large settlements – see Kidlington, above – have very limited services, perhaps because of proximity to a large city (in this case, Oxford).

Administrative status: Before the revision of local government, some small towns – e.g. Montgomery, population 900 – had administrative control over a large county. Even today, Stornoway, administrative centre of the Western Isles, has a population of 5,000.

Rural settlement can, itself, be classified.

Q. 1. Make a classification of the rural settlement types of western Europe. [NI]

In all questions asking for a classification, you must:
(a) state the basis of the classification: size, function, shape, etc.
(b) give examples from each class
(c) note any settlements which do not fit your classification.
You can choose from a number of classifications.

Classification by size

Settlement	Population
Isolated dwelling	1 – 10
Hamlet	11 – 100
Small village	101 – 500
Large village	501 – 2,000

Classification by location

1) Spring-line villages, e.g. Alfriston, Sussex.
2) Scarp-foot villages, where flat land and shelter are available, e.g. Skanevik, on Skanevikfjord, Norway.
3) Villages on south-facing slopes – notably in the Swiss Alps, where the **adret** (sunny, south-facing) slope is preferred to the **ubac** (shaded, north-facing).
4) Villages on defensive sites, notably the French villages of the Puy-de-Dôme.
5) Dry point sites. Examples range from Chelsea (*eye* = Saxon for 'island') to the *terpen* (mounds) of the Low Countries, e.g. Antwerp.

6) On good agricultural land. Fertile areas tend to have a greater density of villages than infertile areas.
7) Along routeways, particularly at lowest bridging points, e.g. Warkworth (Northumberland) on the River Coquet.

Classification by form

Four major forms are shown in Fig. 118:

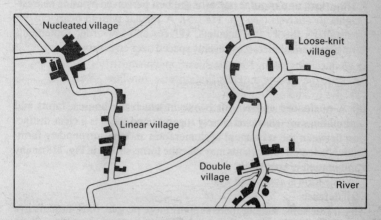

Fig. 118 *Village forms (after Whynne-Hammond)*

Use your local O.S. sheet to find examples.

Settlement patterns

We saw on p. 31 that geographers differ when they define 'settlement pattern'. Charles Whynne-Hammond's recognition of two types of settlement pattern – nucleated and dispersed – would not appear to provide enough material for Question 2.

Q. 2. With reference to named examples selected from more than one region, outline and justify a classification of rural settlement patterns.

[WEL]

For this question, you might consider a classification based on the relationship of the settlements to each other, e.g. (a) clustered; (b) linear; (c) random; (d) regular.

(a) **Clustered villages** are seen in their extreme form in Yorubaland, Nigeria. Here, the villages are so close together that densities of over 100 persons/km^2 are recorded.

(b) **Linear villages** may run along (i) the base of a scarp, e.g. the South Downs; (ii) a river, e.g. French-Canadian villages along the St Lawrence; (iii) the south slope of an Alpine valley.

(c) **Random and regular patterns** are best perceived by using nearest-neighbour analysis (see pp. 114–15). A regular pattern bears out W. Christaller's theory that hamlets, villages and low-order settlements form a numerical hierarchy, evenly spaced over an isotropic plain.

Nucleated and dispersed settlement

(a) A **nucleated settlement** is one in which the houses, farms and outbuildings are clustered closely together and there is a clear distinction between the settlement agglomeration and the surrounding farm-land. Nucleated settlements may take the forms shown in Fig. 118 or any combination of these four.

Nucleation is associated with:
  (i) defence
 (ii) fertile soils: smaller fields support more people; thus, farmers live within easy reach of their fields and enjoy village amenities
(iii) concentration of water supplies into limited locations
(iv) culture: New England village forms resemble those of European villages.

(b) **Dispersed settlement** is a pattern of settlement where most of the population live in scattered farms, houses and cottages. There is an absence of villages, *perhaps* because of:
  (i) freedom from invasion: favours an outward spread of homesteads
 (ii) poor land, e.g. in highlands or arid lands: necessitates large hold-ings
(iii) farming systems – market gardening and dairying
(iv) abundant water supply
 (v) culture: Welsh lowland settlement, e.g. Anglesey, is much more dispersed than English
(vi) history: (a) dispersed settlement is associated with the break-up of large estates; (b) the U.S. system of land allocation laid out farms on a grid plan.

The coefficient of dispersion, C, expresses the degree of scatter of a rural population. For a parish,

$$C = \frac{p \times n}{P}$$

where p = population *not* living in largest village
 P = total population of a parish
 n = number of settlements.

The higher the value of C, the more dispersed the population.

Q. 3. Discuss the relative importance of physical and other factors in influencing the location and pattern of rural settlement. [SUJB]

Question 3 requires a definition and examples. You would be advised to study in detail the settlement pattern of your local area (not more than 100 km^2), most notably for WEL and CAM.

Q. 4. In many advanced nations town and country are becoming less mutually distinct. Explain how and why. [NI]

The difficulties of distinguishing between town and country (urban and rural) were discussed at the beginning of this chapter. This is the 'how' of Question 4. The 'whys' include:
– decentralization of offices and factories (p. 294)
– commuting
– suburbanization (p. 266)
– out-of-town superstores/hypermarkets
– increase in second-home ownership
– improved rural infrastructures.

19. Central places

A place for everything, and everything in its place.
(Samuel Smiles, *Thrift*)

A central place, defined on p. 62, may be a village, town or city. Villages are discussed in Chapter 18.

Towns

Questions on towns are predominantly concerned with central-place theory (see below), but other themes occur.

Classification

Q. 1. *(a)* *Suggest ways in which towns may be classified.*
     (b) *Discuss the problems encountered in trying to classify towns.*
        Illustrate your answer by referring to specific examples.

[SCO. T]

(i) Size
Two classes may be recognized: 2,001–10,000 – small town; 10,001–100,000 – large town. This is an arbitrary grouping, adding little to our knowledge. Market Harborough (pop. 14,527) provides better retail services than Oadby (pop. 19,530), as the latter is part of the built-up area of Leicester.

(ii) Location
Towns are rarely thus classified, but it is possible to recognize:
(a) *fall line/zone towns* (e.g. Philadelphia, Baltimore, Washington) along a line of knick points on the eastern Appalachian Piedmont
(b) *defensive towns* – grown up around a castle (Edinburgh) or fort (Fort William)
(c) *towns in fertile agricultural land* – usually have evolved from a village

(d) *towns at route junctions* – many towns are classed as route centres, but which came first: town or routes? Probably both evolved together

(e) *gap towns* – Dorking (Surrey) is the classic example

(f) *lowest bridging points* – Wareham (Dorset) is at the head of navigation of the River Ware.

Since all the settlements in the above list grew for many other reasons, such a classification is too simplistic, and fails to include towns with no clear physical locational factor. You should know the precise physical details of one town – perhaps within the local area, as suggested on p. 325.

Q. 2. With reference to specific examples wherever possible, discuss the influence of natural features of the landscape upon the siting and physical growth of towns. [JMB; part]

(iii) Function

If a larger percentage of the population is engaged in some economic activity than is found nationally, a town can be classified by function (this reflects the idea of location quotients, pp. 117–18). Thus Oxford clearly *is* a university city, even though the university is not the major employer. Some town functions are: administrative, dormitory, educational, financial, industrial, market, tourist; but many towns have several functions.

Central-place theory

Walter Christaller (1893–1969) postulated that central places provide **central goods** – from tractors to teacups – and **central services** – from hospitals to hairdressers. **High-order** places offer a wide array of goods and services, serve a large area and occur less frequently than **low-order** places, with limited goods and services, and small complementary regions.

Christaller demonstrated that a group of similar central places would have hexagonal complementary regions, with the central places arranged in a regular triangular lattice. You should be able to reproduce Fig. 119, which shows this development:

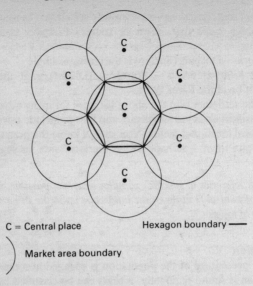

C = Central place   Hexagon boundary ——

    Market area boundary

Fig. 119 *Hexagon formation*

Three cases were discussed (see Fig. 120):

1) the **market principle** case. One higher-order place serves a total of two lower-order neighbours – either it dominates two places or shares a portion of the trade of several places with a competitor, e.g. one-third of all six places: $\frac{1}{3} \times 6 = 2$. This is the k = 3 system (central place, 1, + dependent places, 2 = 3)

2) the **traffic principle** case. With better transport, as many dependent places as possible will lie on direct routes to the high-order place, which can now serve itself and three other places; i.e. k = 4 (either wholly, or in shared parts, as above)

3) the **administrative** case produces a k = 7 system, since this arrangement maximizes the number of settlements dependent on any one central place, and eliminates the sharing in k = 3 and k = 4.

Christaller further postulated that, for each system, the high-order places would themselves be dependent on even higher-order places, and that these networks would interlock. In every case, places of similar order are equally spaced; the higher the order of a place, the further it will be from its equivalent, competing place. YOU MUST BE ABLE to recognize and explain the k = 3, k = 4 and k = 7 systems outlined above.

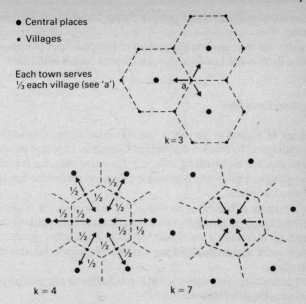

● Central places
• Villages

Each town serves
⅓ each village (see 'a')

k = 3

k = 4   k = 7

Fig. 120 *The three smallest systems of Christaller's central-place model*

Many of the limitations of the model arise from the assumptions that Christaller made:
1) an isotropic plain with
2) evenly distributed purchasing power and
3) the same travel costs in any direction;
4) consumers buy from the nearest possible place, thereby
5) minimizing movement;
6) all parts of the plain are served;
7) no central place earns excess profit.

You can best show that these assumptions do not hold good by applying them to a country or region with which you are familiar. Thus, for Northern Ireland candidates, in answering Question 3, part (b):

Q. 3. (a) What are the principal features of the settlement patterns produced by central-place theory?

(b) Consider the likelihood of finding such a pattern in the settlement geography of Northern Ireland. [NI]

1) name relief obstacles
2) outline regional variations in prosperity

3) name areas with every expensive/cheap transport to high-order centre.

Add to this the disruption to the pattern of (a) specialized centres, e.g. ports like Belfast and Londonderry, and (b) the border with Eire.

Range and threshold

The range of a good or service is the maximum distance over which people will travel to achieve that object. Christaller expected people to travel further for high-order goods, e.g. fur coats, than for low-order ones, e.g. milk. This is why high-order places are spaced further apart than low-order places.

The threshold of a good or service is the minimum level of demand (usually measured in terms of population: threshold population) that is required to maintain a particular activity. High-order goods, e.g. fridges, require a high threshold population and compete for sites in the central place.

It is particularly important for JMB candidates to put central-place theory into a regional context.

A modification of Christaller's model

Lösch also used hexagonal service areas, but experimented by over-laying tracings of the settlements derived from various 'k' systems; that is, he assumed that the market, traffic, administrative (and other) cases would all exist together. He produced a pattern of settlement closely resembling that surrounding Indianapolis.

The rank–size rule

In the models of Lösch and Christaller, as in real nations, there are many small towns (low-order places), fewer medium-sized towns and a few high-order centres. There is, in fact, a fairly regular relationship between city rank and city population size.

The rank–size rule, formulated by Auerbach, is given on p. 115. From it, town size can be predicted, using the formula:

$$Pn = \frac{P_1}{n}$$

where Pn is the population of the nth town
$\qquad$ P_1 is the population of the largest city.

On ordinary graph paper, a plot of rank against size produces a backward J-shaped curve. On logarithmic graph paper this should, in theory, become a straight line. In real life, three types of graph are produced:

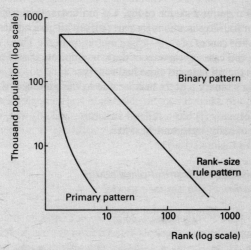

Fig. 121 *Settlement hierarchies*

1) a *stepped order*, where a number of settlements of the same size exist at every level;
2) the **binary pattern**, where a number of settlements of the same size occur only at the upper end of the hierarchy (e.g. Australia); and
3) the **primary pattern**, where the largest city is very much bigger than the second-ranking city. This first city is then called the **primate city**, attracting a disproportionately large share of the population, economic activity and social functions of the nation. Primary pattern can be seen as an acute agglomeration (p. 334) of high-order functions.

Fig. 44, p. 130, shows the rank–size relationship for the cities of two countries. Fig. 44a shows the primate pattern which some geographers associate with:

(a) developing nations: Iran, Colombia, Peru, Venezuela are among the nations to show this pattern (but India does not); or

(b) industrial nations which once had a large empire. This type of primary is shown in England (London), Austria (Vienna) and so on.

Fig. 44b shows a stepped hierarchy which some geographers associate with a federal state.

Q. 4. (a) Explain what you understand by the 'urban rank–size'.

(b) Contrast countries with different rank–size distributions and suggest explanations for the differences shown. [OXF]

Question 4 requires a sketch of Fig. 121 to illustrate point (a). Be very tentative in your explanations for part (b); not all geographers agree on this topic. For causes of rural–urban migration in the Third World, see p. 264. In the case of capitals of former empires, consider the total population the primate city once had to serve.

Australia's binary pattern may be due to the presence of its federal capitals.

West Germany (i) has a federal structure, and (ii) was, until 1871, composed of many independent states.

Settlement size and central-place status

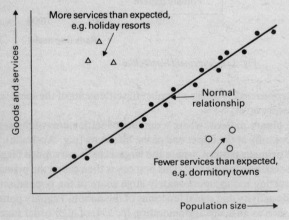

Fig. 122 *Central-place status and population size (after Garner)*

Methods of measuring centrality are discussed on pp. 62–4. Status does not always correlate with size, as Question 5 indicates.

Q. 5. Discuss the factors which might disrupt the expected close relationship between settlement size and central-place status.   [LON]

Fig. 122 suggests some answers to Question 5, but you must find real-world examples.

20. Cities

> You will not find new lands, nor find another sea.
> The city will follow you.
> (C. P. Cavafy, *The City*)

Throughout the world, cities are spreading over new land. Commuters have moved to the suburbs and the city has followed them.

Urbanization is the process whereby an increasing proportion of the population becomes concentrated into towns and cities. This increases both the number and the size of towns and cities.

Urbanization in the developed world

This is, in part, due to rural depopulation (pp. 264–6). Other factors include:

(i) Agglomeration economies
i.e. the savings that can be made by serving a large market distributed over a small area. Industries are thus attracted to cities.

(ii) Urban multipliers
Consider these theoretical figures: 100 industrial jobs are created. Each worker brings a family of 3: increase $= 100 \times 4 = 400$. For every 10 people 1 job is created in service industries, therefore new service jobs $= 400/10 = 40$. These 40 bring *their* families: $40 \times 4 = 160$. Therefore the total population increase from 100 industrial jobs $= 400 + 160 = 560$. In fact, more service jobs are created for the families of the service workers . . . and so on.

This does not automatically happen, but it illustrates the multiplier effect of one industry upon others.

Q. 1. Discuss the principal factors which contribute to the development of urbanization. [O and C]

Split this into four: (a) developed-world push; (b) developed-world pull (above); (c) Third World push; (d) Third World pull (all on pp. 264–5).

City structure in the Western world

Q. 2. Show how historical, cultural and physical factors affect the internal structure of cities in the Western world. [O and C]

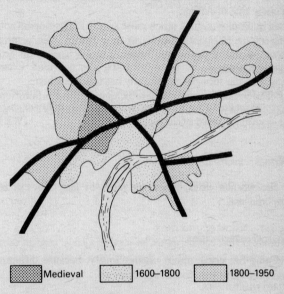

| | Medieval | | 1600–1800 | | 1800–1950 |

Fig. 123 *The development of Warwick*

Fig. 123 shows how Warwick has grown. First (1066) a fortified mound, then a residential town, today Warwick is a centre for tourists and small industry. Note the way development has avoided the river.

You *can* learn about Warwick in preparation for the examination, but the purpose of this section is to show you how you can make a sketch of a city you already know well.

Urbanization in the Third World

Since 1950 urbanward movement in the Third World has been immense. It is caused by (a) rural depopulation, and (b) high natural increase, reflecting the youth of the in-migrants.

Third World urbanization differs from that in the developed countries:

1) The dominant target is the primate city. Bangkok contains over half Thailand's population, and accounted for 60% of all urban growth in Thailand from 1960–70.
2) Circulatory movements are common. In-migrants may remain in the city for weeks or years, and then return to their community. This is especially true of Africa.
3) Urban unemployment is much more severe in developing countries: incomers are frequently worse off than before. This results in the growth of shanty towns and imposes severe strains on transport, water and sanitation.

Q. 3. With reference to specific examples, outline the effects of rapid urban growth on the social and economic geography of towns and cities in the 'less developed' areas of the world. [WEL; half]

Zoning

Within the world's cities, there are more or less clear-cut zones of different land-use.

Zoning in Western cities

Much zoning has come about unconsciously, because different land-users have different locational requirements:

(i) The C.B.D. needs to be at the most accessible point in the city because its high-order functions depend on a large market area: the better the transport, the larger the market area. Shoppers will not walk far from the centre; until recently businessmen needed face-to-face contact. All this points to a compact C.B.D. at the terminus of major route systems.

(ii) Industry cannot outbid the administrative, financial and retail users of the C.B.D. (p. 267), but needs a near-central location. Also of importance is flat land: for building sites and easier road, rail and canal links.

(iii) Residential requirements vary. ALONSO assumed that all urban households need (a) access to work in the city centre, and (b) dwelling space. The poor cannot afford high commuting costs, so are confined to housing which is near the centre, but is densely crowded (to cover high rents per hectare). The rich can live in the lower-density outer areas and afford to commute. Should they not want spacious homes and gardens, they can outbid the poor for more accessible locations. In this way, many erstwhile working-class areas – Islington and Camden Town in London, for example – are becoming **gentrified**: taken over and improved by the richer middle classes. Alonso's ideas are at the heart of Question 4.

Q. 4. Attempt to explain the apparent paradox that low-income families frequently reside in inner-city areas where land values are high. [LON]

There scarcely seems enough to write about for Question 4. When a question is as simple as this, back it up with named examples – preferably from an area you know – and good sketch maps, with an indication of the scale involved.

Recently, planners have consciously tried to develop land-use zones. See 'New Towns', pp. 365–6.

Zoning in Third World cities

This is generally more extreme than in the developed world. Many African towns have developed around several separate nuclei (Fig. 124):

(i) traditional towns: tightly packed courtyard houses with irregular streets

(ii) European (colonial) towns: layout usually rectilinear with greater facility for modern transport. C.B.D. located here, or close by

(iii) immigrant quarters: areas of new housing accommodating migrants from rural areas, often shanty towns

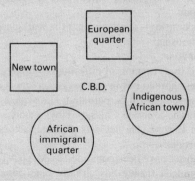

Fig. 124 *Model of composite elements of an African city (from Clarke)*

(iv) new towns: better-class housing projects for civil servants and company officials.

Changes in city structure

Q. 5. Identify and account for the major changes that have taken place in the internal structure of Western cities during the last thirty-five years.

[NI]

Spontaneous deconcentration, the spillover of central-city populations into the suburbs and then into the rural fringe, has been a common feature of Western cities since the Second World War. Why?
1) Industries, increasingly footloose (p. 266), are moving to cheaper locations with better amenities – space, clean air, etc.
2) Higher crime-rates, traffic, noise and dirt are causing disenchantment with city living. The city centre is in decline, with more than its fair share of the old, the sick, the unemployed and the poor.
3) Retailing is shifting to suburban sites: superstores, hypermarkets, etc. Shoppers go by car, and parking is easy.

Models of urban land-use

BURGESS believed that towns expand evenly outwards from the core. At any one time, several concentric zones are identified (Fig. 125a):
1) the C.B.D.
2) **the transition zone**: industrial premises; old private houses which are being converted into offices, warehouses or multi-occupied dwellings, often slums
3) working-class housing – relatively near the workplaces in (1) and (2)
4) middle-class housing
5) the commuter zone.

HOYT argued that, because of differing requirements (pp. 336–7), land-use groupings spread out in wedges or sectors (Fig. 125b). Once established, these sectors are perpetuated. His evidence was the variation in land values he found in Chicago. Hoyt's model applies more to the U.S.A. than Europe. He neglects physical factors, historic traditions, and decentralization.

These two theories have been combined by MANN (Fig. 125c).

The **multiple nuclei theory** has already been touched upon with reference to the Third World (p. 337). In the West, city growth is seen as

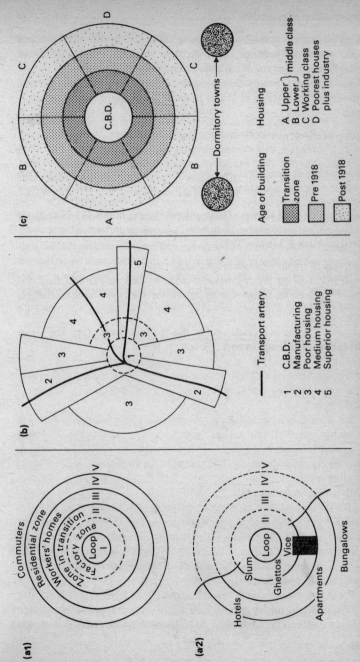

Fig. 125 *Urban models: (a) Burgess, (b) Hoyt and (c) Mann*

(a1)

Commuters
Residential zone
Workers' homes
Zone in transition
Factory zone
Loop
I II III IV V

(a2)

Hotels
Slum
Ghettos
Loop
Vice
Apartments
Bungalows
II III IV V

(b)

—— Transport artery

1 C.B.D.
2 Manufacturing
3 Poor housing
4 Medium housing
5 Superior housing

(c)

C.B.D.
A B C D

Dormitory towns

Age of building

Transition zone
Pre 1918
Post 1918

Housing

A Upper } middle class
B Lower
C Working class
D Poorest houses plus industry

taking place from several cores; among these may be industrial estates, ports, transport termini, once-separate villages, route junctions (notably where ring roads cut radial routes) and major roads.

Questions on urban models are very common. Almost all require you to describe the major models and assess how well they represent reality. Thus:

Q. 6. *(a)* *Briefly describe and account for the pattern of major land-use zones in one named town or city.*

(b) *Outline one model of urban land-use zones and suggest reasons for the differences between the pattern of zones you have described in (a) and the model.* [WEL]

A fieldwork-based answer is best; otherwise, see the study of Bradford quoted in Charles Whynne-Hammond's *Elements of Human Geography* (George Allen & Unwin, 1979).

Q. 7. *(a)* *Explain why urban land values vary.*

(b) *Analyse the relationship between land values and land-use patterns, in one named large town or city you have studied.*

[WEL]

Question 7 requires a discussion of the bid-rent theory (pp. 266–7) in part (a), and fieldwork in part (b): see pp. 65–6.

21. Problems of resource development

> A culture is no better than its woods.
> (W. H. Auden)

A **natural resource** is any feature of the physical environment that is of value to man. Given this definition, Question 1 becomes much simpler: just exemplify the different ways in which man uses climate.

Q. 1. To what extent can climate be considered a natural resource?

[LON]

Resources have been classed as:

(a) **non-renewable**: materials which, like coal, occur in a finite amount. Once used, more cannot be made

(b) **renewable**: living organisms procreate, creating new resources, but it is important to remember that all living things take energy from the sun via photosynthesis. There is a roughly constant amount of solar radiation available to the earth. Photosynthesis can convert 5% of this – but when all the possible solar energy has been photosynthesized there can be no increase in the production of renewable resources. Thus *there is a limit to renewable resources* just as there is a limit to non-renewable resources.

If the ecosystem producing the renewable resource is damaged beyond repair then the resource may also be lost. Forestry would be a good example to develop for Question 2.

Q. 2. Why are 'renewable' resources closely linked to the concept of balanced ecosystems? [O and C]

Q. 3. With the aid of examples, outline a classification of natural resources. By reference to any one natural resource (excluding fisheries) discuss the problems associated with its management. [AEB]

A classification diagram (see that for migration, p. 259) is required here. Start with the renewable/non-renewable division and sort out the following into the appropriate groups and sub-groups: scenery; climate; water; natural vegetation (forestry and food resources); marine resources; minerals (ferrous and non-ferrous); fuels (fossil fuels, H.E.P., geothermal power, wind and wave power).

Water

Water is 'used' in two ways:
1) **consumptive**: where it is incorporated into some new material/organism
2) **non-transformational**: no change occurs, e.g. swimming.

Man's 'consuming' uses of water include:

(a) DRINK, FOOD, SANITATION: Amount varies with development: Karachi: 90 litres/day/head; U.S.A.: 635 litres/day/head.

(b) INDUSTRY: Used as a raw material and as a coolant. Theoretically coolant water can be recycled, but there is a substantial daily loss to the atmosphere.

(c) AGRICULTURE: Water supplies need to be controlled and conserved in areas of apparently abundant supply. Thus, in the U.K., 700 mm/annum would seem to be adequate for agricultural purposes, but it is frequently not enough, because:
  (i) there are other water users (see above, (a) and (b)). In the London area, water suppliers can meet demand from people, industry and market gardening only by recycling water
 (ii) intensive agriculture needs more water:
    – dairy cows: 37 litres/day/capita
    – extensively farmed sheep: 4 litres/day/capita
(iii) apparently abundant precipitation can fail – e.g. U.K., summer 1976; summer 1984.

Where water supplies are inadequate, irrigation is used, but see pp. 282–3 for the need for very careful management.

Non-transformational uses include:

flotation (logs in Finland, barges on the Mississippi; recreation; H.E.P.

Multi-purpose river projects

Q. 4. Consider, with appropriate examples, some of the physical and human problems that arise over competitive or conflicting interests when large-scale multi-purpose schemes associated with rivers and their basins are undertaken. [O and C]

Problems include:

1) growth of water plants, which increase losses by transpiration. The Sudanese spend $1.5 million/annum clearing water hyacinth
2) downstream of the dam, water is often cooler and silt-free: nutrients which were once supplied by Nile silt must now be provided by (expensive) fertilizers. Fishing off the Nile Delta has fallen dramatically
3) large dams may trigger seismic movements (Konya Dam earthquake, 1967)
4) health hazards may increase (pp. 282–3)
5) populations have to be resettled (p. 282).

For each of these points decide *whose* interests are conflicting.

Countryside problems

Table 54 summarizes problems and some solutions for one specific area.

Table 54. An Area of Outstanding Natural Beauty: the Chilterns and South Downs

Problem	Remedy
Too many tourists: White Horse being eroded by feet; car parks deface scenery	Fence off fragile features; plant trees around car parks
Ploughing of downland grasses for crops; irrigation sprays and tanks change scenery	None – there is no legislation to control agricultural change
Forestry Commission coniferous plantations change scenery, e.g. Britwell Plantation	None – no forestry legislation – but forests can be an asset if picnic places and camp sites are provided

Be prepared to summarize problems and remedies for one named National Park and one named area of Heritage Coast (see Fig. 126, overleaf).

Forestry

Man's uses of timber include:

(a) *fuel:* 46% of the world's wood production in 1976 was burned, often as charcoal, for fuel

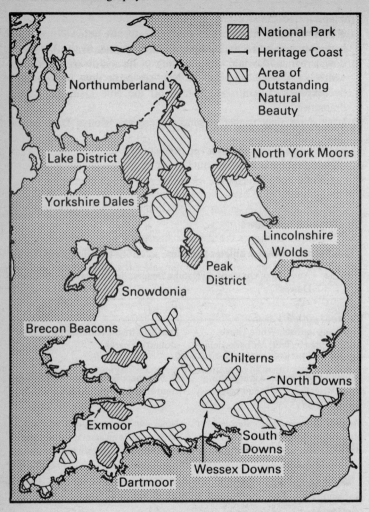

Fig. 126 *National Parks, Heritage Coasts and Areas of Outstanding Natural Beauty in England and Wales*

(b) *lumber*: for construction, furniture, etc.
(c) *paper*: nearly all paper is converted to ash and CO_2 although recycling is perfectly possible. (The profligacy of the West's use of paper is illustrated by the story of the old lady who cried so much at the sight of a felled forest that she used up a whole box of Kleenex!)

Environmental consequences of forestry

1) Mineral nutrients are removed permanently.
2) Transpiration is reduced, surface water increases, accelerating soil erosion.
3) Soil-binding roots are removed, accelerating soil erosion. (Extensive deforestation in Asia has led to silting and choking of high-yield Green Revolution crops.)
4) Fire control changes the species balance.
5) Logging roads can initiate gullying.
6) Clearance of the major forests may alter the hydrological and CO_2 balances of the whole world.

Forest conservation

This may be achieved by:
(a) a ban on logging (very difficult to enforce)
(b) selective burning to maintain the species balance
(c) selective logging
(d) re-afforestation.

Estuaries

Estuaries are a battleground.

A. Conservationists argue that estuaries:

1) are biologically highly productive
2) are a vital habitat for migratory wildfowl
3) are a 'nursery' habitat for young fish
4) are very fragile ecosystems.

B. Oil refiners like estuarine sites because they provide:

1) flat, reclaimable land
2) large quantities of easily available water
3) deep-water tanker berths.

C. Nuclear power developers like estuarine sites which are:

1) relatively far from densely populated areas
2) suppliers of cooling water.

But refineries can pollute sites (salt marsh at Fawley, near South-ampton, was destroyed); nuclear power stations discharge warm water into the sea, changing the habitat; nuclear leakages occur (Three Mile Island, Pennsylvania); and any building and reclamation destroys the natural estuarine habitat.

The wildlife of the Severn estuary is threatened by:

1) three nuclear power stations: Oldbury, Hinkley Point and Berkeley
2) one oil refinery: Bristol
3) industrial growth at Avonmouth.

Minerals

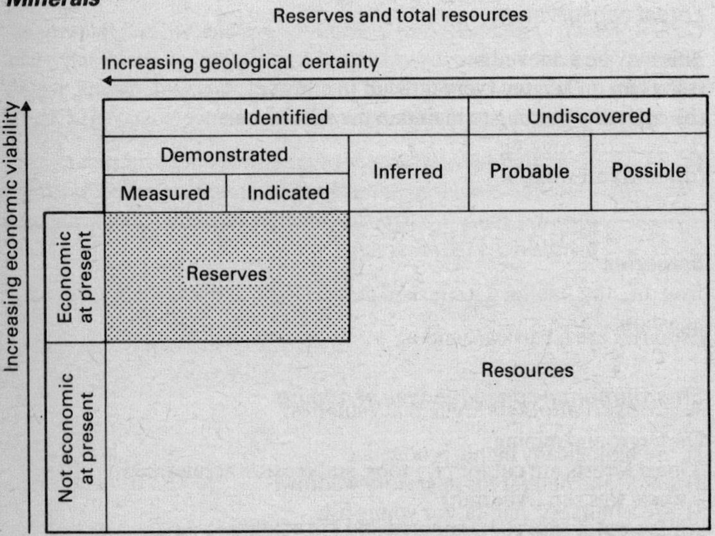

Reserves and total resources

Increasing geological certainty

Increasing economic viability		Identified			Undiscovered	
		Demonstrated		Inferred	Probable	Possible
		Measured	Indicated			
	Economic at present	Reserves				
	Not economic at present				Resources	

Fig. 127 *Resources and reserves as a function of geological knowledge and economic viability*

Q. 5. With the help of Fig. 127 discuss the changing importance and potential of any one mineral resource in terms of the economic and geographical conditions of its availability. [O and C]

Fig. 127 shows that 'reserves' are defined as economically viable and geologically proven. 'Resources' are thought to exist, but it would not be economically profitable to develop them. This is illustrated by oil. The existence of North Sea oil was confirmed in 1969. New technology had to be developed to extract the oil, but it was the huge price increases of OPEC (Organization of Petroleum Exporting Countries) oil in the 1970s which made North Sea oil economically viable. When oil prices fell to below $35 a barrel in 1982, there were serious fears that North Sea oil would be too expensive. Other marginal producing areas include:
– oil shales in Wyoming, Utah, Colorado; Irati valley, south-west Brazil
– oil: Prudhoe Bay, Alaska; Novyy Port, U.S.S.R.

Mining techniques

A few Boards (notably Scottish Alternative Higher) ask technical questions about minerals, which are beyond the scope of this book.
    Two sample questions are given here:

Q. 6. 'Metallic minerals, coal measures, petroleum and natural gas deposits tend to be associated with distinct types of rocks and rock structures.' Discuss and illustrate the above statement, giving widely selected named and located examples in each case. [SCO. A]

Q. 7. (i) Explain briefly the origins of the alluvial deposits of tin.
(ii) Describe the different methods of mining required to extract the two types of deposit, and the different environmental problems which are created. [SCO. A]

Iron ore, tin, kaolin, gypsum and gravel might similarly be the subject of questions.

Environmental consequences of mining

Underground mining:
– local forests are cut for pit props; soil erosion accelerated
– waste tips slip (Aberfan)
– mine waters are contaminated and kill wildlife.
Devastation of this kind can be seen from the lower Swansea valley to Copper Hill in Tennessee.

Q. 8. Discuss the effects on communications, population distribution, social structure and the social services when minerals are exploited in a hitherto remote and thinly peopled part of the world. [SUJB]

The development of the Prudhoe Bay oilfield is an excellent example to use:

COMMUNICATIONS: Since oil is moved by the Alaska Pipeline (Prudhoe Bay to Valdez), and since transport by amphibious aircraft is common, no new routes have developed.

POPULATION DISTRIBUTION: Many of the indigenous Indians and Eskimos have moved to work at Prudhoe Bay or Valdez, but very few Americans have migrated permanently to Alaska. Oil extraction creates few permanent jobs, but some new towns have developed.

SOCIAL STRUCTURE: The indigenous inhabitants who moved to the oil termini left behind a life of trapping and hunting. In the past, Eskimos and Indians have suffered badly from contact with Americans. Alcoholism and suicide rates are higher in both groups than the national average. Similar problems may occur in Alaska, and are thought to relate to the breakdown of traditional social structures.

SOCIAL SERVICES: There is no doubt that the living standards – notably welfare, education and health provision – of the 43,000 native people have risen substantially as a result of Prudhoe Bay oil drilling.

Submarine minerals

The sea's mineral resources can be divided into two:
 (i) *Dissolved in the water*, notably common salt, evaporated from the sea in, e.g., the South of France. No serious ecological damage is reported, but oil and sewage pollution of the Mediterranean may threaten this activity.
(ii) *On the sea-bed*: sand and gravel are dredged in the Texas Gulf.
   (a) The quantities of silt released alter the ecological balance because, coupled with the high turbidity, light for photosynthesis is cut out, with drastic effects on the phytoplankton at the base of the food chain.
   (b) Disturbance of bottom sediments causes an increase of micro-organisms which secrete poisons and cause 'red tides'. There is no antidote to this poison, which may be ingested by eating mussels after a 'red tide'.

(c) Removal of sediment may increase tidal scour and erosion. Offshore oil and gas are exploited up to depths of 2–2.5 km. The major fear here is of oil pollution, which taints fish and shellfish, and kills birds and tidal-zone flora and fauna. Even the methods used to clean up the oil – detergents and steam-cleaning – can kill, especially the **benthos**: the flora and fauna at the bottom of the sea.

Energy

Questions on this topic are very common. Three major themes emerge:

A. World distribution

You should know for two major fuels:
 (i) the main features of present world distribution (see Fig. 128)
(ii) the changes in the volume and location of production which have occurred during the twentieth century.

Table 55. World power consumption, 1900–75

| Energy source | % contribution to total energy used | | | |
	1900	1925	1950	1975
Coal	85	61	44	27
Oil and natural gas	3	12	33	55
H.E.P. and nuclear	<1	1	2	5

Table 56. Changes in coal production (production in thousand metric tonnes)*

Rank	1913	1962
1	U.S.A. (510)	China† (510)
2	U.K. (320)	U.S.A. (520)
3	Western Europe (–)‡	U.S.S.R. (380)

* *Note also* the development of India's coalfields, centred on Jharia, Damodar valley.

† China's coal comes from the north-western loess plateau, Manchuria and Szechwan.

‡ Data unavailable.

H.E.P. was first developed in North America, e.g. Kitimat, Canada; Grand Coulee Dam, U.S.A.; and Europe: Narvik, Norway; Schaffhausen, Switzerland. After the Second World War the U.S.S.R. greatly increased production in the valleys of the Dnieper, Volga, Yenisey, Angara and Vakhsh. Japan emerged as one of the world's greatest

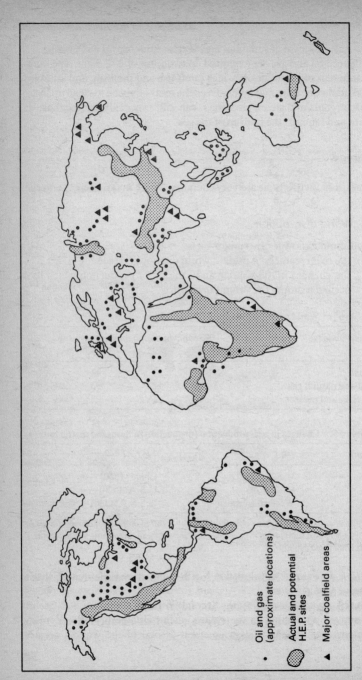

Oil and gas
(approximate locations)

Actual and potential
H.E.P. sites

Major coalfield areas

Fig. 128 *World distribution of power sources*

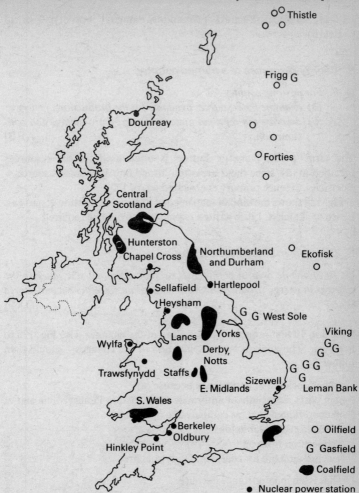

Fig. 129 *U.K.: energy resources*

producers of H.E.P. Since 1960, less developed countries have begun to generate H.E.P.:

– Malaysia: Chenderoh Dam; Abu Bakar Dam
– Africa: Akasombo Dam (Ghana); Kariba, Zambezi River; Owen Falls, Nile, Aswan High Dam

351

– Latin America: Yaciretá (Argentine–Paraguay border); Tucuruí (Brazil).

B. Energy resources of a named country

Q. 9. For any one country
    (a) examine the resources available for the production of energy;
    (b) describe the regional pattern of energy production and con-
          sumption.   [AEB]

The term 'primary energy source' is often used for the resources specified in (a), since these are often turned into a secondary source = electricity. (Hence primary energy budget, p. 130.)

Fig. 129 shows the kind of map needed to answer Question 9, part (a). Learn to sketch it. Little written explanation would be required.

C. Changes in energy production

Q. 10. For one area of continental or subcontinental size, analyse the changes in energy production and consumption since the Second World War.   [OXF]

Question 10 first requires a description of the changes. Use Fig. 130 to help you. The analysis – an explanation of the changes – should then follow.

Coal has declined in importance because of:
– high costs, especially of anthracite from eastern Pennsylvania and of all deep-mined coal (as compared to open-cast)
– exhaustion of older fields
– competition from oil
– lowered demand for coal, e.g. fewer coal fires.

Oil has risen in importance because:
– it is easy to transport
– demand has soared with the increasing importance of diesel-fuelled ships and trains; aircraft; motor vehicles.

Natural gas
– is cheaper than coal-made gas
– has become more available with new gasfield discoveries
– is easily transported by pipeline.

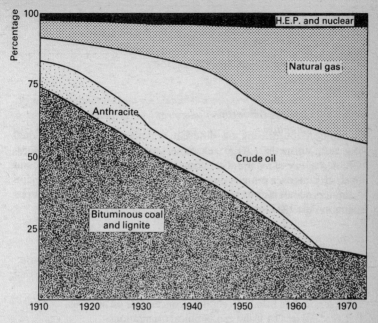

Fig. 130 *U.S.A.: changing fuel consumption*

353

22. Themes in regional geography 1: The developed countries

Variations between Boards

In addition to focusing on different regions (or avoiding regional geography altogether; AEB), examiners ask very varied types of question. *At the time of writing*, Cambridge questions are highly specific, and those of London most generalized – this does not mean that London examiners do not require specific information. Data-response questions appear on the JMB regional papers.

Stimulus- and data-response JMB questions

1) Do the essays first: candidates tend to waste time on data-response.
2) Familiarize yourself with the place-names of your set regions so that you can name them from the examination maps.
3) Describe data briefly if required; concentrate on analysis.
4) Locate places by using geographical orientations.
5) Double-check any arithmetical calculations.

Despite the variations, there are certain major themes within regional papers. The next two chapters identify these themes and give some examples to illustrate them. In this chapter, examples will be taken from U.K., western Europe, the Soviet Union and U.S.A. – always in that order. Throughout, you must select the relevant region, and follow up the examples or, better still, find your own examples.

Theme 1: The physical environment

Relief

Practise drawing sketch maps to show the following:

U.K.:

MOUNTAINS: North-West Highlands; Grampians; Southern Uplands; Cumbrian Mts; Pennines; Cambrian Mts; Cotswolds; Chilterns; North,

South and Berkshire Downs; Exmoor, Dartmoor; Antrim and Mourne Mts

RIVERS: Clyde, Forth, Trent, Ouse, Avon, Severn, Thames

LOWLANDS: Vale of York, Cheshire Plain, the Fens

Western Europe:

MOUNTAINS: Pyrenees, Massif Central, Alps, Vosges, Schwarzwald, Eifel, Taunus, Harz, Hunsrück, Apennines

RIVERS: Loire, Garonne, Seine, Rhône, Meuse, Rhine, Weser, Elbe, Po, Tiber

LOWLANDS: Paris Basin, North German Plain, Maremma

Soviet Union:

MOUNTAINS: Caucasus, Panin, Altai, Sayan, Trans Baykalian, Sikhote Alin, Kamchatka, north-east Siberian, Ural

RIVERS: Volga, Syr Darya, Irtysh, Ob, Yenisey, Lena

LAKES: Caspian Sea, Aral Sea, Balkhash, Baykal

LOWLANDS: West Siberian Plain

U.S.A.:

MOUNTAINS: Alaska, Mackenzie, Rocky, Cascade, Sierra Nevada, Wasatch, Ozark, Appalachian, Allegheny

BASINS AND PLATEAUX: Great Basin, Colorado, Snake and Columbia plateaux

RIVERS: Yukon, Mackenzie, Columbia, Colorado, Rio Grande, Missouri, Mississippi, Ohio

LAKES: Winnipeg, Huron, Superior, Michigan, Erie, Ontario

Climate

Add to your sketch maps the following isotherms and isohyets:

U.K.: Jan. 4°C, July 16°C; 750 mm

Western Europe: Jan. 5°C, July 20°C; 1,000 mm

Masterstudies: Geography

Soviet Union: Jan. −10°C, July 20°C; 500 mm

U.S.A.: Jan. 0°C, July 20°C, 30°C; 500 mm

This is the *absolute minimum* of physical background. You will need it for questions on agriculture and settlement. (All the questions in this and the next chapter will apply to your chosen region in its entirety, or to one country within that region.)

Q. 1. In what ways does the physical environment restrict patterns of agriculture in your chosen region? [NI; part]

*Q. 2. Analyse the present-day distribution of population in any one country in the prescribed region.** [WEL; part]

Physical factors will be only one influence in Question 2, but they must be noted with accurate figures and place-names.

Q. 3. To what extent has the physical geography influenced the nature and distribution of:
(a) agricultural activities, and
(b) manufacturing industries of any one country? [SCO.T]

Do not neglect natural vegetation – notably forests – in Question 3. See 'To what extent?', p. 124.

Theme 2: Regional differentiation

A. Regions

Formal regions are areas with sets of similar geographical attributes which differentiate them from other areas. Examples include:
– East Anglia and the Fens, the South-West Peninsula
– Provence, North German Plain, the Mezzogiorno
– Baltic Provinces, Urals
– New England, Great Plains.
You would be advised to know two regions really well, both for detailed answers:

Q. 4. Assess the relative importance of (a) the physical environment and (b) distance from markets, as factors influencing the type of agriculture.

* Your chosen region.

356

(You may illustrate your answer by reference to either one detailed area or two less detailed areas.)

and as examples for questions on types of region:

Q. 5. (i) *Distinguish between 'functional' and 'uniform' ('formal') regions.*
    (ii) *Discuss the geographical uses to which these types of regions can be put.*   [NI]

A **functional region** is delimited as a result of *human* activity. **City regions**, i.e. a city and its urban field, are one example.
  Other functional regions:
– administrative
– cultural: Ulster: Protestant, Catholic; Belgium: Flemish and Walloon; atheist and Muslim Soviet Republics; U.S.A.: 'Black', various European descents, e.g. Jewish, etc.
– agricultural: Vale of Evesham; Languedoc, Rhine gorge, Friesland, Flanders, Italian Riviera; Ukraine, steppes; 'Corn Belt', Great Valley (California).

Q. 6. *What are the problems involved in dividing a country into a scheme of functional regions?*   [LON]

1) The boundaries of functional regions are difficult to determine because landscape changes are usually gradual. Look up any of the functional agricultural regions named above in two or more regional geography books; how similar are the boundaries?
2) A river may form a functional region and yet be a political divide, e.g. Rhine rift valley (France and West Germany), the River Bug marshland (Poland and Russia), St Lawrence valley (Canada and U.S.A.).
3) Functional regions may overlap. This is true of urban fields and agricultural and industrial regions.

B. Regional variations within one country

(a) Regional variations exist because:
1) the physical endowment varies. Give relief and climate and resource details to illustrate this
2) development processes cause inequalities.
  Myrdal claimed that:
1) development will occur where there are natural advantages

357

2) **cumulative causation** takes place (see Fig. 131)
3) the **backwash effect** occurs: other regions lose skilled labour and capital to the growth region
4) as the national economy expands, the **spread effect** of the growth area may encourage growth in other regions.

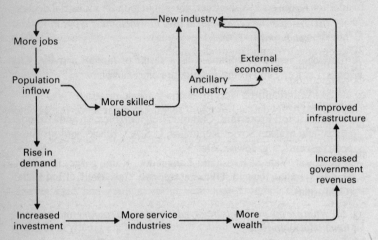

Fig. 131 *Myrdal's process of cumulative causation (from Chorley, R. J., and P. Haggett*, Models in Geography, *Methuen, 1967)*

Some growth regions	Backwash effect on . . .
West Midlands, 1945–75	South and central Wales
Randstad Holland	Friesland
Turin	Calabria
Maryland	New York State

Many believe that the free movement of goods and people within the E.E.C. has encouraged regional inequalities.

(b) *Regional variations are undesirable* to governments because:
1) regional inequality can cause political instability: South Wales miners (among others) confronted the U.K. government in 1984
2) people migrate from poor to rich regions, e.g. from Calabria to Turin, creating problems of rural depopulation (p. 265) in Calabria and inner-city problems (p. 338) in Turin
3) 'problem regions' are created.

C. Problem regions

Q. 7. Select two contrasting areas within the prescribed region where economic problems since 1960 have been particularly severe, and suggest reasons for these difficulties. [WEL; adapted]

In addition to the backwash effect, you might look for industrial decline due to:
1) fall/change in demand (world recession)
2) low productivity and outmoded methods
3) automation
4) competition
5) decline in agricultural workforce due to mechanization.

FRIEDMANN defined problem regions in different terms. He did not attempt to explain why variations in development took place, but where they would occur in relation to each other. According to his definition:

Core regions are urban industrial areas with high levels of industrial input (p. 294), complex economic infrastructures and high growth rates.

Upward-transition regions border the cores, and are greatly influenced by them.

Resource-frontier regions are areas outside the upward-transition regions where new settlement and development occur.

Downward-transition regions are the most peripheral (furthest from the cores). They have stagnant or declining rural economies.

See Table 57 (overleaf) for examples on all scales.

Q. 8. 'Within many countries there are signs of a developed or developing centre and a less developed periphery.' Illustrate this statement and consider its relevance in terms of regional development strategies.

[O and C]

D. Regional development strategies

For reasons listed above, governments try to introduce policies aimed at reducing inter-regional variations in well-being.

Table 57.

Scale	Core	Upward transition	Resource frontier	Periphery Downward transition
City	C.B.D.	Suburbs	Rural/urban fringe	Ghettos. Inner city*
National: U.K.	South-east	East Anglia	Shetlands†	Scottish Highlands
U.S.A.	Florida	'The South'	Alaska‡	New York State
Continental: Europe	Benelux, North Germany	Bavaria	S.W. France?	Southern Italy
Global	Eastern U.S.A., western Europe	N.I.C.s (p. 318)	Siberia, Alaska	Less developed countries

* Often closest to core
† Further from core than Highlands ⎫ contradict Friedmann's model.
‡ Further from core than New York State ⎭

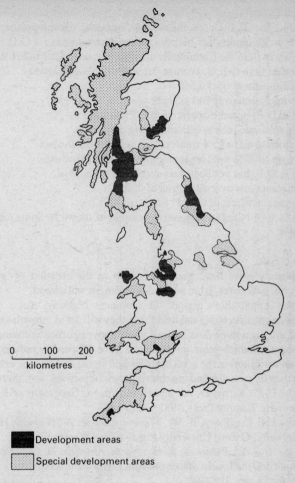

Fig. 132 *U.K. development areas*

In the U.K.:
The government designated Development Areas (considerably shrunken by the government of 1983; therefore most textbook maps will be out of date). Certain grants and concessions are available to industries willing to locate in these areas.

The E.E.C.:

In 1973, the E.E.C. established a Regional Development Fund (R.D.F.). To qualify for benefits, an area should have a G.D.P. per capita lower than the Community average plus *one* of the following:

1) a higher than E.E.C. average dependence on agriculture
2) unemployment over 3.5%
3) out-migration over 10/1,000 per year.

The R.D.F. became operative in 1975. It can:

1) help to create jobs in manufacturing or services
2) contribute up to 15% total cost of an industrial project
3) give up to 30% total costs of improving infrastructures.

The R.D.F. has not been very successful because of:

1) disagreements over allocation of funds
2) the greater effect of C.A.P. funds (p. 373)
3) the lack of belief in regional development shown by some member states.

In the U.S.A.:

Friedmann's ideas have been picked up in the creation of 'growth poles', i.e. new cores, from which development will spread.

In the Appalachian region, 'development highways' (new roads) have been constructed in the belief that they will act as 'growth axes'.*

You will need more detail than is given above in order to discuss both the measures which some governments have adopted to reduce inter-regional variations in the level of social well-being and also the extent to which they have succeeded in achieving their objectives. See, therefore:

– *for the U.K.*: Kirby, D. A., and H. Robinson, *Geography of Britain*, University Tutorial Press, 1981, Chapter 20
– *for the E.E.C.*: Ilbery, B. W., *Western Europe: A Systematic Human Geography*, Oxford University Press, 1981, Chapter 10
– *for the U.S.A.*: Paterson, J. H., *North America: A Geography of Canada and the United States*, 6th edn, Oxford University Press, 1979, Chapter 15, pp. 299–302.

Soviet authorities do not admit to more than slight variations in wage rates, or to any unemployment. However, some economists believe that living costs are lower and conditions are better in the Central Asian republics, but incomes higher in the Baltic areas – Lithuania, Latvia, Estonia.

* Axes: plural of axis.

Q. 9. Discuss the importance of industrialization as a basis for regional economic development. [NI]

You can answer this by quoting Myrdal (see pp. 357–8) and describing the multiplier effect (p. 296). Another theorist who believed that industrialization was the key to economic development was ROSTOW, who saw development in stages:

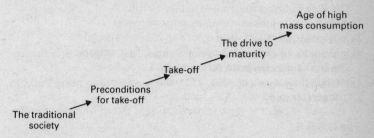

Fig. 133 *Rostow's stages of development*

But some L.D.C.s are finding that over-emphasis on industrialization can be dangerous since food production has been neglected.

Theme 3: Population

Population structure

Q. 10. Write an explanatory account of the population geography of one country in the specified region. [NI]

Do not limit yourself to distribution of population for a question like this. Population structure also includes: growth; migration (pp. 264–7); and composition: (a) be prepared to sketch an age–sex pyramid (progressive, stationary or regressive – pp. 255–6), and (b) note ethnic variations.

Ethnic variations

In the U.K.:
Apart from the old divisions of Scots, Welsh, Ulstermen and English, three more recently settled groups are:
(a) citizens of Eire, who make up 1.4% of the total population, located mainly in London

(b) Europeans: European Jews, Germans and Poles, but notably Italians, particularly in the south-east: London and Bedfordshire

(c) new Commonwealth citizens – from the West Indies, Pakistan, India and Sri Lanka, and Asians from Kenya and Uganda. These have settled in the centres of the large conurbations.

Note how these three groups bear out Ravenstein's second 'law' (p. 267).

In Europe:

Ethnic minorities tend to be:

(a) nationals of former European colonies, e.g. Algerians in France, South Moluccans in the Netherlands

(b) migrant workers (pp. 262, 272), the biggest group being Turks in West Germany.

The U.S.S.R.:

In terms of social geography, this is not one nation but many: Armenians, Byelorussians, Estonians, Georgians, Latvians, Lithuanians, Mongols, Tartars, Ukrainians, and so on.

In North America:

The French speakers are a large minority (30%) in Canada. *U.S. minorities* include Blacks, no longer only in the South, but mainly confined to ghetto areas in the cities; Mexicans in California and Texas, and Puerto Ricans in New York.

Internal migration in the developed world

Five trends can be seen:

1) *A marked rise in population numbers* since the Industrial Revolution.

2) *Rural depopulation.* Rural areas losing population include:
– Scottish Highlands, central Wales
– Corrèze (Massif Central), Ardennes (Belgium), Drenthe (Netherlands), Calabria (Italy)
– North and South Dakota, Maritime Provinces.

3) *Urbanization.* Conurbations grew up in:
– West Midlands, South Lancashire
– north-east France, Sambre–Meuse, Randstad Holland, Ruhr, Milan

– Moscow–Gorky; Sverdlovsk–Chelyabinsk–Magnitogorsk
– 'Megalopolis': e.g. Boston–New York–Philadelphia–Baltimore–Washington.

You must know the historical development of the cores of a megalopolis (or conurbation), the reasons for its development, and its economic and social problems.

4) *Dispersal from conurbations* (decentralization). Examples of this trend are:
– London, Merseyside, Tyneside
– Lille, Namur, Duisburg–Dortmund, Genoa
– New York, Detroit, Chicago.

5) *A move to better amenities*. In the U.K. this is one reason for the 'drift to the south'. In 1931, 38% of the population lived south of the Severn–Wash line; in 1971, 43%.

In the U.S.A. there is a move to the 'sun belt', stretching from the Carolinas to California.

Q. 11. (a) *On an outline map of one country, mark the areas of high population density and explain their location and distribution.*
(b) *Assess the extent to which the distribution of areas of high population density is a legacy of the past.* [WEL]

Q. 12. (a) *Explain the main features of the pattern of population change.*
(b) *Discuss the effect of the population changes shown, on the local national economy.* [WEL]

Theme 4: Settlement

New Towns

New Towns have been established:

(i) **to receive overspill population from conurbations** and provide balanced employment. This is the U.K. ideal, initiated by the Abercrombie plan of 1944.
1946–50: Towns, e.g. Stevenage, Cwmbran, East Kilbride, were planned on neighbourhood units (c. 5,000 people), with low housing densities and some land-use zoning.

1951–60: Towns, e.g. Redditch, Cumbernauld, had increased housing densities, more flats, more private enterprise and more centralization of facilities, with efficient public transport and road systems.

1961–70: Towns, e.g. Milton Keynes, Irvine, Ballymena, are linked with pre-existing settlements. Industry is dispersed throughout residential areas.

1971 → : Amalgams of existing towns are planned. Oakengates, Wellington and Dawley were merged into Telford (Shropshire).

CRITICISMS OF THE U.K. NEW TOWNS:
– social amenities are lacking
– shopping facilities are inadequate
– rents are high
– architecture is uniform and ugly
– resettled people often commute to the conurbation from which they moved (particularly around London).

In western Europe, *Dutch New Towns*, like Grevilingenstad, are also built to relieve congested cities; but the Ruhr structure plan illustrates a second aim of New Towns:

(ii) to relieve unemployment

The Ruhr Planning Authority (the S.V.R.) has initiated several New Towns, among them Wulfen and Marl, together with zones of industrial development, new transport links, area parks and anti-pollution measures. Unemployment and pollution levels have been reduced and new science-based industries have moved in.

(iii) to house workers in developing areas

Soviet New Towns account for 14 million people and are associated with state-guided industrialization (Magnitogorsk) or agricultural development like the irrigation schemes of the Arun Delta, for which the New Town of Nukus is the centre.

In the U.S.A. there are over 140 New Towns, more than a quarter of them in California. Private enterprise is more important than in Europe or the U.S.S.R. Within Minneapolis–St Paul there is the new town of Cedar-Riverside: this idea of a 'town within a town' seems to be peculiar to the U.S.A.

Soviet urbanization

Since the state controls development so firmly, the U.S.S.R. has not shared in the migratory trends of the developed world (pp. 259–67). Candidates specializing in the U.S.S.R. will find Question 13 a useful basis for revision.

Q. 13. Discuss the influence of government policies on the patterns and processes of urbanization in the Soviet Union. [OXF]

Theme 5: Rural aspects

These have been favoured by London examiners from 1979 until the date of writing (1984).

Rural settlement densities

Question 4, p. 249, asks if rural population density is related to physical geography. To answer this:

1) Give examples of rural areas with densities below 6 persons/km^2 where physical factors hamper settlement:
   – Scottish Highland region
   – Massif Central
   – Caspian coastlands
   – Nevada.

   Find out the physical reasons for low population densities: climate, relief figures, soil types, resource base.

2) Locate areas of prosperous, but extensive, farming where mechanization has played a part in low population densities: south-eastern steppes, North and South Dakota.

3) Locate areas of prosperous agriculture which have resulted from a favourable environment and have high population densities:
   – Fenland: nearly 100/km^2
   – Médoc (50–100/km^2); the Börde Loess area
   – Moldavian Republic
   – Sacramento valley.

   Again, give climate and relief figures, soil types.

4) Finally, note the areas of intensive agriculture which are not physically favoured, but where demand or technology has stimulated agriculture:

– Lea Valley (north London)
– interior Flanders
– Moscow–Gorky region
– San Joaquin valley.

Note the details of physical difficulties, how they have been over-come and why.

Recreation and rural areas

Q. 14. 'The value of rural areas is much more than value as farmland.'
Critically examine this statement with reference to one area or more.

[LON]

You should first mention the agricultural value of the farming areas of your selected region. Table 58 gives some details.

Table 58.   Agricultural value of various regions

	% G.D.P. from agriculture	% employed in agriculture	% arable	% permanent pasture	
			Land-use		
U.K.	3	2.7	29.4	47.2	I
France	5	1.3	34.4	25.6	E
West Germany	3	7.3	32.6	21.6	I
Belgium and Luxembourg	2.5	9.8	27.4	24.0	I
Netherlands	6	6.6	22.6	34.4	E
Italy	8	15.8	40.6	17.4	I
U.S.S.R.	17	23	under 10%		I
Canada	4	3.5	7.6		E
U.S.A.	3	3.0	25.0	32.0	I

I = Net importer of food   E = net exporter of food

Rural areas are of value both as producers of agricultural wealth and as areas of employment.

With decreases in working hours and increasing affluence, the countryside is an important area for recreation. Recreational use of rural areas is seen in:
(a) general outdoor recreation areas, with easy access to towns
(b) 'natural' environmental areas: unspoilt countryside with provision for visitors, such as camping, caravan and picnic sites
(c) unique areas – in the U.K., Areas of Outstanding Natural Beauty,

National Parks and Heritage Coasts. Access must be restricted if these are not to be spoilt by visitors
(d) primitive or wilderness areas, notably in North America, from which humans might be barred for ecological reasons
(e) historic sites – specialized sightseeing points, e.g. Stonehenge, Hadrian's Wall.

Theme 6: Agriculture

Agriculture and physical geography

Q. 15. 'Diverse physical environments underlie regional contrasts in agricultural geography.' Discuss, with specific examples from one country.   [OXF; adapted]

You must be able to draw a map of the agricultural regions of the country or countries you are studying.* Draw to the same scale a summary map of the physical geography (pp. 354–6). You can then show how physical controls have affected agriculture, referring constantly to your maps. In addition, show how some agricultural areas have been influenced by human factors, notably demand.

Changes in agriculture

Q. 16. With reference to various locations in the specified area, explain the following trends in agriculture:
  (i) There has been a loss of agricultural land.
 (ii) There are fewer farms than ten years ago.
(iii) The number of persons employed in agriculture has fallen.
(iv) Agricultural production has risen.   [SCO. A]

(i) Loss of agricultural land
The pressure on agricultural land is great:
– population increases imply more housing, often at the rural/urban fringe
– new towns are extravagant of space and eat up land
– motorways make big demands on land.
  In the U.K., motorway construction consumed land equivalent to the area of Dorset between 1972 and 1980.

* The U.S.A. is often split into two regions – east and west of the Mississippi – for such questions.

The Dutch, with the highest rate of national increase of any country in western Europe, will need new houses for a million people. Pressure on land is great and building will be permitted only in restricted areas – along main routes, between Amsterdam and Flevoland and on the island of Voorne.

The U.S.A. lost 19 million ha of farm acreage, between 1966 and 1976, to construction. Furthermore, government policy encouraged a decrease in acreage.

(ii) Decline in farm numbers

There has been a trend towards a larger scale in farming. Small farm units have been amalgamated to make them more viable, a trend encouraged by U.K. and E.E.C. grant aid. In Britain in 1961, the biggest-size group of farms was under 2 ha; by 1971, the largest group was 20–40 ha. Farm consolidation schemes have existed in all West European countries.

The French Service du Remembrement, starting in 1941, aimed to redistribute land in larger parcels (in 1891, the average French farm was 0.36 ha). The policy has had varied success; the north-east has benefited most, the west least. Similar policies were adopted in Germany where the system of divided inheritance had caused fragmentation, most severely in the south-west. Progress has been very slow.

Farms are becoming larger in the U.S.A., notably in the Great Plains states of North and South Dakota. The American government, however, is committed to the survival of the family farm as a political ideal, in contrast to the huge collectives of Communist countries. Nevertheless, some speculators have engrossed large areas.

After land consolidation, the region becomes more productive, because mechanization is most effective on large farms. A less beneficial side-effect is that, in the U.S.A., farmers can make a living by cultivating large areas of low-yielding, poor land – which probably ought not to be cropped at all.

Socially, the effects vary. When farm people leave the land they may retain their old social contacts – as in the American Mid-West. On the Great Plains, however, many communities face extinction. Schools close, railway lines lose money and so are closed, and the trackside grain elevators – a basic function of the community – are redundant. See rural depopulation, pp. 264–5.

(iii) Decline in agricultural employment

1) This is the result of mechanization. British farms are among the most mechanized in the world. In East Anglia, thousands of miles of hedges have been uprooted to create larger fields, better suited to machinery. The labour force has been drastically reduced. The French government has promoted mechanization, with limited success in the backward areas. Interestingly, Paterson* claims that the drift to the cities is the major factor in the decreasing agricultural workforce of the U.S.A., and mechanization has enabled productivity to rise in spite of this. The U.S. 1970 farm population was one-third of the 1911 figure. Canada has a less marked decrease.

2) The West German government provides financial inducements for older farmers to leave agriculture. Pensions are granted to farmers over 55 if they agree to retire.

(iv) Increasing agricultural productivity

Land consolidation and mechanization have been very important. Other factors are high-yielding crop strains – U.S. sorghum yields doubled in the 1950s – and the use of fertilizers, selective weed killers and insecticides. Areas of greatly increased agricultural output include:

1) *The Orkney Islands*. Crofters have bought up land from out-migrants and reclaimed moorland to increase farm unit size. Stocking ratios, i.e. numbers of beasts per hectare, are very high; fodder crops are grown with the aid of fertilizers, sheep are kept on moorland, and poultry are intensively reared.

2) *Languedoc*, which is being transformed by irrigation, land reclamation and new farms. The biggest project is the Alès to Pézanas canal: in all, 400,000 ha of Languedoc have been newly irrigated. Co-operative marketing schemes have helped farm incomes.

3) Irrigation has similarly been important in *Tashkent–Samarkand*. The fertile loess soils and long hot summers favour 'oases' of irrigated farming, producing cotton, wheat, rice, fruit and vegetables.

4) Modern *Californian* agriculture is marked by:
   - irrigation (California is the leading irrigation state, with 3 million irrigated hectares)
   - mechanization
   - specializations – constantly changing to suit consumer demand
   - large-scale organization of processing and marketing.

   The major products are fruit, vegetables and wine.

---

* Paterson, J. H., *North America: A Geography of Canada and the United States*, 6th edn, Oxford University Press, 1979.

371

Intensive agriculture and the environment

Q. 17. Write an essay on intensive agriculture and its environmental impact. [NI]

Sedentary (fixed) agricultural systems permanently manipulate the ecosystem: the natural biota are removed, and considerable effort is needed to keep weeds and pests (remnants of the original biota) at an acceptable level.

Side-effects of intensive agriculture include production of farm wastes. Fertilizer wastes introduce high levels of nitrogen and phosphorus which may lead to **eutrophication**: raised phosphorus levels cause plankton 'blooms', more nitrogen encourages algal 'blooms'; both deplete oxygen, fish populations change completely, midges and worms increase, offensive scums form.

Pesticides don't always kill pests only: every year in the U.S.A. 58 million toxic bird carcasses have to be destroyed.

Careless use of intensive techniques has led to salination (p. 283), notably in southern California, where water tables have fallen and salt-water is invading the aquifers of the coastal valleys.

Soil erosion is common where steep slopes are cultivated; soil is compacted by heavy machines; soil is acidified after drainage (e.g. Camargue). 'The intensification of agriculture inevitably reduces the quality of wildlife in rural areas.'*

Soviet agriculture

Measures to increase farm size and boost output began in 1927 with the introduction of **collectivization**: state seizure of land, which is then leased in large units to large groups of several hundred share-holder farm workers. By 1933, most of the land was forcibly collectivized, but millions died in the process, mostly of hunger.

Agricultural employment is high (25%) in the U.S.S.R. in spite of the partial failure of the Virgin Lands Programme of the 1960s.

* Simmons, I. G., *The Ecology of Natural Resources*, Edward Arnold, 1981.

The Common Agricultural Policy (C.A.P.) of the E.E.C.

It has been difficult to establish the C.A.P. because of variations between:
1) the relative importance of agriculture in states (Table 58, p. 368)
2) the proportion of agricultural land
3) farming methods
4) crop types
5) price support levels.

  One aspect of the C.A.P. is to neutralize differences in price levels within the Community, by setting guaranteed prices. The effects have been:
(a) the encouragement of inefficient and marginal farmers to stay in production
(b) overproduction, particularly of livestock products. Surplus goods have to be:
   – stored ('mountains' and 'lakes')
   – exported cheaply: in 1973, 200,000 tonnes of ridiculously cheap butter went to the U.S.S.R.
   – destroyed.

Other problems stemming from the C.A.P. are:
(a) the more agricultural countries gain more – France received over £600 million more than it paid in between 1962 and 1976
(b) there remain too many farmers.

  C.A.P. priority zones are either:
1) hill farms
2) suffering from severe depopulation
3) problem areas, e.g. poor infrastructure, destruction of the countryside.

Help has been given but success has been limited.

Q. 18. With reference to any two of the priority agricultural zones, compare efforts made to improve agricultural production and analyse the level of their success.   [WEL; half]

E.E.C. specialists will need detailed examples, which are beyond the scope of this book.

Theme 7: Industry

A. Location

You must know the nature and distribution of industry in your chosen region. Practise drawing sketch maps. You may get a very simple question:

Q. 19. With reference to one named industrial region within the prescribed region, describe and account for the present-day structure and distribution of manufacturing industry. [WEL]

More often, you will need to select material from this basic information to illustrate your arguments, for example:

Q. 20. Discuss and exemplify the factors which have affected the growth and location of industry in developing countries.

Remember that no single factor is entirely responsible for any industrial location as you use information from Table 59.

B. Steel production

Learn steel and one other industry. Steel features prominently in examination questions, and you may also use material on the steel industry in questions which ask about 'one major manufacturing industry'.

The British steel industry

Many small plants grew up where both coal and iron ore were mined: South Wales valleys, Teesside, Don valley, Clyde valley. These were least-cost locations in an industry based on bulky raw materials.

Economies of scale led to the concentration of the industry into fewer but larger plants, e.g. Port Talbot, Cardiff, Ebbw Vale and Newport in South Wales. As local ores became exhausted, ore was imported and coastal locations with deep-water harbours – Port Talbot, Immingham, Teesside and Hunterston – became important. The Jurassic ores of the limestone escarpment were developed, notably at Corby, Northants. Falling demand due to world recession and competition led to large-scale closures – Ebbw Vale, Corby, Shotton, Cleveland and Consett – and reductions in the workforce at Port Talbot, Llanwern and Sheffield.

The future of some remaining plants is in doubt, notably Ravens-

Table 59. Some factors in industrial location

	U.K.	Western Europe	U.S.S.R.	U.S.A. and Canada
Power	Alumina processing, Burntisland (H.E.P.)	Nitrates: 'fixing' N_2; Alpine Italy (H.E.P.)	Aluminium smelting, Zaporozhye (H.E.P.)	Aluminium smelting, Kitimat (H.E.P.)
Raw materials	Chemicals, Northwich – Warrington* (local salt, coal)	Chemicals, Leverkusen* (local lignite, Ruhr coke)	Chemicals, Slavyansk* (local sodium salts)	Oil refining, Houston, Texas*
Markets	Cement, Medway*	Food processing, The Hague	Food processing, Gorky	Motor assembly, Los Angeles
Labour	Marine engineering, Sheffield (skilled labour)	Motor assembly, Bochum (redundant miners)	Akademgorodki (academic townships)	Electronics, Stamford, Conn. (skilled labour)
Transport	Pottery, Stoke (canals†)	Light industry, Saarbrücken (canalization River Saar, 1975)	Tractors, Volgograd (Volga–Don Canal)	Warehousing and wholesaling, Atlanta, Ga.
Agglomeration economies	West Yorkshire	Ruhr	Donbas	Great Lakes
Government policy	Motor assembly, Halewood, Liverpool	Iron and steel, Taranto	Iron and steel, Oskol, p. 377	Aerospace, Huntsville, Ala.

* Least-cost location.
† Factor no longer operating.

craig – too far from ore supplies and markets ('peripheral location'). By the time you read this, Ravenscraig and Llanwern could be closed.

Western Europe*

The pattern has been similar here. Early coal-and-ore sites included north-east France (Valenciennes, Maubeuge), Lorraine and St Étienne; the Ruhr (Remscheid and Solingen); the Saar (Saarbrücken and Neunkirchen, using Lorraine ores); the Sambre–Meuse region (Liège).

In 1952, the European Coal and Steel Community (E.C.S.C.) was established with six members: France, West Germany, Belgium, Netherlands, Luxembourg and Italy. Tariffs were removed and a single large market created, freight rates were lowered, grant assistance was given and western Europe became a major steel producer. The nineteenth-century steel areas (above) suffered rationalization, and growth was outstanding in the Netherlands (IJmuiden) and Italy (Genoa, Milan and Turin), previously non-producers. Electric steel smelting has freed the steel industry from the coalfields. Coastal (tidewater) locations accounted for 20% of E.E.C. steel by 1975. Two areas predominate:

1) North Sea coast: Dunkirk, Zelzate, Maasvlaakte, IJmuiden, Bremen, Ravenscraig
2) Mediterranean coast: Fos, Cornigliano, Piombino, Bagnoli, Taranto.

U.S. steel industry

See pp. 299–300.

Soviet steel

By contrast, tidewater locations are relatively unimportant in the U.S.S.R. Early steelworking was based on iron ore in the Ukraine (Tula, Yelets, Lipetsk) and the Urals (Sverdlovsk and Nizhni Tagil), but production was low before the Russian Revolution. State power and modern technology have transformed the situation. Production of steel was 4 million tons in 1928, 65 million tons in 1960, and 148 million tons in 1980.

Modern developments are still ore-centred:
(a) Ukraine: notably at Zhdanov and Krivoy Rog, using Krivoy Rog ore, Donbas coal and Dnieper H.E.P.

* For more detail, see Ilbery, B. W., *Western Europe: A Systematic Human Geography*, Oxford University Press, 1981, pp. 97–9.

(b) Urals: Magnitnaya (Iron Mountain) ores, coal from the Kuznetsk Basin (1,600 km to the east) and Karaganda. Magnitogorsk is a major centre.

(c) K.M.A. – the Kursk Magnetic Anomaly (mostly in Belgorod, despite the name) – is the largest iron-ore deposit in the world. Direct reduction techniques at Oskol concentrate and smelt ores by natural-gas ovens and electric ore processes. The resulting iron is cheaper and better than the product of coke ovens and blast furnaces. K.M.A. ore is concentrated at Zheleznogorsk and Gubkin and sent to Cherepovets, 250 km north of Moscow, where production is based on Vorkuta coal and Urengoy natural gas. Kola ore is also used.

The only significant tidewater works is in the Soviet Far East at Komsomolsk-on-Amur, using imported pig-iron and scrap.

Clearly the key to the pattern of Soviet steel is the presence of major ore reserves, giving independence from imported ores: in strong contrast to Europe and the U.S.A.

Q. 21. 'Soviet industrial development has been extended into progressively more difficult physical environments.' Explain and illustrate with specific reference to locational changes in either:
(a) the iron and steel industry, or
(b) coal and lignite production. [OXF]

C. Decentralization of industry

See 'Decentralization', p. 294; 'suburbanization', p. 266; 'New Towns', p. 365.

D. Industry and port locations

1) Oil refining seeks port locations (pp. 298–9).
2) Iron and steel like tidewater sites (p. 300).
3) A port is a break-of-bulk point – the location at which a cargo is transferred from one form of transport (sea, in this case) to another (road, rail or pipeline). Consequently, since commodities have to be 're-packed', the port is a logical place for processing to take place before distribution inland.
4) Ports have good transport facilities to the hinterland.
5) Coastal sites often have access to cheap, flat land.
6) Water is readily available.
7) Large ports also provide markets.

Some ports and port industries

LONDON:* processing imports – grain, sugar, oil, timber, building materials, paper; also motor assembly

LE HAVRE: import processing – oil, petrochemicals, vegetable oils, food processing; also engineering, cement

HAMBURG: import processing – chemicals, oil, soap, tobacco; also electrical engineering, shipbuilding, beer

EUROPOORT: import processing – oil and petrochemicals; fertilizers

ANTWERP: import processing – oil, chemicals, vegetable oil, sugar, soap, margarine, chocolate, rubber; also metallurgy, engineering, vehicle assembly

GENOA: shipbuilding, steelmaking, electrical engineering

LENINGRAD: engineering, chemicals, food, textiles – but the raw materials are mainly Soviet-produced

ASTRAKHAN: engineering, food-processing, again from Soviet raw materials

PHILADELPHIA: import processing, carpets and textiles, rubber (Trenton), chemicals (Wilmington)

MONTREAL: import processing – chemicals; also rolling-stock, meat-packing, leather and fur working, paper, electrical engineering

Pick out the market-orientated industries in the list above.

Q. 22. Choose any two ports in the prescribed region. In each case:
(a) draw an annotated sketch map illustrating the port's situation and chief lines of communication;
(b) write an account of the main factors which have contributed to the port's growth and development.   [SCO. T; adjusted]

---

* Candidates frequently forget that London is an industrial area.

Theme 8: Energy

A. The decline of the coalfields

Q. 23. (a) Describe the main changes in the distribution of the coal industry in any one country within the prescribed region since 1960.

(b) State what you consider to be the most important reasons for the changes you describe; justify your choice and illustrate your answer with examples. [WEL]

Throughout western Europe and the U.S.A., the nineteenth-century coalfields are in decline because:

(i) more accessible deposits – 'exposed' coalfields – have been worked out

(ii) demand for coal as a raw material has fallen – notably in the iron and steel industry: to produce one ton of pig-iron:
- in 1760, 8–10 tons of coal were required
- in 1860, 4 tons
- in 1900, 2 tons
- in 1950, 1.3 tons.

Direct reduction methods (p. 377) need no coal.

(iii) demand for coal as an energy source has fallen. Oil, nuclear and water (hydro-electric) power are now used to produce electricity, in addition to coal. Ships and trains are diesel-fuelled, houses are increasingly heated by gas, oil and electricity where once the coal fire dominated.

The results are that:

1) employment in coal mining has plummeted

2) new pits are highly mechanized or worked by open-cast methods to cut costs.

Table 60. Trends in U.K. coal mining

Pre-1960 centres	Developments since 1960
Northumberland and Durham	Employment: 1964: 119,000 1975: 38,000
Derby and Nottingham	Western collieries exhausted; new automated collieries on concealed field
South Lancashire	Geologically difficult; closures; few pits survive

379

Table 60 continued

Pre-1960 centres	Developments since 1960
North Wales	—
South Wales	Pit closures led to removal of branch railways. Car ownership low, poor bus service. Severe regional problems
Staffordshire	—
Warwickshire	Declining
Kent	—
Leicestershire	Thick, low-grade coal increasingly worked. Vale of Belvoir mining opposed by conservationists
Ayrshire, Lanarkshire, Fife, Midlothian	—
South Yorkshire	Major eastward shift to the concealed field (Selby). Labour force remained constant

Table 61.   Western Europe: coal mining

Europe	Mining areas in decline	New developments
France	North-east, Massif Central	—
West Germany	Southern Ruhr	Mines now on concealed field – up to 1,000 m deep. Contraction halted by 1973–4 oil crisis. Mechanization, new techniques – most efficient coal industry in Europe: 6.5 tonnes/man-shift
Belgium	Sambre–Meuse: 1965: 11.39 million tonnes 1977: 0.79 million tonnes	Campine (Kempen): 1965: 10.07 million tonnes 1977: 6.27 million tonnes
Netherlands	South Limburg coalfield closed	

In the Soviet Union

The relative importance of coal is declining:

percentage of energy provided by coal:

1940: 69

1960: 56

1980: 24

but actual production is still rising:

coal production in millions of tonnes:

1940: 166

1960: 513

1980: 716.

The major coalfields are: Donbas, Kuznetsk, Urals, Karaganda and Ekibastuz, Eastern Siberia, Yakutsk, Pechora Basin, Norilsk, Moscow Basin, Far East.

In the U.S.A.

The Appalachian fields have suffered. Pennsylvania anthracite production has fallen continuously from 1916 (98 million tons) to 1975 (6 million tons). The mining of bituminous coal has shifted from southwest Pennsylvania to West Virginia and thence to eastern Kentucky. Nevertheless, Appalachia, with thick horizontal seams, easily mined, dominates U.S. coal production, and the Birmingham field, to the south, has increased in output.

Low-grade reserves exist in western U.S.A.: lignite in North Dakota, lignite and bituminous coal in Montana. Coal is mined in Wyoming, Utah, Colorado, New Mexico and Washington.

The 1973–4 oil crisis provoked the U.S. government to launch Project Independence: 'to take us to the point where we are no longer dependent upon potentially insecure foreign supplies of energy'. One of its aims was to increase domestic coal consumption. This has not happened because:

  (i) Appalachian coal, with a high sulphur content, is banned by many states on grounds of air pollution

 (ii) cheap open-strip techniques are falling foul of conservationists (but still account for 40% of U.S. production)

(iii) western deposits (see above) are too remote from markets.

The U.S. coal industry has been subject to 'wild economic gyrations'* and the miners have suffered:

employment in coal mining:

in 1950: 415,000

* Paterson, op. cit.

in 1970: 125,000
in 1975: 200,000 (post oil crisis).
In spite of the rise in employment in 1975, Appalachia is the most depressed region in the U.S.A.

B. Alternative sources of energy

Coal has suffered severe competition. Table 62 summarizes the qualities of other primary energy sources.

Table 62. Energy sources

Source	Advantages	Disadvantages
Petroleum (oil)	Easily transported: supertanker and pipelines	Pollutant. Developed nations are heavily dependent on OPEC states. Non-renewable
Natural gas	Clean, easily controlled (provides 16% of world's energy with capacity for increase)	Non-renewable
H.E.P.	Renewable resource. Clean. Cheap to operate. Can be developed in association with irrigation	Restricted to areas with: (i) constant water supply (ii) suitable sites for dam construction. High development costs
Nuclear power	Small quantities of fuel needed. Abundant supply of fuel	Very high development costs. Danger of radioactive leakage. Difficulties of nuclear waste disposal
Solar power	Inexhaustible	Of restricted use in cloudy climates. Inconvenient: very large structures needed
Wind power	Inexhaustible	Intermittent nature of source
Tidal power	Inexhaustible	Expensive, but two schemes exist: Rance Barrage (Brittany); Newfoundland
Geothermal power	Significant and cheap in Iceland, New Zealand	Difficult to develop

Q. 24. (a) *Discuss the relative merits of traditional sources of energy (water, coal, oil, gas).*

    (b) *Describe the alternative sources of energy which are currently being developed.*   [SCO. A]

Theme 9: Transport

Transport and the physical environment

Again you must have details of the physical geography: draw a labelled sketch map. On it, mark the major road, rail and water systems.

Q. 25. For one country within the prescribed region, describe the main effects of the physical environment on the railway network. How have the railways contributed to regional specialization in economic activity?

Motorways or waterways could be substituted for railways.

Theme 10: The role of governments

Throughout this chapter, references have been made to government action:
– to reduce regional inequalities, pp. 361–2.
– to establish industry and relieve unemployment in New Towns, pp. 365–6
– in precise locations: Table 59, p. 375
– in the steel industry, pp. 374–6
– in the U.S.S.R., pp. 376–7
– in the coal industry, p. 381.

23. Themes in regional geography 2: The less developed countries

Here are no Hottentots without religion, civil society or articulate language.
(Preface to *A Voyage to Abyssinia*, trans. Dr Johnson)

Johnson was praising, in 1739, a book which did not speak of 'Third World' peoples as if they were idiots. Yet, in 1981, examiners still complained of the 'sweeping, paternalistic tones' in which candidates wrote about less developed countries. Do not be condescending about Third World peoples, *especially* if you fail to spell their place-names properly.

Theme 1: Causes of underdevelopment

Before you tackle this, you must know the indices of underdevelopment.

Q. 1. What would you regard as the distinguishing characteristics of a 'developing country'?   [LON]

Table 63.   Indicators of development

	Developed countries	*Less developed countries (L.D.C.s)*
Birth rate	13/1,000	over 30/1,000
Death rate	12/1,000	over 15/1,000
Infant mortality rate	under 50/1,000	50–150/1,000
% workers in agriculture	under 5%	over 50%
Daily calorie intake	nearly 3,000	2,200 or less
% of calorie requirement	over 120%	80–90%
Daily protein consumption	over 85 gm	below 65 gm
% having secondary schooling	over 80%	under 20%
Literacy rate	over 80%	under 25%
Electricity consumption/head	over 5.4 watt-hours	under 0.4 watt-hours
G.D.P. per capita	over $2,000	$100–1,000

Explanations of underdevelopment include:

1) the nations concerned have yet to go through the D.T.M., pp. 253–5
2) nations have yet to achieve 'take-off', p. 363
3) underdeveloped nations lack resources. Supporting evidence for this comes from the much higher G.D.P. per capita shown by OPEC states, e.g. Libya, $7,422; Saudi Arabia, $6,155; Venezuela, $2,794. (Examples in this chapter will always be given in the order: Africa, Asia, Latin America)
4) underdeveloped nations lack capital (productivity is strongly linked with investment); skilled labour, demand; economies of scale, which cannot be applied in areas of low demand
5) the less developed countries are at the periphery of Myrdal's model, pp. 357–8. Trade figures illustrate this:

% world trade, 1971	
E.E.C.	42
U.S.A.	17
Canada	12
Non-E.E.C. Europe and Russia	10
Japan	7
Remainder of Asia	7
Latin America	5

Q. 2. To what extent does the theory of national cores and peripheries provide an explanation of the unequal regional development in any one developing country? [AEB]

6) some geographers see Third World peoples as caught in a 'poverty trap' (see Fig. 134, overleaf)
7) there are physical constraints on development in L.D.C.s.

Physical constraints on development

Relief
Relief can form barriers to the development of road, rail and water transport. For your chosen region, locate on a sketch map the following features:

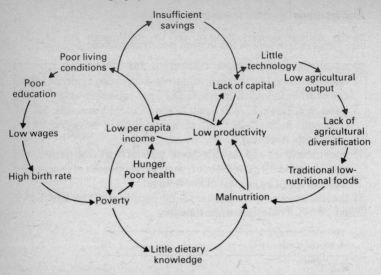

Fig. 134 *Circles of poverty and ill-health*

AFRICA: Atlas, Adamawa Highlands, Fouta Djallon, Ethiopian High-lands, East African Highlands, Matopo Hills, Bié Plateau, Mitumba Chain (Zaïre), Komaso Highlands (Namibia). Nile (plus cataracts 3–6), Senegal, Gambia, Niger (plus rapids below Bamako), Benin, Volta, Zaïre (plus Inga and Kisangani Falls), Oubangui (plus Bangui Falls), Zambezi (plus Victoria Falls, Kariba gorge, falls below Cabora Bassa Dam), Cunene, Limpopo. Add the swamplands of Okavango, Makgadikgadi, Sudd, and the Niger 'delta' in Mali.

ASIA: Zagros Mts, Hindu Kush, Himalayas, Chin Hills, Annamatic Chain, Central Highlands (Vietnam), Cameron Highlands (peninsular Malaysia). Indus, Ganges, Brahmaputra, Irrawaddy, Salween, Menam, Mekong, Hong (Red).

LATIN AMERICA: Cordillera Occidental, Cordillera Central, Cordillera Oriental, Cordillera de Mérida (Andes), Bolivian Plateau, Guiana Highlands, Sierra Pacaraima, Borborema Plateau, Brazilian High-lands, Serra da Mantiqueira, Serra do Mar, Sierra de Córdoba, Mato Grosso plateau. Orinoco, Magdalena, Amazon, Negro (Brazil), Madeira, Araguaia, Parnaíba, São Francisco, Paraná, Paraguay, Río de la Plata, Colorado.

Tropical soils

Fig. 135 shows the soils of the tropics, greatly simplified:

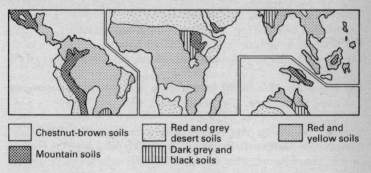

☐ Chestnut-brown soils	Red and grey desert soils	Red and yellow soils
▨ Mountain soils	▥ Dark grey and black soils	

Fig. 135 *Tropical soils*

Poor soils include:

Desert soils: grey or red soils with almost no humus, and frequent concentrations of salt at or near the surface. Irrigation and fertilizers are necessary if they are to be cultivable.

Laterites (p. 226) often have a hard crust which will not support vegetation.

Ferraltitic soils occur below tropical rain forest. Deeply weathered, they contain free iron oxide and alumina, but they lose their fertility quickly after forest clearance.

Ferruginous soils: associated with savanna.

Good soils include:

Tropical black earths (vertisols). These have developed over base-rich rocks (e.g. calcareous rocks or basalts). They occur in areas with a marked dry season, during which they become hard. In the wet season, they are sticky and difficult to work.

Chestnut soils occur on the desert margin and contain humus. Thus, only water is needed to make them productive.

Q. 3. 'In the developing world, river valleys are often negative areas as regards settlement and economic activity.' How far is this true of the area or areas you have studied? [LON]

'Negative settlement areas' means regions of low population density. Check a population density map against the relief map of your region. Is the statement true?

Reasons for avoiding river valleys include:
(a) disease: bilharzia (pp. 282–3), river blindness, malaria
(b) flooding: notably in Bangladesh; also in Somalia
(c) exposed sites: no defence against adversaries, slave traders (West Africa)
(d) vegetation. Many of the great tropical river systems are covered by tropical rain forest. Give details (pp. 234–5).

Densely populated river valleys include the Niger delta, Nile valley, Indus valley, Ganges–Brahmaputra, Irrawaddy delta, Mekong and Red deltas, Lower Paraná, Plate estuary. Find out how these regions support high populations. Give density figures.

Question 2 of this chapter indicated a pressing problem:

Theme 2: Inequalities in development

Q. 4. Fig. 136 shows a relationship often believed to apply to countries undergoing economic development.
(i) Explain briefly what this relationship is.
(ii) Suggest the reasons that may underlie the relationship. [NI]

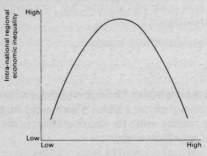

Fig. 136 *See Question 4*

Fig. 136 illustrates Myrdal's model: read again pp. 357–8.

Regional disparities increase after development plans have been initiated because:

1) new projects tend to be located in the economically most attractive and profitable places. This intensifies the core–periphery pattern
2) some development specialists believed that growth should be located where economic progress would be maximized, rather than dispersing it, which might involve higher costs and lower returns
3) any development based on high technology benefits some groups to the exclusion of others.

These points, together with the unequal distribution of physical advantages, will help you with Question 5, but you must LOCATE AND NAME less-developed and better-developed areas:

Q. 5. 'Unbalanced regional development is an inevitable feature of the development process.' Discuss this statement with reference to regional patterns of development in one country in the prescribed region. [WEL]

This is an excellent revision question: too many candidates write as if the entire Third World were equally densely populated and equally underdeveloped.

Q. 6. For two named countries within the prescribed region, suggest how inter-regional contrasts in economic development might be reduced.

[WEL; adapted]

Such contrasts are reduced if economic development programmes are adopted for deprived areas. You must know the details of such programmes:

THE HADEJIA JAMA'ARE RIVER-BASIN DEVELOPMENT is located in Bauchi state, Nigeria. An 11-km dam is to create a 235-km^2 lake on the Bunga River, with H.E.P. turbines. Below the dam, the Kawali diversion scheme will regulate water flow and reduce seasonal flooding.

THE SERENJE RURAL SERVICE DEVELOPMENT (Zambia) has set up or provided rural shops, a women's development group, a farm co-operative, a community development demonstrator, radio farm forum groups, a primary school clinic, a grinding mill, and a shared tractor. This development, in the view of the World Bank, may be more successful because, for a project to succeed:
(1) 'the technological package must be appropriate to the resources and technical conditions found at the farm level'*
(2) 'the technological package must be consistent with the human attributes, attitudes and abilities of the region'.*

* World Bank Staff Working Paper No. 295, *The Technology of Rural Development,* c. 1978.

THE INDIAN PLANNING COMMISSION, in the Third Five Year Plan, stated (for the first time) that regional planning was as important as national planning. Steel mills were located in the deprived areas of Orissa and Madhya Pradesh.

THE MEKONG PROJECT includes Thailand, Laos, Cambodia, Khmer Republic and Vietnam. Twenty-six countries are helping; some examples are:
– Australia: geological surveys of dam sites
– Mekong Committee (countries involved): flood forecasting and demonstration farms
– Netherlands and U.S.A.: resettlement problems
– Canada: fisheries research
– UNESCO: farm education in Laos
– WHO:* malarial studies.
In addition, power stations and pumping works are planned. The major drawback seems to be the military offensives dominating this part of Asia.

THE 'ASSAULT ON THE AMAZON' (Brazil, 1970s) measures included:
1) the construction of the Transamazon Highway from Recife to the Belém–Brasilia Highway, which was completed as a two-lane dirt road by the late 1970s. This was to provide a route for the migration of poor north-eastern farmers and landless labourers, thus relieving population pressure in the north-east
2) colonization schemes
3) the economic development of fifteen selected areas.
But:
– lumbering, and mining and energy projects (Trombetas, Carajás and Tucuruí) have been more successful
– major rivers have been inadequately bridged
– flash floods and landslides block roads
– speculators and agribusinesses have bought up land, often instead of poor farmers
– surviving indigenous tribal groups have suffered; and have attacked colonists.

VENEZUELA has tried to generate industrial growth at Ciudad Guayana by:
 (i) road construction
 (ii) power provision: H.E.P. at Macaguan and Guri

* World Health Organization.

(iii) industrial development: steel, aluminium, iron-ore reduction and paper and pulp.

'The Ciudad Guayana scheme has been moderately successful in establishing an . . . industrial centre . . . but few South American governments could afford or manage such a large and costly project.'*

Venezuela can afford this 'peripheral' development because of her oil revenues (Venezuela produces 40% of the world's oil).

Theme 3: Hunger and food: the Brandt Report recommendations

In addition to increasing output, the Commission recommends:
(a) better food-storage facilities
(b) agrarian reform
(c) international emergency reserves
(d) increases in food aid
(e) liberalization of trade in food and agricultural products between developed countries ('North' in Brandt parlance) and L.D.C.s ('South')
(f) support by developed countries for international agricultural research.

Theme 4: Climate

Climate is deemed to play a more important role in the agriculture of the L.D.C.s than in the developed world; perhaps because L.D.C.s do not have the technological expertise to overcome climatic restraints.

Aridity

IN AFRICA: the proportion of thorny species in the woodland increases, grasses are shorter and plants are more specialized in their adaptation to drought conditions as the desert margins are approached. Thence, vegetation is confined to the edges of storm-water channels and temporary lakes; date-palms, tamarisk and acacias can obtain soil water at depth.

Man has (i) introduced grasses and drought-resistant trees, like poplar and Australian wattle, notably in southern Africa. He has also (ii) cleared vegetation by overgrazing. Strips of bush or grass separated

* Bromley, R.D.F. and R., *South American Development: A Geographical Introduction*, Cambridge University Press, 1982.

by wide, bare zones are common in the Sahel zone (brousse tigre)* and have been attributed to overgrazing or climatic deterioration.

Cattle (about 30/km^2), sheep and goats are pastured on the semi-desert. In the dry season, the herds remain near lakes and flood plains, moving to the watersheds in the rainy season. In this way, they take advantage of the grazing and avoid water-borne diseases, especially tsetse. The routes followed vary according to

– weather
– patterns of sedentary cultivation: manure is welcomed in the dry season
– state governments and taxation authorities.

The Fulani are nomads who live on milk. The Kanuri are partly nomadic.

IN ASIA: nomadic groups are found in Central Asia, Afghanistan and parts of Pakistan, e.g. the Pathans. They travel between summer pastures and winter camps.

BRAZILIAN nomads are mainly to be found in the Sertão do Nordeste.

The vegetation is thorn scrub – the caatinga, with sandy, saline soils and bare rock pavements. The dominant economy is semi-nomadic subsistence cattle rearing (only 10% of Brazil's cattle) with equal numbers of sheep and goats. The vaqueros (north-eastern cowboys) tend herds of up to 2,000 head, which droughts can cut by half. The stock are driven from Recife to Fortaleza and to Crateús. Wages are very low and many vaqueros also cultivate small plots.

Areas of seasonal rainfall
You must understand WHY rainfall is seasonal and uncertain.

MUCH OF AFRICA experiences rain at the **intertropical convergence zone (I.T.C.Z.)**, which lies between the two sets of trade winds. The strength of the convergence and its north–south movements vary enormously: rainfall is very unreliable in consequence.

SEASONAL RAINFALL IN ASIA is dependent on the monsoon (pp. 217–23).

NORTH-EAST BRAZIL is wracked by drought because:
 (i) the land mass projects seawards into the South Atlantic high-pressure system where the stable, descending air is dry
 (ii) the I.T.C.Z. is retarded in summer by the South Atlantic anti-cyclone.

* Grove, A. T., *Africa*, Oxford University Press, 1978, p. 36.

In March 1984, *The Times* reported a sixth successive drought year in north-east Brazil, causing almost total loss of crops, rises in infant mortality to 250/1,000, deaths of children, adults and cattle, and out-migration of thousands of people. The Brazilian government estimates that 25 million people have been affected, 15 million (11% of Brazil's population) suffering directly from hunger and thirst.

Q. 7. For one major climatic hazard experienced in the prescribed region,
(a) explain why it occurs;
(b) assess its economic and social impact and the effectiveness of measures taken to combat it. [WEL]

The UNESCO scheme: planning against drought

This proposes a change from nomadic to sedentary cattle farming, to reduce the dangers of catastrophic drought. A circle of land 20 km in diameter will centre on a deep well, providing water in the dry season. Several grazing areas 10 km out, centred on artificial, rainwater-fed ponds, encircle the well and support cattle in the rainy season. A village is sited near the well where cultivation will be possible. The grazing areas will be used in rotation. *This scheme has yet to be implemented.*

Remember that, in the tropics, high evapo-transpiration further reduces available moisture.

Many questions centre on the agriculture response to seasonal rainfall. Details of nomadic movements in response to wet and dry seasons have been given. Sedentary agriculture shows a similar close correlation with climate:

Table 64. Subsistence farming

	Jan.–March	April–June	July–Sept.	Oct.–Dec.
West Africa (Hausa)	grazing on stubble: cattle, sheep, goats (0 mm)	millet, cow peas (550 mm)	groundnuts (475 mm)	irrigation: onions, pepper, sugar cane, rice (100 mm)
India (Bihar)	harvest rabi,* irrigate (75 mm)	sow kharif,† rice, maize (480 mm)	harvest kharif crops (905 mm)	sow rabi, wheat, barley, pulses, irrigate (139 mm)

* Spring crop   † Autumn crop

Note the rainfall totals for the two regions in Table 64: 1,125 mm and 1,599 mm respectively. In Britain, this is ample. But there are also losses through evapo-transpiration, and seasonal fluctuations. In India, if the monsoon fails:

1) there is not enough water for rice
2) maize, wheat and barley fail
3) there is no food: villagers must earn money by stone-breaking for building roads, canal-digging and tank construction to buy food from government reserves. Few die of starvation; but many, especially children, die from malnutrition diseases.

Q. 8. Examine the view that it is seasonality of rainfall rather than amount of rainfall which causes so many economic problems. [OXF]

Of course, monsoons can cause flooding . . .

Q. 9. The monsoon can be a mixed blessing to Indian farmers. Discuss. [SCO. T]

Theme 5: Agriculture

Subsistence farming

Q. 10. 'Subsistence farming often represents a close adjustment to the physical environment.' Discuss, with reference to specific examples. [LON]

BUSH-FALLOWING SYSTEMS IN GHANA

(i) Food farms in the forest region mimic the ecology of the rain forest (pp. 234–5): maize grows straight up (like the 40-m layer); cocoyams, shorter, spread broad leaves (like the 30-m continuous canopy); groundnuts spread at ground level (like the 8-m under-storey layer). As with the species in the rain forest, the crops are scattered.

(ii) Land rotations allow the crops to pick up nutrients from the decaying litter layer; the soil is low in nutrients. (Do *not* talk about 'goodness' in the soil!)

(iii) Vegetation is cleared by burning *in situ*. Since the bulk of nutrients are in the vegetation, these are kept on the land.

(iv) Crops – like the forest trees – are planted and harvested at various times. This, together with point (i), means that there is continuous cover; soil erosion is avoided.

When yields drop, the plot is abandoned until it regains its fertility. Native oil palms and shea butter trees are cropped where they have grown naturally and sold for cash.

SHIFTING CULTIVATION IN NORTHERN THAILAND is very similar to the Ghanaian system. The cropped area is known as a swidden; the following sums up the pattern of activity:

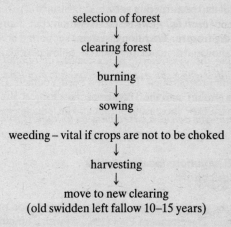

selection of forest
↓
clearing forest
↓
burning
↓
sowing
↓
weeding – vital if crops are not to be choked
↓
harvesting
↓
move to new clearing
(old swidden left fallow 10–15 years)

The main crops are: dry rice, maize, millet, grain (chickpeas). Rubber is a cash crop.

IN BRAZIL, shifting cultivation is known as **roça**. The pattern of 2–3 years of cultivation followed by a long fallow period is the same as in Ghana and Thailand. Manioc, rice and beans are the staples; pepper and tobacco are cash crops. In most systems, special crops of vegetables are grown near the house and manured by household wastes.

Decline of subsistence agriculture

The decline of nomadism is due in part to:
1) droughts: West Africa, 1973; north-east Brazil, 1978–84
2) serious overgrazing that reduces the carrying capacity of the land. Masailand pasture has deteriorated (East Africa), the Sahel borders are experiencing desertification. Desert Iraq was once a densely populated area. In the Sertão do Nordeste (Brazil), the area of bare rock is increasing
3) governments trying to stabilize nomads because movements of

animals interrupt and threaten sedentary agriculturalists

4) irrigation schemes transforming traditional grazing lands, e.g. from Lake Chad; in Abu Dhabi; by the POLONORDESTE programme in Brazil

5) lorries representing strong competition as a transport mode for camel-keeping nomads in Africa and Arabia

6) new work opportunities attracting nomads – Libyan pastoralists move to oil and construction sites.

The decline of bush fallowing results from:

1) population pressure. Traditional systems supported around 23/km^2. As population and demand for food rise, fallow periods are cut short: yields fall

2) government programmes: 'Operation Feed Yourself' (Nigeria), the Fifth Plan (India), and the Transamazonica Project aim to commercialize agriculture, increasing output and introducing cash crops.

The Green Revolution: local examples

Re-read pp. 283–4.

IN NIGERIA: the government gave the Green Revolution priority in the Fourth National Development Plan (1981–5) with a funding of $11,944 million. Nigerian food output had fallen by 12% per capita (1969–73), as people moved into oil-related jobs and imports of 'luxury' foods soared with the new prosperity.

The Green Revolution has failed to meet targets because:

1) imports – especially rice – undercut local product prices

2) price levels have fallen, making the effort worthless for small farmers

3) farmers dislike new methods

4) promised fertilizers and equipment have failed to arrive.

Rice production sums up the situation:

production in 1980 = 1.09 million tonnes

1981 = 1.2 (10% rise),

but imports in 1981 = 0.6 million tonnes.

IN INDIA AND PAKISTAN: low levels of nutrition (average calorie intake in 1971 was under 2,200 per capita per day) and high infant mortality (50–100/1,000), coupled with a desire to improve rural conditions, made the Green Revolution attractive. *But*:

1) peasants dislike new methods

2) 'miracle' rice is low in protein
3) poor tenants were evicted to make way for the necessary improvements in irrigation that the new varieties demand
4) the small owner-occupier cannot afford the new technology. He has to sell land to raise capital. Eventually he may be squeezed out.

IN BRAZIL: the problem area is the north-east, drought-ridden and over-populated at 12–25 inhabitants/km^2. Developments have included:
(a) a multi-purpose river project on the São Francisco river
(b) credit to buy new crop strains
(c) movement of population from the area.

Nevertheless, the region remains poor; development has concentrated in a few areas, principally on the coast, and regional inequality has increased. The region is still not proof against drought (see pp. 392–3).

Commercial agriculture

(i) Extensive pastoralism
This only occurs with any significance within the Third World in Latin America.

THE CERRADO REGION OF BRAZIL comprises Mato Grosso and Goiás: an area of high grass-covered plateaux and ranges with forest in the valleys. Winters are 'dry' (May–Oct., 125–250 mm; 20°C) and summers wet (1,000–15,000 mm; 25°C), and the acid soils produce grassland of low nutritional value. Much of the cerrado is inaccessible. Cattle are mostly unimproved 'zebu': low-yielding and prone to disease. The POLOCENTRO programme aims to develop the cerrado by increasing the cultivated areas and promoting pastoralism and forestry.

(ii) Extensive arable farming

THE GEZIRA SCHEME is the most successful arable scheme in the African L.D.C.s, summarized by Fig. 137 (overleaf).

THE DECCAN PLATEAU is India's main cotton-producing area. The soils are deep, heavy and moisture-retentive (**regurs**: Indian term for 'black cotton soils'). Rainfall is 600–1,000 mm, mainly in summer, and irrigation is not used. The major production unit is the peasant farm.

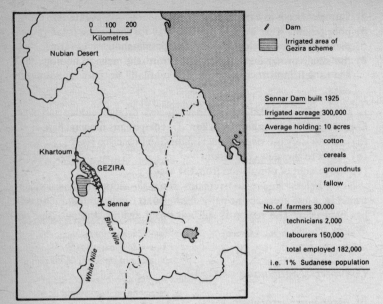

Fig. 137 *The Gezira scheme*

EXTENSIVE ARABLE FARMING IN LATIN AMERICA is exemplified by the estancias of Argentina and Uruguay. The pampas is flat, fertile, and well watered (500–700 mm, July 10–15°C, Jan. 15–25°C). Wheat production dominates but cattle are also reared. The large estancias are owner-occupied, so that they have been able to resist the growth of agribusiness on the pampas.

Plantation agriculture

A **plantation** is a large farm in tropical and subtropical areas which is used for specialist production of one crop (**monoculture**). Plantations were usually introduced by Europeans because:
1) economies of scale make farming more profitable
2) division of labour (p. 280) increases efficiency
3) there is a long delay between planting and harvesting tree crops, and large units of production are necessary as security against loans until the crop can be sold

4) Europeans could organize indigenous labour to operate this profitable system
5) plantations were much more profitable than indigenous farms
6) first-stage processing can be carried out in attached factories, thus reducing transport costs.

Table 65. Some examples of Third World plantations

Continent	Producing area	Crop	Effect on the economy
Africa	Liberia (White Plains – Ganta)	Rubber	Firestone Co. provided H.E.P., schools, churches, hospitals, brickworks. Rubber = 13% export earnings (1973)
	Kenya (Kericho, Limuru)	Tea	Brooke Bond Liebig: 5,500 ha of tea, 12 tea factories. Tea = 14% exports (1974). Number of small tea farms rising
Asia	Malaysia	Oil palm	Replacing rubber because of competition from synthetic rubber. 16% Malaysian exports: world's leading producer. Many Chinese immigrants to plantations. Estate villages
	Java (Indonesia)	Coffee	Dutch planters forced Javanese to work plantations. 50% of Javanese landless by 1940. Poverty. Coffee now only 2% agricultural output of Indonesia
Latin America	Brazil (São Paulo, Paraná)	Coffee	Despoiler of land, continually moving, leaving poor pasture behind. Coffee 25% export earnings. Large-scale European immigration to coffee areas
	Brazil (irrigated northern coastlands)	Sugar	Created port facilities but little other infrastructure. Plantation owners' taxes benefited armed forces and wealthier classes. Plantation wages very low

Theme 6: Industry and mining

Mineral resources as a locating factor

Q. 11. With reference to named areas within the prescribed region, assess the extent to which the location and exploitation of mineral resources have affected the present-day location of manufacturing industry. [WEL]

You would be wise to choose examples where there is a restricted range of minerals in a few locations:

MAURITANIA has been transformed economically by the opening of haematite deposits in 1963. The ore is dry with few impurities. Ore-related developments include the Kedia d'ldjil–Nouadhibou railway and the construction of townships at each end of the railway. No associated manufacturing industry has developed. Copper was mined at Akjoujt, but mining stopped when world prices fell. Gypsum from the Nouakchott area is used for cement-works in Senegal.

Thus, despite ore reserves, no significant manufacturing industry is found in Mauritania.

LIBERIA has iron ore in the Bomi Hills, on Mount Nimba and in the Bong Hills. The ore has led to the development of three railway lines and a little industry: beneficiation of ore at the Bomi Hills mines and at Buchanan. An iron and steel plant is planned at Robertsport. Some diamonds are mined. In 30–40 years the ore will have gone, and Liberia will have little to show for it.

WEST MALAYSIA produces one-third of the 'free' world's tin, which accounted for 15% of Malaysian exports (1974). The ore occurs in alluvial deposits. The main field is in the Kuita valley. Tin is concentrated at the mines and smelted at Penang and Butterworth. Industry is developing at Petaling Jaya (food processing, textiles; not tin-related), but only 8.7% of the West Malaysian labour-force is in manufacturing.

INDIA is one of the few L.D.C.s to have coal. Fig. 138 summarizes the mineral reserves and developments of the Damodar valley, the major industrial area of South-East Asia.

Other steel mills are at:
1) Rourkela, using local ores. Coal is brought 280 km from the Damodar valley. Fertilizers are a by-product.
2) Bhilai: local ores and limestone. Coal is railed 600 km.
3) Bhadravati: local ore, locally produced charcoal.

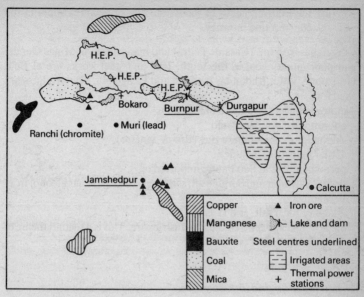

Fig. 138 *The Damodar valley*

The Damodar valley iron is used in the engineering industries of Calcutta, including cars, and the railway works at Jamshedpur. Other Indian manufactures include aluminium (Damodar valley), zinc, cement and cotton yarn. India is unusual in the size and extent of her industries, and yet only 9.5% of the workforce are in manufacturing.

VENEZUELA has petroleum and natural gas (Maracaibo) and iron ore south of the Orinoco. Mineral-based developments include:
1) oil refining and chemicals at El Tablazo on the oilfield
2) fertilizers at Maron (near Puerto Cabello)
3) the Guayana industrial complex.
   Oil revenues ($13,000 million in 1971) have permitted:
(a) light industry: food, cars, textiles, clothing at Carácas, Maracay and Valencia
(b) the Guayana industrial complex:
   (i) steel is made, using local ore (from Cerro Bolívar), European and Japanese coking coal and H.E.P.
   (ii) aluminium is smelted at Ciudad Guayana (see p. 391), using Jamaican bauxite

401

    (iii) the housing needs of the workers have meant a boom in the construction industry.

BRAZIL has iron ore (Casa de Pedra) and manganese, in Minas Gerais, and poor-quality coal in the south. Iron and steel works are at Belo Horizonte, Volta Redonda, Ipatinga and Picaguiera. The products are used for:
– motor vehicles: Greater São Paulo
– aircraft: Greater São Paulo
– shipbuilding: Guanabara Bay (Rio de Janeiro).
   Other industries include:
– petrochemicals at São Paulo: imported oil
– Bahia: Salvador and Sergipe oil, salt from Alagôas, sugar alcohol from Pernambuco
– Alagôas: local salt, and H.E.P.
Note how market-centred these industries are. This is a second theme of industry in the L.D.C.s

Urban location and industry

The spatial concentration of manufacturing in the Third World is remarkable:

IN AFRICA: Egypt and Nigeria contribute 40% of the total value added by manufacturing.

IN ASIA: India is a major manufacturing nation, but 70% of all industrial employment is in six of the twenty-three states, especially Maharashtra and West Bengal. Hong Kong has 41% of its labour force in manufacturing.

MANUFACTURING IN LATIN AMERICA is largely confined to six core areas: see Fig. 139.

   This concentration can be explained by:
 (i) outstanding natural resources; but industrialization is not the automatic result of resources; see Mauritania, Liberia, West Malaysia, all on p. 400.
(ii) the presence of urban areas. Most industries operate most efficiently in large factories (internal economics of scale). Factories are often best sited in cities because:
   – agglomeration economies operate, hence

CENTRAL VENEZUELA
Carácas, Valencia

CENTRAL COLOMBIA
Bogotá, Medellín, Cali

LIMA

SOUTH-EAST BRAZIL
São Paulo, Rio de Janeiro
Belo Horizonte

CENTRAL CHILE
Santiago, Valparaiso

RIVER PLATE
Buenos Aires, Montevideo
Rosario

Major core areas

Fig. 139 *The major core areas of Latin America*

– linkages are easier
– demand is high
– influential politicians and administrators can be contacted most
easily.

Few of these industrial areas are major industrial exporters: none of
the African states; Korea, Hong Kong, China, India and Singapore in
Asia; Brazil only in Latin America. The crucial problem for Third
World countries is the hostility of developed countries, who see imports
from L.D.C.s as a threat to their own industry, and check them by
quotas, price controls and subsidies to domestic producers. Consequently most L.D.C.s supply only their domestic markets. Their industrial growth has been based on the idea of **import substitution**: the
manufacture of hitherto imported manufactures, often behind a tariff
wall, in order to save foreign exchange. Food, drink and tobacco,
textiles and clothing tend to be the first to be substituted and these tend
to seek urban locations.

403

Theme 7: Population

Growth

Q. 12. Discuss the implications of population growth for the rate and distribution of economic development in one country. [WEL]

Table 66.   Population growth and growth of G.N.P. per capita

Country	Annual population growth (%)*	G.N.P. per capita: annual rate of growth, 1960–70 (%)†
Ghana	2.8	−0.4
Sudan	3.2	1.0
India	2.2	1.2
Malaysia	2.8	3.1
Brazil	2.8	2.4
Venezuela	3.1	2.3

* Source: *Universal Atlas*, George Philip.

† Source: Dickenson, J. P., *et al.*, *A Geography of the Third World*, Methuen, 1983.

Table 66 seems to show that high rates of population increase do not correlate with low increases in G.N.P. Note Ghana and Malaysia; Sudan and Venezuela.

You should be aware that population increases are not spread evenly over any country – make a note of areas of high increase, and areas of population loss, for at least one country within your prescribed region.

Since industrialization is very much city-based in the Third World, one might think that urbanization would be an aid to industrial growth. However, 'it is generally true that the accumulation of population in Third World cities has outstripped by a large margin the capacity of their manufacturing economies to absorb labour'.* Squatter settlement, based on begging, stealing, prostitution, and legal and illegal street peddling, is the result.

Distribution

Q. 13. Critically examine the view that population distribution in the developing world is more closely related to physical features than to economic conditions. [LON]

* Dickenson, J. P., *et al.*, *A Geography of the Third World*, Methuen, 1983.

To answer Question 13, you must draw for at least two states a 'physical features' map (p. 386) and a simplified map of population density: high, medium and low (with figures, if possible). The economic factors to be considered are commercial agriculture, industry, transport and urbanization.

You may well conclude that the two sets of factors operate, to some extent, in unison.

A simpler question on the same theme is:

Q. 14. (a) *Describe in some detail the density distribution of population in one L.D.C.*
(b) *Explain the factors which have influenced the present distribution, and indicate changes taking place aimed at helping to solve some of the demographic problems of the country concerned.* [SCO. A; adapted]

Maps – as above – are again necessary. Use one of the regional development strategies outlined on pp. 389–91 to help in answering part (b).

Migration

You should be able to provide examples of the following migrations: rural–urban, rural–rural, rural–extractive industry, seasonal, and hazard-response migration. In each case, state the origin, the destination, the cause and the consequences.

Population and technology

Q. 15. How are technological change and population geography interdependent? [NI]

Technological change is a change in practical and/or industrial areas. Some changes discussed in this book are the generation of H.E.P., establishment of industry, irrigation, application of fertilizers, insecticides and pesticides, breeding and use of new crop and animal strains. Find relevant examples for one or more L.D.C.s. Peter Haggett* has shown that technological innovation is interlocked, not only with population, but with capital formation and natural resources (Fig. 140, overleaf).

* *Geography: A Modern Synthesis*, p. 506.

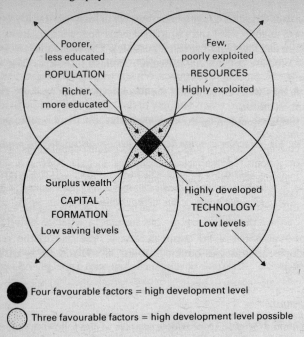

Four favourable factors = high development level

Three favourable factors = high development level possible

Fig. 140 *Major factors in economic development (from Haggett)*

National unity

Q. 16. For an appropriate country, examine the factors which hinder the development of national unity. [LON]

Physical factors are easily dealt with, especially if you can draw a 'physical features' map. Do not neglect the sheer force of distance in a large country: give an indication of the scale involved.

'Human factors' almost certainly refers to the problem of **plural societies**, i.e. multiracial societies. These are not confined to the Third World, but are very common there, especially in Black Africa, because:

(i) a colonizing power has made an artificial political unit which gathers together several indigenous tribes. The Biafran War (Nigeria, 1966–7) was caused by the desire of the Ibo peoples to secede from non-Ibo Nigeria (comprising many tribes). Rioting in the non-Muslim south of mainly Muslim Sudan severely disrupted a scheme to develop irrigation from the White Nile in 1974. The

Eritrean (and Tigréan) people are still fighting a war of liberation in Ethiopia

(ii) the descendants of European colonists remain in the ex-colony. Problems of white minority rule occurred in Kenya, Angola and Algeria, among many others. Violence against white farmers is still a feature of terrorism in Zimbabwe (probably because the developed world reacts strongly to the killing of White by Black and much less so to Black–Black massacres, i.e. there is more political impact)

(iii) colonial powers brought in non-indigenous populations, as slaves or indentured labourers. Examples include Asians in Kenya, Uganda, the West Indies, and Chinese over most of South-East Asia

(iv) different ethnic groups inter-married, with happy results in the case of the mestizos of Brazil, but forming a separate group in the Republic of South Africa.

A second human factor which causes disunity is uneven regional development. Regional development schemes (pp. 389–91) aim to dissipate feelings of inequality which can ignite political unrest.

Theme 8: Transport and trade

Limited and inadequate transport networks are both a cause and an effect of low levels of economic activity. Questions on transport systems tend to be very straightforward, usually asking for the influencing factors. Such questions tend to be very badly done; for two reasons:

1) candidates lack detailed factual knowledge on the nature and existence of transport networks. Do not attempt transport questions without this knowledge

2) simple questions like this require a strong plan. Taking each form of surface transport in turn (rivers, roads, railways), go through, factor by factor. You should include:

(i) Relief

African rivers* pose navigational problems because of:

(a) rapids: name and locate them. Congo railways were built along unnavigable reaches

---

* For an excellent summary of West African rivers, see Senior, M., *Tropical Lands: A Human Geography*, Longman, 1979.

(b) swamps, p. 386.
(c) seasonal fluctuations in volume, resulting from seasonal rainfall
(d) the possibility of drying up and/or flooding.

Asia has several major river systems. Flooding apart, physical constraints are fewer than in Africa, yet the value of river-borne traffic is negligible.

Similarly, the Amazon is navigable for 5,000 km in the flood season, but only the Orinoco is significantly used.

Railways do not care for gradients; yet, in Africa, lines run over 2,000 m O.D. between Addis Ababa and Djibouti; Mombasa and Kampala. Several lines run above 3,000 m in Latin America: Bogotá (Colombia); Quito (Ecuador); Cerro de Pasco, Huancayo and Cuzco (Peru); La Paz, Oruro and Uyuni (Bolivia); and in two Chile–Argentina links: Antofagasta–Salta and Valparaiso–Mendoza. Clearly relief barriers will be overcome if the economy justifies the cost.

Roads are less sensitive to relief; but where relief inhibits economic development, all-weather roads are few in number.

(ii) Drainage and climate obviously affect river transport (see above), but tropical rainfall can cause landslides, and floods wash away bridges and sections of road and track.

High temperatures and humidity can cause severe maintenance problems.

(iii) Vegetation
Road construction in the tropical rain forest is desperately difficult; railway building is harder, but lines do run through the rain forest in: Ivory Coast, Ghana, Cameroon, Gabon, Zaïre; Malaysia, Thailand, Vietnam, Java.

(iv) Natural resources provide the key to the building of many railways over mountains and through tropical forest. Find out where minerals and forest resources have been responsible for lines in the list above.

(v) Commercial agriculture has stimulated other lines in the list: identify the crops.

(vi) Development plans now frequently include the improvement of transport networks – examples are given on p. 390. See also 'Density of networks' (below). Of the surface modes of transport, rivers are most often examined.

A typical JMB question on rivers would combine two fields of geographical knowledge: hydrology and regional geography. Question 17 would require more detail. Candidates are fairly sound on H.E.P. and irrigation, but tend to neglect transport.

Q. 17. Discuss, with examples, the economic importance of rivers in the prescribed region. [OXF; adapted]

Density of networks

In the Third World there are fewer kilometres of roads or railways, per head or per km^2, than in the developed world because:
1) there are fewer foodstuffs to be moved where a high proportion of the population is in subsistence agriculture
2) low levels of industrialization generate little freight
3) low incomes generate little demand for manufactured goods
4) low literacy reduces movement of newspapers and mail.
'Physical and economic isolation are closely related.'*

Ports

Question 18 picks out the dominant theme:

Q. 18. For two major ports in the prescribed region,
(a) outline the main characteristics of the trade of each port;
(b) compare and contrast the nature of the ports' hinterlands and the links between the ports and their hinterlands. [WEL]

Trade

London examiners are keen on trade questions. It is important to note that agricultural exporters are at risk from:
 (i) climatic hazards
(ii) policies of the developed world:
    (a) the C.A.P. decision to become self-sufficient in sugar, through beet growing, was a body blow to Third World cane growers
    (b) the U.S.A. and Canada have increased grain exports to relieve

* Dickenson *et al.*, op. cit., p. 214.

409

their own problems of surplus; with increases in supply, prices
fall

(iii) increases in supply from other L.D.C.s.

You should include the risks of exporting renewable agricultural
produce in discussing Question 19.

*Q. 19. 'A developing country is at risk so long as its economy relies on
the export of non-renewable resources.' Discuss.* [LON]

Appendix 1: Index of geographical terms

Page numbers in italics indicate a diagram or table.

Appendix 2: Important geographical authors

Page numbers in italics indicate a diagram or table.

Appendix 3: Place-name index

Page numbers in italics indicate a diagram or table.

MORE ABOUT PENGUINS, PELICANS, PEREGRINES AND PUFFINS

For further information about books available from Penguins please write to Dept EP, Penguin Books Ltd, Harmondsworth, Middlesex UB7 0DA.

In the U.S.A.: For a complete list of books available from Penguins in the United States write to Dept DG, Penguin Books, 299 Murray Hill Parkway, East Rutherford, New Jersey 07073.

In Canada: For a complete list of books available from Penguins in Canada write to Penguin Books Canada Ltd, 2801 John Street, Markham, Ontario L3R 1B4.

In Australia: For a complete list of books available from Penguins in Australia write to the Marketing Department, Penguin Books Australia Ltd, P.O. Box 257, Ringwood, Victoria 3134.

In New Zealand: For a complete list of books available from Penguins in New Zealand write to the Marketing Department, Penguin Books (N.Z.) Ltd, Private Bag, Takapuna, Auckland 9.

In India: For a complete list of books available from Penguins in India write to Penguin Overseas Ltd, 706 Eros Apartments, 56 Nehru Place, New Delhi 110019.

THE PENGUIN ENGLISH DICTIONARY

The Penguin English Dictionary has been created specially for today's needs. It features:

* More entries than any other popularly priced dictionary
* Exceptionally clear and precise definitions
* For the first time in an equivalent dictionary, the internationally recognised IPA pronunciation system
* Emphasis on contemporary usage
* Extended coverage of both the spoken and the written word
* Scientific tables
* Technical words
* Informal and colloquial expressions
* Vocabulary most widely used *wherever* English is spoken
* Most commonly used abbreviations

It is twenty years since the publication of the last English dictionary by Penguin and the compilation of this entirely new *Penguin English Dictionary* is the result of a special collaboration between Longman, one of the world's leading dictionary publishers, and Penguin Books. The material is based entirely on the database of the acclaimed *Longman Dictionary of the English Language*.

1008 pages   051.139 3   £2.50 ☐

PENGUIN REFERENCE BOOKS

☐ **The Penguin Map of the World** £2.50

Clear, colourful, crammed with information and fully up-to-date, this is a useful map to stick on your wall at home, at school or in the office.

☐ **The Penguin Map of Europe** £2.95

Covers all land eastwards to the Urals, southwards to North Africa and up to Syria, Iraq and Iran * Scale = 1:5,500,000 * 4-colour artwork * Features main roads, railways, oil and gas pipelines, plus extra information including national flags, currencies and populations.

☐ **The Penguin Map of the British Isles** £1.95

Including the Orkneys, the Shetlands, the Channel Islands and much of Normandy, this excellent map is ideal for planning routes and touring holidays, or as a study aid.

☐ **The Penguin Dictionary of Quotations** £3.95

A treasure-trove of over 12,000 new gems and old favourites, from Aesop and Matthew Arnold to Xenophon and Zola.

☐ **The Penguin Dictionary of Art and Artists** £3.95

Fifth Edition. 'A vast amount of information intelligently presented, carefully detailed, abreast of current thought and scholarship and easy to read' – *The Times Literary Supplement*

☐ **The Penguin Pocket Thesaurus** £1.95

A pocket-sized version of Roget's classic, and an essential companion for all commuters, crossword addicts, students, journalists and the stuck-for-words.

PENGUIN REFERENCE BOOKS

☐ **The Penguin Dictionary of Troublesome Words**   £2.50

A witty, straightforward guide to the pitfalls and hotly disputed issues in standard written English, illustrated with examples and including a glossary of grammatical terms and an appendix on punctuation.

☐ **The Penguin Guide to the Law**   £7.50

This acclaimed reference book is designed for everyday use, and forms the most comprehensive handbook ever published on the law as it affects the individual.

☐ **The Penguin Dictionary of Religions**   £4.95

The rites, beliefs, gods and holy books of all the major religions throughout the world are covered in this book, which is illustrated with charts, maps and line drawings.

☐ **The Penguin Medical Encyclopedia**   £4.95

Covers the body and mind in sickness and in health, including drugs, surgery, history, institutions, medical vocabulary and many other aspects. Second Edition. 'Highly commendable' – *Journal of the Institute of Health Education*

☐ **The Penguin Dictionary of Physical Geography**   £4.95

This book discusses all the main terms used, in over 5,000 entries illustrated with diagrams and meticulously cross-referenced.

☐ **Roget's Thesaurus**   £2.95

Specially adapted for Penguins, Sue Lloyd's acclaimed new version of Roget's original will help you find the right words for your purposes. 'As normal a part of an intelligent household's library as the Bible, Shakespeare or a dictionary' – *Daily Telegraph*

PENGUIN TRAVEL BOOKS

☐ *Arabian Sands* **Wilfred Thesiger** £3.50

'In the tradition of Burton, Doughty, Lawrence, Philby and Thomas, it is, very likely, the book about Arabia to end all books about Arabia' – *Daily Telegraph*

☐ *The Flight of Ikaros* **Kevin Andrews** £3.50

'He also is in love with the country . . . but he sees the other side of that dazzling medal or moon . . . If you want some truth about Greece, here it is' – Louis MacNeice in the *Observer*

☐ *D. H. Lawrence and Italy* £4.95

In *Twilight in Italy, Sea and Sardinia* and *Etruscan Places,* Lawrence recorded his impressions while living, writing and travelling in 'one of the most beautiful countries in the world'.

☐ *Maiden Voyage* **Denton Welch** £3.50

Opening during his last term at public school, from which the author absconded, *Maiden Voyage* turns into a brilliantly idiosyncratic account of China in the 1930s.

☐ *The Grand Irish Tour* **Peter Somerville-Large** £4.95

The account of a year's journey round Ireland. 'Marvellous . . . describes to me afresh a landscape I thought I knew' – Edna O'Brien in the *Observer*

☐ *Slow Boats to China* **Gavin Young** £3.95

On an ancient steamer, a cargo dhow, a Filipino kumpit and twenty more agreeably cranky boats, Gavin Young sailed from Piraeus to Canton in seven crowded and colourful months. 'A pleasure to read' – Paul Theroux

PENGUIN TRAVEL BOOKS

☐ *The Kingdom by the Sea* **Paul Theroux** £2.50

1982, the year of the Falklands War and the Royal Baby, was the ideal time, Theroux found, to travel round the coast of Britain and surprise the British into talking about themselves. 'He describes it all brilliantly and honestly' – Anthony Burgess

☐ *One's Company* **Peter Fleming** £2.95

His journey to China as special correspondent to *The Times* in 1933. 'One reads him for literary delight . . . But, he is also an observer of penetrating intellect' – Vita Sackville West

☐ *The Traveller's Tree* **Patrick Leigh Fermor** £3.95

'A picture of the Indies more penetrating and original than any that has been presented before' – *Observer*

☐ *The Path to Rome* **Hilaire Belloc** £3.95

'The only book I ever wrote for love,' is how Belloc described the wonderful blend of anecdote, humour and reflection that makes up the story of his pilgrimage to Rome.

☐ *The Light Garden of the Angel King* **Peter Levi** £2.95

Afghanistan has been a wild rocky highway for nomads and merchants, Alexander the Great, Buddhist monks, great Moghul conquerors and the armies of the Raj. Here, quite brilliantly, Levi writes about their journeys and his own.

☐ *Among the Russians* **Colin Thubron** £2.95

'The Thubron approach to travelling has an integrity that belongs to another age' – Dervla Murphy in the *Irish Times*. 'A magnificent achievement' – Nikolai Tolstoy

PENGUIN TRAVEL BOOKS

☐ *Remote People* **Evelyn Waugh**   **£2.95**

Writing with typical brilliance, remorseless observation and wit,
Waugh describes his travels as a journalist in Ethiopia and British
Africa, 1930–31.

☐ *The Stones of Florence* and *Venice Observed*
  Mary McCarthy   **£3.50**

In these travelogues, published together here, Mary McCarthy
evokes the local life, the colour, sights and character of two marvellous cities, the brightest jewels in Italy's crown.

☐ *First Russia, Then Tibet* **Robert Byron**   **£3.95**

First published in 1933, this richly personal view of Russia, India and
Tibet assured Robert Byron's reputation as a wonderfully sharp and
stimulating arm-chair travelling companion.